CW00435090

Features of a Form that Works

Data-entry fields easily distinguishable from their labels, neatly aligned, falling in normal reading order

A clearly labeled form

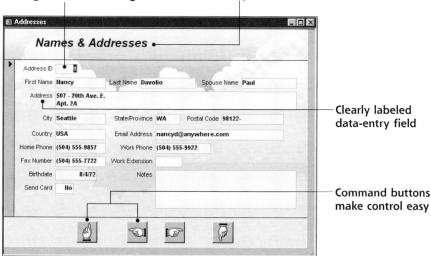

Clearly labeled data-entry field

Command buttons make control easy

Access Chart Type Icons as They Appear On-Screen

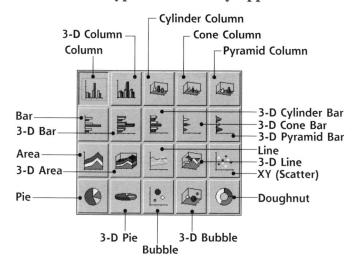

Cylinder Column

3-D Column
Column

Cone Column

Pyramid Column

Bar
3-D Bar

3-D Cylinder Bar
3-D Cone Bar
3-D Pyramid Bar

Area
3-D Area

Line
3-D Line
XY (Scatter)

Pie

Doughnut

3-D Pie

3-D Bubble

Bubble

Chart Types in Access

Chart Type Icon	Type of Chart
	Column
	3-D Column
	Cylinder Column
	Cone Column
	Pyramid Column
	Bar
	3-D Bar
	3-D Cylinder Bar
	3-D Cone Bar
	3-D Pyramid Bar
	Area
	3-D Area
	Line
	3-D Line
	Pie
	3-D Pie
	XY (Scatter)
	Bubble
	3-D Bubble
	Doughnut

DISCOVERY CENTRAL

DISCOVER
ACCESS 97

DISCOVER ACCESS 97

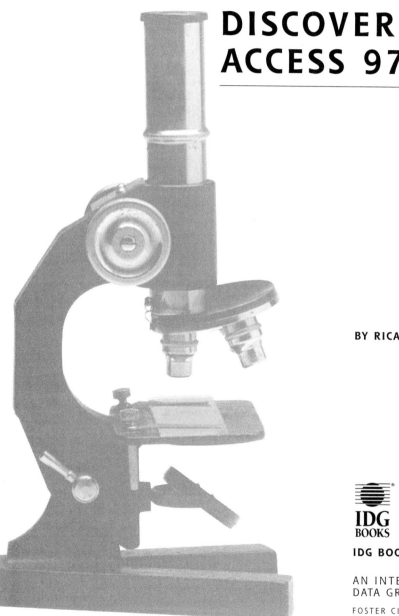

BY RICARDO BIRMELE

IDG BOOKS WORLDWIDE, INC.

AN INTERNATIONAL
DATA GROUP COMPANY

FOSTER CITY, CA • CHICAGO, IL •
INDIANAPOLIS, IN • SOUTHLAKE, TX

Discover Access 97

Published by
IDG Books Worldwide, Inc.
An International Data Group Company
919 E. Hillsdale Blvd., Suite 400
Foster City, CA 94404

http://www.idgbooks.com (IDG Books Worldwide Web site)

Library of Congress Catalog Card No.: 96-80028

ISBN: 0-7645-8026-4

Printed in the United States of America

10 9 8 7 6 5 4 3 2 1

1B/RX/QU/ZX/FC

Distributed in the United States by IDG Books Worldwide, Inc.

Distributed by Macmillan Canada for Canada; by Contemporanea de Ediciones for Venezuela; by Distribuidora Cuspide for Argentina; by CITEC for Brazil; by Ediciones ZETA S.C.R. Ltda. for Peru; by Editorial Limusa SA for Mexico; by Transworld Publishers Limited in the United Kingdom and Europe; by Academic Bookshop for Egypt; by Levant Distributors S.A.R.L. for Lebanon; by Al Jassim for Saudi Arabia; by Simron Pty. Ltd. for South Africa; by Pustak Mahal for India; by The Computer Bookshop for India; by Toppan Company Ltd. for Japan; by Addison Wesley Publishing Company for Korea; by Longman Singapore Publishers Ltd. for Singapore, Malaysia, Thailand, and Indonesia; by Unalis Corporation for Taiwan; by WS Computer Publishing Company, Inc. for the Philippines; by WoodsLane Pty. Ltd. for Australia; by WoodsLane Enterprises Ltd. for New Zealand. Authorized Sales Agent: Anthony Rudkin Associates for the Middle East and North Africa.

For general information on IDG Books Worldwide's books in the U.S., please call our Consumer Customer Service department at 800-762-2974. For reseller information, including discounts and premium sales, please call our Reseller Customer Service department at 800-434-3422.

For information on where to purchase IDG Books Worldwide's books outside the U.S., please contact our International Sales department at 415-655-3172 or fax 415-655-3295.

For information on foreign language translations, please contact our Foreign & Subsidiary Rights department at 415-655-3021 or fax 415-655-3281.

For sales inquiries and special prices for bulk quantities, please contact our Sales department at 415-655-3200 or write to the address above.

For information on using IDG Books Worldwide's books in the classroom or for ordering examination copies, please contact our Educational Sales department at 800-434-2086 or fax 817-251-8174.

For press review copies, author interviews, or other publicity information, please contact our Public Relations department at 415-655-3000 or fax 415-655-3299.

For authorization to photocopy items for corporate, personal, or educational use, please contact Copyright Clearance Center, 222 Rosewood Drive, Danvers, MA 01923, or fax 508-750-4470.

IDG BOOKS is a trademark under exclusive license to IDG Books Worldwide, Inc., from International Data Group, Inc.

ABOUT IDG BOOKS WORLDWIDE

Welcome to the world of IDG Books Worldwide.

IDG Books Worldwide, Inc., is a subsidiary of International Data Group, the world's largest publisher of computer-related information and the leading global provider of information services on information technology. IDG was founded more than 25 years ago and now employs more than 8,500 people worldwide. IDG publishes more than 275 computer publications in over 75 countries (see listing below). More than 60 million people read one or more IDG publications each month.

Launched in 1990, IDG Books Worldwide is today the #1 publisher of best-selling computer books in the United States. We are proud to have received eight awards from the Computer Press Association in recognition of editorial excellence and three from *Computer Currents'* First Annual Readers' Choice Awards. Our best-selling *...For Dummies*® series has more than 30 million copies in print with translations in 30 languages. IDG Books Worldwide, through a joint venture with IDG's Hi-Tech Beijing, became the first U.S. publisher to publish a computer book in the People's Republic of China. In record time, IDG Books Worldwide has become the first choice for millions of readers around the world who want to learn how to better manage their businesses.

Our mission is simple: Every one of our books is designed to bring extra value and skill-building instructions to the reader. Our books are written by experts who understand and care about our readers. The knowledge base of our editorial staff comes from years of experience in publishing, education, and journalism — experience we use to produce books for the '90s. In short, we care about books, so we attract the best people. We devote special attention to details such as audience, interior design, use of icons, and illustrations. And because we use an efficient process of authoring, editing, and desktop publishing our books electronically, we can spend more time ensuring superior content and spend less time on the technicalities of making books.

You can count on our commitment to deliver high-quality books at competitive prices on topics you want to read about. At IDG Books Worldwide, we continue in the IDG tradition of delivering quality for more than 25 years. You'll find no better book on a subject than one from IDG Books Worldwide.

John Kilcullen
CEO
IDG Books Worldwide, Inc.

Steven Berkowitz
President and Publisher
IDG Books Worldwide, Inc.

Eighth Annual
Computer Press
Awards 1992

Ninth Annual
Computer Press
Awards 1993

Tenth Annual
Computer Press
Awards 1994

Eleventh Annual
Computer Press
Awards 1995

Welcome to the Discover Series

Do you want to discover the best and most efficient ways to use your computer and learn about technology? Books in the Discover series teach you the essentials of technology with a friendly, confident approach. You'll find a Discover book on almost any subject — from the Internet to intranets, from Web design and programming to the business programs that make your life easier.

We've provided valuable, real-world examples that help you relate to topics faster. Discover books begin by introducing you to the main features of programs, so you start by doing something *immediately*. The focus is to teach you how to perform tasks that are useful and meaningful in your day-to-day work. You might create a document or graphic, explore your computer, surf the Web, or write a program. Whatever the task, you learn the most commonly used features, and focus on the best tips and techniques for doing your work. You'll get results quickly, and discover the best ways to use software and technology in your everyday life.

You may find the following elements and features in this book:

Discovery Central: This tearout card is a handy quick reference to important tasks or ideas covered in the book.

Quick Tour: The Quick Tour gets you started working with the book right away.

Real-Life Vignettes: Throughout the book you'll see one-page scenarios illustrating a real-life application of a topic covered.

Goals: Each chapter opens with a list of goals you can achieve by reading the chapter.

Side Trips: These asides include additional information about alternative or advanced ways to approach the topic covered.

Bonuses: Timesaving tips and more advanced techniques are covered in each chapter.

Discovery Center: This guide illustrates key procedures covered throughout the book.

Visual Index: You'll find real-world documents in the Visual Index, with page numbers pointing you to where you should turn to achieve the effects shown.

Throughout the book, you'll also notice some special icons and formatting:

 A Feature Focus icon highlights new features in the software's latest release, and points out significant differences between it and the previous version.

 Web Paths refer you to Web sites that provide additional information about the topic.

 Tips offer timesaving shortcuts, expert advice, quick techniques, or brief reminders.

 The X-Ref icon refers you to other chapters or sections for more information.

Pull Quotes emphasize important ideas that are covered in the chapter.

 Notes provide additional information or highlight special points of interest about a topic.

 The Caution icon alerts you to potential problems you should watch out for.

The Discover series delivers interesting, insightful, and inspiring information about technology to help you learn faster and retain more. So the next time you want to find answers to your technology questions, reach for a Discover book. We hope the entertaining, easy-to-read style puts you at ease and makes learning fun.

Credits

ACQUISITIONS EDITOR
John Osborne

DEVELOPMENT EDITOR
Ralph Moore

COPY EDITOR
Chris Katsaropoulos

TECHNICAL EDITOR
Robert Wazeka, Ph.D.

PROJECT COORDINATOR
Phyllis Beaty

QUALITY CONTROL SPECIALIST
Mick Arellano

GRAPHICS AND PRODUCTION SPECIALISTS
Ritchie Durdin
Elsie Yim

PROOFREADER
David Wise

INDEXER
Steve Rath

BOOK DESIGN
Seventeenth Street Studios
Phyllis Beaty
Kurt Krames

About the Author

Ricardo Birmele has been a husband for 23 years, a father for 16, and a terrible — excuse me, terribly famous — author for 12. He has written review articles for most of the larger computer magazines as well as books on such diverse computer subjects as desktop publishing, databases, and software programming. Writing and photographing in the Pacific Northwest, Birmele spends his free time working with the United States Coast Guard Auxiliary where he is an intrepid Aviator and the 13th District Information Services Officer. You can send fan mail to his Internet email address at birm@olex.com.

THIS BOOK IS DEDICATED TO THE GOOD LORD, WHO MADE IT POSSIBLE; TO MY FRIEND AND DARLING WIFE BEVY, WHO MADE IT PLEASANT; AND TO MY SONS CHRIS AND MISHA, WHO MADE IT NECESSARY.

Acknowledgments

The way the trade book industry works in the United States, the author is an awful lot like a journeyman craftsman of days gone by. While he works alone, his efforts are actually a contribution to a project as part of a team. Each new book represents a new project and a new team.

Every now and again, an author has the great fortune to be able to work as part of an excellent team, and that is the case with myself and *Discover Access 97*.

The project started with John Osborne, IDG Books Acquisitions Editor. This man is the epitome of calm professionalism, with a gently firm guiding hand. Coolness and excellent capability under pressure is defined by Ralph Moore, Development Editor. When things went wrong, he was always steadily and professionally "there," solving the problems. We could not have been more fortunate than to have Robert Wazeka, Ph.D., a true friend of mine who would rather be known as the unassuming "Waz," for Technical Editor. His sardonic, acuminate comments pointed out the inevitable holes with humor and good sense. Too bad he's a liberal Democrat. Chris Katsaropoulos, Copy Editor, is incredible in his ability to work accurately at extraordinary speed and with unfailing attention to the constantly changing details. If the information in this book is clearly presented, then it's largely due to his efforts.

It's been a privilege working with you guys. A very rare privilege.

—*Ricardo Birmele*
Buckeley, Washington
February 1997

CONTENTS AT A GLANCE

PART THREE—FLEXING OUR MUSCLES

CONTENTS

INTRODUCTION

Well, how do you do, and thank you for buying this book. You are about to take a journey I wandered not all that long ago. Certainly not so long ago that I've forgotten it — allegations of my senility proffered by my teenage sons notwithstanding.

When one lives the glamorous life of an author, one tends to live much in one's imagination. (With all those "ones" in that sentence, you might get the subliminal message that the glamorous life is actually more of a solitary life — and you'd be correct). That being the case, I don't have the pleasure of your physical company, and so I've had to form a mental image of you. Here's what I see:

You are reasonably intelligent, with an active curiosity and an average to above-average ability to read English. You're at the point — either professionally or personally — where you need to know more about Microsoft Access and databases. Chances are good that you've got something of a life and so don't want to spend much (or waste any) time learning *this* subject. You're not a child to whom one can talk down, and you expect respect for your intellect and abilities.

Well, friend, you've come to the right place. In this book, I'm going to show you how to use Microsoft Access 97. If you've never even heard about databases, then you still have nothing to fear. In this book, I'll take you right from knowing nothing at all about databases to actually creating one. It's not as difficult as some computer nerds would have you believe. I mean, *I* was able to pretty well master the subject — and I'm not all that bright. Good looking, certainly; but not all that bright.

Discover Access 97 is divided into three parts, as explained in the following sections.

Part One: Beginnings

We start with an overview of Access, continue with a look at its Help system (you're never alone), and finish with your creating a useful little address book. Along the way, you'll come to understand the basic difference between data and information and how that difference guides your implementation and use of databases generally, and Access particularly.

Part Two: Getting More Than Our Toes Wet

This is where I get to show you in some easy detail all about Access itself. We start by taking a close look at the datasheet, where Access shows you your data arranged in rows and columns. Then I teach you a bit of what you'll want to keep in mind as you begin to design your own databases. Together, we learn about and use each of Access's database tools such as queries (where you form questions that turn your data into information), relationships (which make Access unlimited in its database usefulness), forms (which make Access easier for you and others to use), and reports (whereby you share your database's information).

Part Three: Flexing Our Muscles

Here's where you develop your intuitive understanding of databases and Access. You'll build on your new databasing skills to learn how to include graphics on your forms and reports, how to make your database's user interface more efficient and pleasing, and how to share data on a network. I even give you a close beginner's look at the Structured Query Language (SQL) that underlies the way Access works.

Discovering Access 97 is a no-nonsense guide to getting started with Access, so turn to the Quick Tour... and get started!

ACCESS 97 QUICK TOUR

KEY GOALS OF THIS CHAPTER:

HOW TO OPEN ACCESS   PAGE   1

HOW TO CREATE A NEW DATABASE   PAGE   2

HOW TO PRINT A REPORT   PAGE   4

HOW TO CLOSE A DATABASE AND EXIT ACCESS
        PAGE   5

To get up and running quickly, let's walk through this simple Access implementation, which will introduce you to most of the basics associated with starting Access and creating and saving a simple document using the Database Wizard.

To begin your Quick Tour of Access 97, follow these simple steps:

 1. First, be sure that Access 97 is installed on your machine (for instructions, see Appendix B, "Installing Access").

2. Move your mouse cursor to the Windows   Start   button and click it. Windows pops up its main menu.

3. Move your mouse cursor to the word   Programs   and click. The Programs submenu pops up.

4. Slide your mouse cursor over to the   Microsoft Access   item and click. Windows looks for Access on your computer's hard disk, loads it, and runs it for you. When you get to the initial dialog box, click   Cancel   to close it (we're not using it for the purpose of our Quick Tour).

5. Click   □   on the Access toolbar. Access displays the New dialog box.

6. Click the Databases tab if you're not already there. Figure QT-1 shows you what should be on your screen at this point.

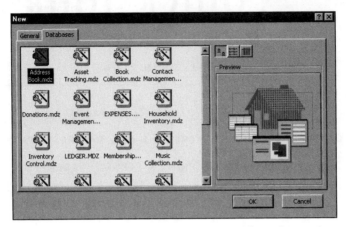

Figure QT-1 The Database Wizard is conjured from the Databases tab of the New dialog box.

7. Double-click the Address Book icon from the display of available templates. Access displays the File New Database dialog box.

8. Three essential bits of information are now required. First, you need to give your new project a name; for this Quick Tour, type the name **Quick Tour** in the File name field. Next, you need to specify what type of file you are creating. Because you are, in fact, creating a database, the default in the Save as type field, Microsoft Access Databases, works for your Quick Tour. Finally, you need to specify where you want Access to store your database. Choose the default location or choose your own location.

9. Click **Create** . In a few seconds, Access proudly presents the Database Wizard, your helpful guide (aside from yours truly) to constructing a finished database.

The next process requires that you actually enter some information into the Database Wizard; then it can construct your database. Without going into too much detail, that's what you'll do next.

To construct your database and add data, follow these simple steps:

1. In the first screen of the Database Wizard, which is shown in Figure QT-2, click the **Finish** button. Doing so will tell the Wizard to create an Address book that contains all the elements — fields, tables, queries, and reports — that the wizard offers as defaults.

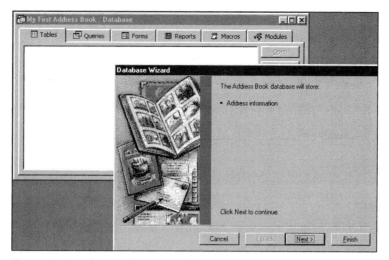

Figure QT-2 The Database Wizard knows all about creating databases.

2. The next window to appear is the switchboard, which is shown in Figure QT-3. To begin entering data into your Quick Tour database, click the button next to Enter/View Addresses. Access then presents you with a form for entering data, which is shown in Figure QT-4.

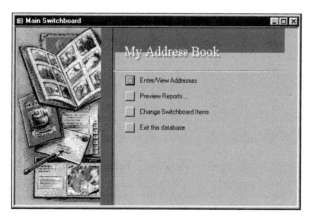

Figure QT-3 An Access switchboard is a push button menu of options for working with your database.

3. For purposes of this Quick Tour, enter your own name, address, and telephone number into this form. When you're done entering this information, click the ⬚ Close button at the very top right of the form — the one with an X on it. Access closes the form and displays again the Main Switchboard dialog box.

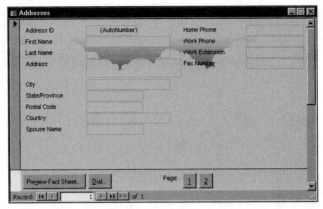

Figure QT-4 Address data is entered and modified in this form.

4. As the switchboard suggests, you have four options at this point:

✳ Enter/View Addresses

✳ Preview Reports

✳ Change Switchboard Items

✳ Exit this database

Click the Preview Reports option so that you can prove to yourself that you have actually created something here. You should now see what's illustrated in Figure QT-5.

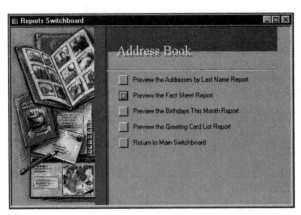

Figure QT-5 Pick an option.

5. You are offered five options: four built-in reports that you can preview, then print, and a way back to the Main Switchboard. For now, however, click the second button on the list — the one for the Fact Sheet report. Access previews the report for you, as shown in Figure QT-6.

Figure QT-6 You first get a preview, then you print.

6. Once you see the previewed report, you can print it by clicking ⎙ on the toolbar.

That's how very easy it is to use Microsoft Access. I'm sure that with this taste, you're raring to get going with the rest of this book. Good! That's just what an author likes to see — um — think. Well, anyway, to get you set up, you need to close this Quick Tour and Access.

To close the Quick Tour and exit Access, follow these simple steps:

1. Close the Print Preview window by clicking the ⎵Close⎴ button at its top right corner. Access again displays the switchboard.

2. Even with the switchboard showing, you can close Access by clicking the close button at the top right corner of its window. Access saves your data almost as soon as you type it in, so it's safe. Also, Access automatically closes any open databases before it closes itself down. Go ahead and close Access by clicking its close button.

Congratulations! You've just created and saved your Quick Tour database, and now you're ready for your adventure with Microsoft Access.

PART ONE

BEGINNINGS

THIS PART CONTAINS THE FOLLOWING CHAPTERS:

CHAPTER **1** YOUR TICKET, PLEASE

CHAPTER **2** WHEN I NEED HELP, I PUSH THE BUTTON

CHAPTER **3** I'D LIKE TO JUMP IN AND GIVE IT A TRY

This part of *Discover Access 97* teaches you all of the basics that you'll need to get working with Access quickly. You'll find a comprehensive overview of getting started with Access, using its various components (including wizards), getting help, and beginning your first project. By the end of this part, you will have all of the information that you need to automatically create and use an Access database.

Like Bill Gates, Jon C. Munson II dropped out of college after only a little more than a year. Now, years later and in his late twenties, Munson is a prime developer at Quality Data Systems (QDS), a consulting firm in Bloomington, MN. Unlike Gates, Munson isn't a billionaire (not yet, anyway), but his career took off when he found a new and better way to utilize one of Gates's own products, Microsoft Access.

Munson was no stranger to computer programming when he took a job as a hardware and software consultant for a health and fitness club back in 1993. He had learned how to program in Basic in the eighth grade, and then learned Pascal in high school and C in college. At the time he started working for the health club, he had learned enough of Access to start building applications.

The assignment Munson had was to develop a facility management database which would be run over a Novell Netware 2.1 network. The database was supposed to manage member and guest demographics as well as check-in procedures.

One of the things Munson noticed about Access was that it could store and utilize graphic images. It seemed like a good idea to him to include photographs (taken with a digital camera) of the club members in their individual records to produce membership cards, but he didn't like the way the documentation told him to do it. After a few trials and errors, he devised his own unique way of inserting and displaying the member photos. When he called Microsoft to check on a few technical points, a very impressed technician at the company told him he was the first person ever to do it that way.

This and other aspects of the way he handled the creation of the health club database were key factors in his getting hired by QDS, Munson says. Started six years ago, QDS now has about 50 employees. Working primarily on five platforms — AS/400, Access, Visual Basic, C++, and SQL — the firm offers database and other information technology consulting to companies ranging from small, local businesses to Fortune 100 corporations.

More recently, Munson has developed a very large tracking database for an importing company. Access, he says, is a very robust and flexible development environment for most of his projects, although it's not a panacea. The tracking application, for instance, outgrew Access's data-handling capabilities and had to be ported to Visual Basic.

"As a beginner designing applications in Access," Munson says, "one needs to be careful. Microsoft made many things in Access very easy, and that is one of its great strengths. But it's also a pitfall for new people. I've seen many examples of poor planning and poor design producing terrible applications."

CHAPTER ONE

YOUR TICKET, PLEASE

KEY GOALS OF THIS CHAPTER:

W e were performing an age-old ritual: Father teaches son to drive the family car in a lonely, deserted space. Just he and I together, bonding. My son was driving the family's "good" car — the one with automatic shift. We had just missed one of two lonely light poles in the parking lot.

Number-one son looked over at me sitting beside him, fixed his brown eyes on me, and said, "Um... oops. Heh heh heh." The car was headed directly for the other light pole. In my best "father calmly teaching" voice I yelled, "LOOK WHERE YOU'RE GOING!!!" With a paint layer's thickness of distance remaining, we missed the second light pole.

Now, this son is one of those people who can simply look at a machine and know how to run it. For someone just learning, he was a very good driver. The problem for him — as it is for someone just getting to know a new software application like Access — was that there were a lot of things going on at once. He had to watch for other cars, remember which pedal stopped the car (he had no problem with the one that made it go), and help unclamp his father's fingers from the arm rests.

As a new user of Access, you may be feeling the same kind of overload. If this is the first time you've actually sat down at a computer to do something, you may feel as though you don't even know where to start. Well — not to worry. Just as driving a car soon became second nature to you, so will your skill at using Access. Both are simply a matter of knowing what you should pay attention to and when. And that's exactly what I'm going to show you.

In this chapter, we walk through the following processes:

* Turn on Access and get it running and ready for you to work with.

* Start up a new database that's got absolutely nothing in it — and then put data into it.

* Learn about Access's parts, such as its database container, tables, menus, toolbars, and such.

* Come to understand a bit about data and how to turn it into information using Access queries, forms, and reports.

When you're done with this chapter, you'll be completely comfortable with your ability to actually accomplish something with Access — just as you can get in your car at any time and easily drive home.

Bringing Access to Life

Before you can use Access, you need to turn it on. Like any other Windows application, you call it up and run it by clicking with your mouse on its name on your Programs menu, or by clicking on the Access icon in its folder from your desktop.

As you get more familiar with Windows in general and Access 97 in particular, you'll probably come to like one way more than the other. For now, however, I'll show you both ways.

Starting from the Desktop

For the first way, start Access from the Programs menu. Here's how you do it:

1. Move your mouse cursor to the Windows **Start** button and click it. Windows pops up its main menu.

2. Move your mouse cursor to the word **Programs** and either click or pause for a moment with the word Programs highlighted. Windows 95 has built into it a facility wherein if you pause on a Start menu item, Windows automatically pops up the associated sub menu. As soon as you click, or if you pause for a moment, Windows pops up the Programs sub menu.

3. Slide your mouse cursor over to the **Microsoft Access** item, (the one including an icon that looks like a key) and click. Check out Figure 1-1

to see what Access looks like in the Start menu. Windows looks for Access on your computer's hard disk, loads it, and runs it for you.

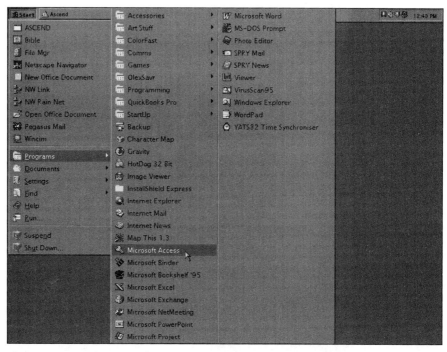

Figure 1-1   Click Microsoft Access to call up and run the program.

Life from a Folder

Another way to load Access is by clicking its icon in its own desktop folder. This may seem a bit more convoluted than the first way, but it's only slightly more involved.

Just closely follow these steps, and it will all work out fine for you:

   1. On your desktop there is an icon labeled My Computer. Figure 1-2 shows you what it looks like. Move your mouse cursor to that icon and click it. Windows opens the My Computer folder, showing you the icons it contains.

   Take a moment now to look at Figure 1-3 where you can see the icons in the My Computer window. Notice that most of them are little representations of disk drives. That's because when you want to use your computer, you usually need to start a program — and programs are stored on hard drives until you need to use them. That seems pretty obvious on its face, but it really isn't. Sometimes people forget that it's not simply their "computer" with which they're working: It's really the software running on their computer.

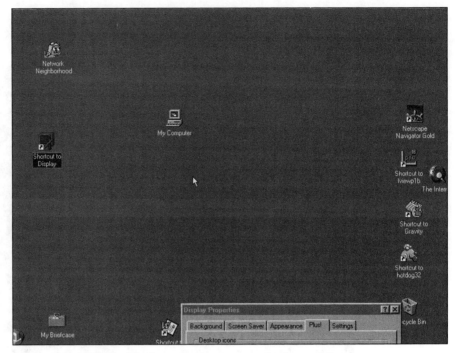

Figure 1-2 Click the My Computer icon to see what's on your computer.

Figure 1-3 My Computer is where you find some often-used folders, as well as all the disk drives connected to your computer.

"Sometimes people forget that it's not simply their computer with which they're working: It's really the software running on their computer."

By the way, your icons may look a bit different from mine. You may have more or fewer icons than you see in Figure 1-3. My computer is connected to a network, and some of my drives are shared with other people who are working with their computers on the same network.

TIP The icons that show a disk drive as though it were being carried by a hand, such as MS dos_6(C:) or Removable Disk (E:) in the figure, represent drives that are shared and so can be used by other people on our network. The lonely icons with no hands are not shared and so can only be used by someone working on my computer.

2. Click the icon of the disk drive that contains your copy of Access. Usually — what we in the computer world call "by default" — it will be in your (C:) drive, so click that one. If you know that it's in a different drive, however, follow your own knowledge. Windows calls up another window showing the icons of all the folders on that drive.

3. Look for a folder labeled MSOffice97, such as the one in Figure 1-4. That is the one Windows creates by default to contain all of the applications in the Microsoft Office suite of programs. Click it and Windows calls up yet another window, this one containing the Microsoft Office folders.

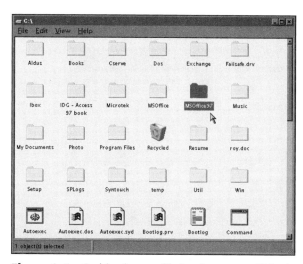

Figure 1-4   C: drive is most likely where you will find Microsoft Office '97.

4. Click the folder labeled Access, like the one shown in Figure 1-5. Windows opens the last window you'll need for this process: the one containing Access and its associated programs and folders.

TIP By the way, don't mistake the folder labeled Data Access for the one more simply labeled Access. The former has to do with sharing data among different kinds of database and application programs; the latter is the one that contains the subject of the present tome.

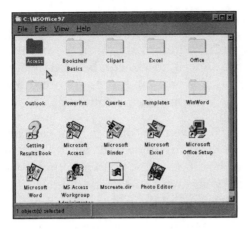

Figure 1-5 The MSOffice97 folder is where you find all the software applications that come on your Microsoft Office 97 disks.

Now would be a good opportunity to look for a moment at the associated programs you see in the folder. As you can see in Figure 1-6, there are a number of different kinds of folders and programs in the window. They break down into five main categories, as outlined in the list that follows.

Figure 1-6 The MSOffice97/Access folder contains all the files — program, data, and supporting — that Microsoft Access needs to run.

✳ Other folders that hold supporting programs such as sample databases or reports, free bitmapped pictures you can use with your databases, a text wizard that helps you bring text data into your databases, and another that helps you work with Internet databases

✳ Application files such as Msaccess (the database application that's the focus of this book) or Wrkgadm (a program that lets you administer a bunch of people who want to use the same database on a network)

* Application help files that hold the information you see when you press F1 to get help

* Support files that have filename extensions such as DLL (a dynamic link library that contains routines and data a program only needs sometimes), GID, or FTS

TIP There's an even faster way to get Access up and running. Open up the MSOffice97/Access folder so that you can see the Msaccess program icon. (Make sure you can see your Windows desktop behind the folder.) Drag that icon off the folder and onto your desktop. Windows copies the Access icon on your desktop and gives it the name Shortcut to Msaccess. From now on, you'll be able to start Access simply by double clicking on your new shortcut icon.

* One of the icons in the Access window is labeled Msaccess and has a golden key in it. That's the one for the Access database application you're learning about with this book, and it's the one you should click to call up the program. Do so, and you see the Access startup screen, similar to that shown in Figure 1-7.

Figure 1-7 This is the first thing you see when you start Microsoft Access.

Now you're almost at the point where the adventure is ready to start. But first, I need to tell you a little bit about the mechanics of how to make Access do your bidding.

Controlling Access

Let's pause here and step back for a moment to look at Access itself. As you know, Access runs under the Microsoft Windows operating system. One implication of this is that it behaves in ways that are similar to every other program that runs under Windows. For example, you control Access by clicking buttons, by making choices from menus, and by communicating with dialog boxes. The following sections clarify what I mean.

Toolbars and buttons

Take a moment to look at Figure 1-8, a picture of Access without a database open. Notice that the mouse cursor is pointing at a small picture of an open file folder. That small picture is a "button" that you can "push" by clicking it with your mouse. The small picture — what we call an "icon" — exists in a row of icons collected together in a toolbar. There are many toolbars within Access. Although you can display them all at once — and confuse yourself no end — it's better to let Access automatically show you the one that's appropriate for the kind of task you are performing.

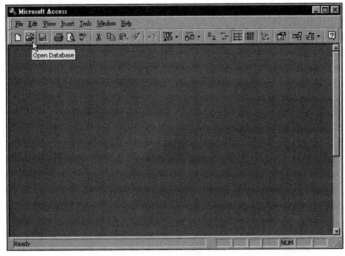

Figure 1-8   Toolbars contain the buttons you click to control Access.

The small window just below the mouse cursor is a *tool tip*: a handy reminder message that Windows pops up when you pause with your mouse cursor on a button. In this case, if you were to click the Open Database button, Access would display a *dialog box* (what we in the biz call dialogs for short) that would let you tell it which file to open.

We'll get to dialog boxes in a moment, but first...

Menus are for choosing from

Now look for a moment at Figure 1-9. What I want you to see starts at the very upper left corner of the picture, where you see the word File. That row of words, File, Edit, View, and so on are what is called a *menu bar*. When you click one of the words, such as File for example, another menu pops down.

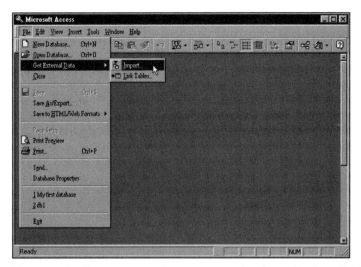

Figure 1-9 Use a menu option when a toolbar button isn't available.

In this case, I did so and then moved my mouse cursor down to Get External Data, where I paused for a moment. Access popped up a sub-menu with two options on it: Import and Link Tables.

That's how menus operate. You start at the top and work your way down by moving your mouse cursor to the option you want and then clicking it. Of course, because this is a Windows product, there are also two kinds of shortcuts you can use.

Look again at Figure 1-9, at the word File in the File menu. Notice that the *F* in File is underlined. That's your indication that you can press Alt+F on your computer's keyboard to do the same thing as clicking on File. The same thing is true of the *N* in New Database. The latter, however, is a bit different in that you can also press Ctrl+N (indicated by the Ctrl+N you see to the right of New Database).

There are two more neat things I want you to know about Access menus. First, notice the icons to the left of some menu options. These correspond to toolbar icons and indicate that you don't always have to go through the Access menu system to do what you want — you may be able to click a toolbar icon, if that's quicker. Second, see how some options aren't quite as distinct as the others. The gray options are made to appear "dimmed," which is an indication to you that while the option may exist on that menu, it isn't available at the moment. For example, the Save option is dimmed here because there's nothing to save right now.

Dialog boxes communicate

Our last little on-screen helper is the dialog box — or dialog boxes, actually, because there are a number of them. And while there are many, you use each of them in the same basic way. You make selections by clicking options, enter information by typing in text boxes, and cause actions to happen by clicking command buttons.

Just as an example — not because we're actually going to use it for something right now — let's look at a dialog box for a moment; the one in Figure 1-10 will do nicely. It's the one you see if you select Save As/Export from the File menu.

Figure 1-10 You use dialog boxes to communicate with Access.

Notice the two circles labeled To an External and With the Current along the dialog box's left side. One is white and the other contains a black dot. These are *radio buttons* that you use to toggle options. When you click one, it is selected and the other is automatically unselected. At the middle bottom of the dialog, you see a rectangle labeled New Name: That is a *text box* into which you type input for Access to use. Finally, there are two command buttons at the dialog's right side. When you click one of these, Access reads what you've typed in the text box, notes the option(s) you've toggled with the radio buttons, and then uses that information to do its work.

Every dialog with which you work in Access will contain one or more of these kinds of controls. You use them in the same way as here — entering different information or making different choices, to be sure — but always in the same way.

Well, with that out of the way, and speaking of dialog boxes, what comes next is especially worth noting.

Starting a New Database

When you first call it up, Access is empty and waiting. It doesn't yet know which of your databases you want to work with today. Look at Figure 1-11 to see how Access prompts you to find out what you want it to do. You tell Access what you want to do by clicking one of the three options in the dialog box. Click:

* **Blank Database** to create a new, blank database. "Blank" in this case means empty. The database has no data and, as yet, no place even to store the data.

* **Database Wizard** to call up a built-in helper that guides you as you create a new database.

* **Open an Existing Database** to do just that. The database will be one that may or may not actually have data in it, depending on whether or not someone's put the data in yet. Even if it doesn't already contain data, the database will have a place to store new data.

If this weren't your first time using Access, you would see in the dialog a list of databases you'd already created. Because we assume this is the first time, however, click the first option: Blank Database. Access cooks for a moment and then displays its File New Database dialog, like the one in Figure 1-12.

Figure 1-11 Access needs to know which database you want: a brand new one or one you've already created.

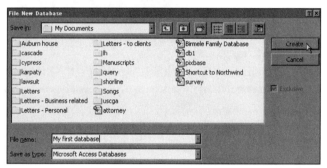

Figure 1-12 The first things to do with a new database are to name it and to save it somewhere on your hard disk.

This dialog is one of the common Windows dialog boxes that all Microsoft Windows-compatible applications use when creating database files. The dialog lets you do three important things:

* Give the file a descriptive name: one that will remind you after six months of not using the database what it is or what kind of data it might hold

* Indicate what type of file the database should be saved as

* Denote a specific location on your computer's hard disk where the file should be saved

DATABASES AND APPLICATIONS

Often, when you hear people talking about Access, you hear them call it a "database application." Then, also, you hear about something called "a database."

This imprecise usage can be confusing, because at first you may not be able to follow the context — and much of English is only understood in context. For example, how many meanings determined by context can you think of for the word "scale?" (I can think of eight right off the bat.)

Here's how to decipher what you're hearing. Microsoft Access is a database application, in that it is software that can accomplish the kinds of tasks you need to control data. Such tasks include:

- Creating a place to store data — and then actually storing it
- Making it easy for you to enter the data you want to store
- Showing the data to you, sorted or arranged in ways such that you can make sense of it
- Calling up smaller subsets of all the data you have stored
- Allowing you to perform calculations on your numerical data
- Printing your data in ways that will make sense to other people

You've probably guessed by now that it's your data — arranged somehow within Access — that is the actual database, and you would be correct in that. To put it in a nutshell: Your database is contained within the Microsoft Access database application.

Follow the next few steps to do just these things:

1. Type **My first database** in the text box labeled File name: to give this first new database a name.

2. Look for a moment at the text box labeled Save as type: just below the one in which you just entered the filename. By default, Access wants to save its files as the file type called Microsoft Access Databases. If your dialog displays something else at this point, click the little arrow button you see at the right end of that text box. Access shows you a list of file types from which you can choose — and you know which one it ought to be, don't you?

3. Finally, because this is an example that you might not want to keep after you've learned Access, save it in your computer's My Documents folder. (If this were an "important" database, you'd probably want to save it in its own folder. For now however, click the Create button you find at the upper right corner of the dialog. Access cooks for a moment and then displays its Database container, like the one you see in Figure 1-13.

Click a tab
to see its
contents

Figure 1-13 This is your database container. It holds all
the different parts of your database
together in one place.

Looking at the Database Container

Do you remember what I said earlier about Access being a container for
databases? Well, here's the proof! This is where the different parts of your
database are organized and stored. What are those parts, you wonder?
I'm glad you asked. Here's a quickie description of the parts:

* **Tables** are the basic unit of an Access database. A database can
  comprise a single table by itself — or it can comprise many tables that
  can be related to each other.

* **Queries** are the tool that you use most often to get actual information
  from your database. Although they look, act, and often feel just like
  tables, they aren't. They are objects that contain subsets of data from
  tables, subsets that you easily define as you create the query.

* **Forms** are your electronic counterpart to the paper forms we all know
  and love to fill out. They show you the data held in a table (or a query),
  usually one record at a time. That makes it easy for you to concentrate
  on one record in particular, without being overwhelmed by the entire
  table or database.

* **Reports** are parts of your database printed out on paper. They are often
  used to transmit information from your database to others.

* **Macros** are programmed instructions for simple, repetitive tasks that
  Access will automatically carry out when you want it to do so.

* **Modules** are more complex procedures written in a programming
  language called Visual Basic for Applications. While extremely useful,
  modules are for more advanced users, and so we won't be going into
  them in any detail here.

Whew! Have you got all that? I know all these things can sound confusing at first — but never fear! They'll make plenty of sense to you as you continue wending your way though this book. For now, though you've got a database, it's no help to anyone if it's empty. Just a little more background and we can remedy that...

Creation Time

As I told you in the previous example, tables are the basic building blocks of Access. So, the next thing you need to do is create one. To do so, click the New button in the database container. Access displays its New Table dialog box, like the one in Figure 1-14.

Figure 1-14 There are many ways to create a new table in your database — just highlight one and click.

The New Table dialog is your open sesame to a new Access database. In later chapters, you'll be working with each of the options you see in the dialog box. For now, however, please just read the bulleted paragraphs below to get some background information to help you better understand each option.

TIP You can create and work with almost any kind of database, but with only one at a time during each Access session.

Looking at the New Table dialog, double-click:

* **Datasheet view** to see a blank datasheet — a kind of grid that enables you to see your data pretty much all at one time.
* **Design View** to see a special kind of dialog that provides you with a systematic way of creating a new database. Incidentally, it's also the dialog that you use to modify the structure of your database if that ever becomes necessary.
* **Table Wizard** to call up a built-in helper that guides you in creating a new table.
* **Import Table** to bring into this database a table (or only the structure of a table) from another database. That other database can be on your computer or on another computer networked to your computer.
* **Link Table** to create a database comprised of one table on your computer that's connected — "linked" — to a table in another database.

Understanding Tables

okey dokey — we're finally at the place where I can show you how to create a quick and simple database. In the New Table dialog, click the Design View option. Access displays a new table in a window it calls design view, like the one shown in Figure 1-15.

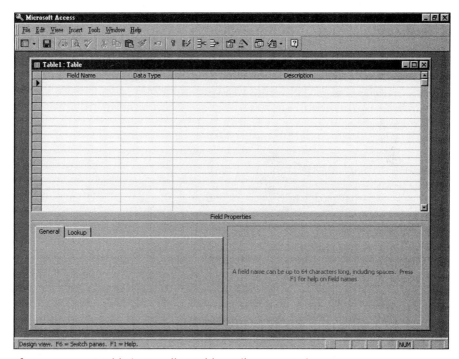

Figure 1-15   A table isn't really a table until you create it.

Your simple database will be a common address book. It will contain a single table that will hold the names and addresses of a few of your many friends. In later chapters, you'll take these same names and addresses and print them out.

Before we get started, there's something more I'd like to tell you. Take a moment and another look at Figure 1-15. Notice that the table is arranged in columns and rows. That fact is very significant as far as databases are concerned, and here's why: The data that has to do with a particular thing is collected into what we call a *record*. Each record is a row in an Access table. If you have a collection of names and addresses for example, each name and address would be analogous to a record.

The individual items of data in a record on the other hand (each one called a *datum*) are held in what are called *fields*. In your address book, each name, city, state, phone number, and so on are fields. And on an Access table, each column is a field.

You can see from the way that you create tables described here that the whole process is really very easy — just like 1-2-3-4, in fact:

1. You decide on the kind of data you want to store.

2. You give it a name.

3. You let Access know what type of data it is.

4. You describe it.

That, friend, is about as complicated as Access gets. And, as you move on to creating more complex tables, you'll find that you'll once again do this same easy task — you'll just do more of it.

Oh, yes... Don't forget to save your work!

I've included Figure 1-16 to help you stay on track as you create your first table.

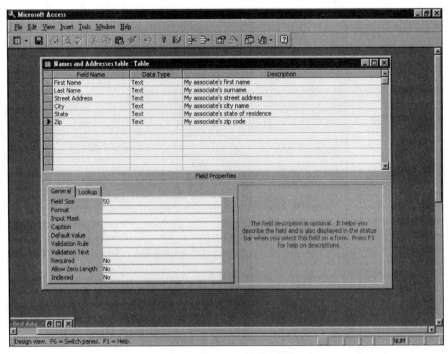

Figure 1-16 This is how your first table should be defined.

You may want to look at Figure 1-16 as you follow these steps:

1. Move your mouse cursor to the first blank area in the column called Field Name. Type **First Name** as the name for the data you're going to store in this field and press Tab . Access keeps your first field name safe and moves your cursor to the next column over, the one labeled Data Type.

2. When Access moves your mouse cursor to the Data Type field, it displays the word Text as the data type for your table's First Name. That means Access will store any character you can type in that field — which is exactly what you want it to do. Press ⌈ Tab ⌉ again to move your mouse cursor to the Description field. (If you're curious as to why Access uses the Text data type here, please see the "How does it know" sidebar.)

3. Type **My associate's first name** as a description for your table's First Name field. I recommend that you always write something actually descriptive. What you put here is what will appear in the Access status bar every time you move your mouse cursor into the First Name field.

4. Repeat the preceding three steps using the information found in Table 1-1.

 TIP Because what you type as a field description is used as a status bar prompt, you'll want to type in a full expression of what a particular field is for. This might mean that what you type seems repetitive, as in the example here. Keep in mind, however, that it won't be repetitive to your users. To them it will be a quickie reminder that might save them the trouble of having to find you and ask, "What's this for?"

TABLE 1-1   Data for Your First Database

Field Name	Data Type	Description
LAST NAME	Text	My associate's surname
STREET ADDRESS	Text	My associate's street address
CITY	Text	My associate's city name
STATE	Text	My associate's state of residence
ZIP	Text	My associate's zip code

There's safety in saving

The next thing you need to do when you create a table is to SAVE IT!

To do so, follow these steps:

1. Click  on your Access toolbar. Because this is the first time you're saving the table, Access displays its Save As dialog box, which looks like the one in Figure 1-17.

Figure 1-17 Enter a full name for the table in the Save As dialog box.

2. Type **Names and Addresses table** in the Table Name text box, and click ` OK `. Access displays a warning box about primary keys, such as the one shown in Figure 1-18.

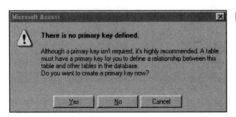

Figure 1-18 You don't need a primary key in a simple table such as the one in this example.

3. A primary key is a kind of unique identifier for a database record. For example, your Social Security number is a unique identifier that is used to identify your own personal records in government databases. For the purpose of our example, however, it's not necessary. Click ` No ` and Access saves your new table under the name you gave it in the previous step.

TIP I'd like to strongly recommend to you that you save your new tables early — right after you've defined its first field, even. And yes, I know that's not the way I showed you in our first example. I had to make a choice between doing it absolutely correctly and doing it clearly, so I chose the latter. I hope you don't mind.

Still and all, when you're doing this work on your own, remember that if you save your work early, it won't matter if later your computer loses power or if you make a mistake. Your table will be intact on your hard disk, and you won't have to repeat your efforts to re-create it. And you won't be found muttering words no one even supposed you knew.

Columns and rows

Click the View button. It's the one at the far left of the table Design View toolbar. Access displays your new table much like the one you see in Figure 1-19. Notice how your field names are arranged along the top of your table, all in a row.

Every Access table is arranged in the same way: Each record is a separate row, and each row is arranged in columns comprising the fields you defined earlier. This is the most basic depiction of data in your database. We call it a datasheet.

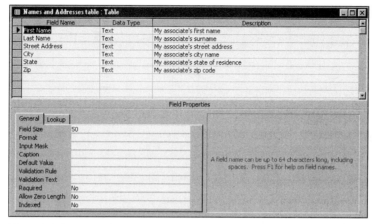

Figure 1-19 Here's an empty table, ready for the filling.

Using Datasheets

Well, now that you've got a datasheet, how about jumping in and using it?

To do so is as simple as typing a letter to your friend, and here are the steps to follow:

1. Move your mouse cursor to the first empty field.

2. Type in your data there and click   Return . Access moves your mouse cursor to the next field in the record.

   If that's the last field in the record, Access saves it and moves your mouse cursor to the first field in the next record.

3. Repeat.

Take a moment and fill in a few records in your new table. You can use the real names of your friends and associates, if you like. Or you can copy my (entirely fictitious) data as delineated in Table 1-2. Look at Figure 1-20 to see what it would look like if you followed my example as I've told it to you.

Figure 1-20 A datasheet can show you all your data at once.

Table 1-2 My Fictitious Data

First Name	Last Name	Street Address	City	State	Zip
JOE	Blow	1234 Main St	Elmwood	WA	25341
JOHN	Doe	3214 Bleeker St	London	OH	49225
IRVING	Thomasen	3940 Snowdon Ave	Harvard	MA	09234
THROCKMORTON	Feeblebottom	4423 Woof Rd	Bothell	WA	98332
SHEILA	Ciaosman	9843 Italy Blvd	Denver	CO	88324

Navigating Your Data

Putting data into records in a database wouldn't do you any good if you couldn't move among the records. Access makes that easy. Look again at Figure 1-20. Notice how there are buttons at the bottom left that bear a striking similarity to VCR controls. Figure 1-21 is an enlargement of those buttons.

Figure 1-21 Here's a close look at the navigation buttons.

From left to right the buttons are:

| ◄◄ | Move to the first record in the database |

| ◄ | Move to the previous record |

| ► | Move to the next record |

| ►◄ | Move to the last record in your database |

| ►* | Create a new record |

All you need to do to move around is click one of these buttons. When you do so, by the way, Access displays the number of the record with which you're currently working in the space that separates the buttons.

Queries Are for Information

Your table is pretty small at this point. What if it were to grow large enough to include the names and addresses of everyone in the U.S.? How could you get meaningful information from that mass of humanity? To get that information, you would create what's called a query: a precise question to Access that lets it know what records you want it to display. I discuss queries in detail in Chapter 6, "I'll Take One of These, and Two of Those." For now, however, I'd like to give you a quickie introduction to what they can do.

Let's say you became curious about who lived in a particular state, the real Washington, for example. Your query would "say" in effect to Access: Select for me the first name and last name of everyone who has WA in their State field. Figure 1-22 shows you the result: only two people, but then it's only a small database.

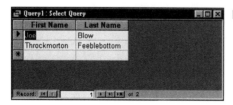

Figure 1-22 A good query shows you just the information you're looking for.

You can use the navigation buttons to move among the records in your query just as you can among records in your entire database. Handy, huh?

Forms Let You Focus

As you can probably tell, although datasheets are extremely useful animals, they can grow from a cute little cub into a large, hairy, and somewhat intense bear faster than you can mix a metaphor — too much of a good thing, in other words. That's where forms come into the picture. They are the way Access shows you a single record at a time. Look at Figure 1-23 to see one of the records from our database as it looks in a simple form.

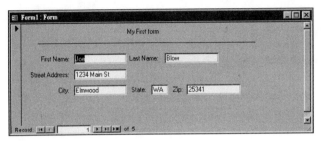

Figure 1-23 A form shows you one record at a time.

You work with your data displayed in a form in the same way as if it were displayed in a datasheet. In other words, to change the data in a field, you simply move your mouse cursor to the field and type in the new data. Access then changes the data in the form's underlying field. The navigation buttons at the bottom of the form work the same way as the corresponding buttons on a datasheet.

 TIP I find the new record button very handy when working with forms, especially when I want to use a form to add data. When you click the button, Access creates a new empty record and puts your mouse cursor right in the first field. Just type in your new record's data and away you go!

Reports Spread the Good Word

The last thing I want to introduce you to is the Access report. This is simply a collection of records from your database printed on paper — or saved to disk for someone else to print. Figure 1-24 gives you an idea of what a report created from the data in your little database might look like.

Although I'm showing you the data direct from your database table in this example, I could have just as easily printed the results of the query created in the previous section of the chapter. It's all the same to Access. And if a chart would help make your point more clear, you can also include one of those (automatically created by Access) in the report. I like it!

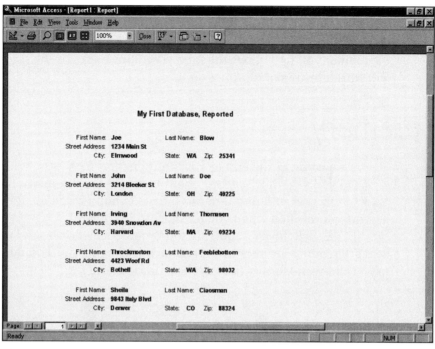

Figure 1-24   Reports show your data on paper.

BONUS

You Can Do This on Your Own

So now that you're ever so much more skillful at working with Access than when you started this chapter, here's something useful and interesting to try: add your friends' telephone numbers to your database.

And in case you need a quickie refresher, here's a simplified step-by-step:

1. Open your new database by double clicking its name in the Windows Explorer.

2. When it opens and you see the switchboard, click the button next to Enter/View Addresses.

3. When you see the Addresses form open on your screen, type in a few names and addresses.

After you've done that, you might find it interesting to click the Preview Fact Sheet button to see what you've just typed in, but in a different form. If you want a permanent copy of the new data printed on paper, click the Print button on the toolbar you find above the form. The Print button is the second one from the left, with a picture of a printer on it.

Summary

So we come to the end of your introduction to Access. What do you think? Do you see what I meant about how it's actually pretty simple if you look at one part of it at a time? In the next chapter, you see how easy it is to get helpful information when you need it.

Oh, yes — I almost forgot. My son is now a safe driver. And with his good student's discount, the monthly insurance payments are enough to keep only a *small* third-world family fully clothed, housed, and fed. I'm told it could be worse.

WHEN I NEED HELP, I PUSH THE BUTTON

2

KEY GOALS OF THIS CHAPTER

Among the responsible parental gifts that my wife and I bought for our children last Christmas, we did surprise them with some of the toys from their wish list. One in particular taught me an important lesson. Nothing too expensive, mind you. Just a contraption they'd had little hearts set on for at least the last six weeks — an eternity in kid years. The kind of toy where on the narrow side of a large box the manufacturer prints a Surgeon General's warning: "Some assembly required."

With a gleam in my eye, I ripped open the first box. My wife clutched herself, moved back, and apprehensively watched. Four excited little munchkin eyes peered from around the door behind her. I poured out all the parts on the floor in front of me. I didn't care where they fell. I was Father Man: Fearless Builder of Toys for My Children.

Bags and parts of all colors fell out of the box. There were tabs and screws and long, thin pieces of metal. At the bottom of the pile was a small printed booklet — the Assembly Manual. But I didn't care! Father Man doesn't *need* directions. Her dark eyes upon me, I felt my wife's unspoken suggestion. "Oh, okay," I said, "I'll give them a look."

The directions in the manual — written on tissue-thin newsprint — were uncertainly translated from some obscure oriental dialect. Printed there, in type barely legible, were those most dreaded words: "Insert tab A into slot B." I tore through the pile of parts. Tabs, I found. And there were plenty of slots. But none was marked with a letter that bore even a Phoenician resemblance to our alphabet. I began muttering dark imprecations.

My wife, hearing me, stood up and gave me The Look. She gathered the children and herded them out of earshot while they happily chanted, "Daddy's saying bad words, Daddy's saying bad words...."

Things are much easier for those of us using Access. For one thing, there are few tabs and no slots to be concerned with. Then again, it's normal for someone first using a software application to occasionally feel lost. In this chapter, I show you how to use Access's Help System. When we're through, you'll understand that you "aren't alone," that you won't get into trouble, break the software, or remain confused as you work with Access.

What Are We Talking About, Here?

Millions of people like you and I have used Windows and Access since the software was introduced. Not that there's anything particularly wrong with these products, but it stands to reason that a good proportion of us have encountered some problem every now and then and have turned to Microsoft for technical support. Over the years, Microsoft has learned a great deal about what's right and what's wrong with its applications. Microsoft also learned a great deal about the different ways users think and so resolve their problems — all to our benefit.

 TIP If you've got a question, Access probably has an appropriate answer waiting. Press F1 and Access displays its Office Assistant.

When you need help, most likely you'll want to learn what that thing you see on the screen actually does, or you'll wonder how to do some task. Microsoft has built into Windows generally — and Access specifically — a number of ways for you to get that help. These include:

* **Office Assistant** comprises a set of animated figures that guide you to the solution of your current problem.
* **Tooltips** are little drop-down boxes that give you the name or function of a particular object on your screen.
* **Overviews** are a special kind of help display that give you a more global perspective on the work at hand.

A WORD ABOUT READING THE MANUAL

When you have a problem with software, you can often call the company to obtain technical support. There, you will speak with a person who, while politely offering advice to you, may ask you if you have read the manual. There's more to this question than first meets the ear.

In the high-tech biz, this question is technically a form of derision. It is often shortened to "Has this person RTFM?" — an acronym for have they "read the fine manual?" That's because many a needless tech support call could have been avoided had the customer only read their manual before picking up the telephone. I'd be willing to bet that using your native intelligence, your manual, and the online help you learn about in this chapter, it's going to be very unlikely that you'll find yourself looking for Microsoft's telephone number.

* **How-to's** are step-by-step instructions that direct you as you accomplish a particular task.

* **Help Topics** are simple, old fashioned presentations of helpful information, one window-full at a time.

On-Screen Help

When I first looked at it, the Access screen looked pretty confusing. All those buttons and things — and no help to be found. Fortunately, this was one of the very first things the designers of Windows fixed. Take a look at Figure 2-1, where my mouse cursor is pointing at a button.

Figure 2-1 Tooltips clue you in to what you see on screen.

"A tooltip appears any time you pause your mouse cursor on an on-screen item for a couple seconds."

Notice that the words Open database appear in a light-colored box next to the mouse cursor. That's what we call a *tooltip*. It appears any time you pause your mouse cursor on an on-screen item for a couple seconds. Access assumes that your pause is one of indecision and so tries to help. Pretty cool, huh?

Navigating the Help System

Let's start with a quick look at help that's available from the Access main menu. At the main menu's far right side, you see the word Help. When you click it, Access displays its Help menu, which is shown in Figure 2-2.

Figure 2-2 Click the word Help to call up the Access help menu.

You'll find five items on the Help menu, each of which is highlighted in Table 2-1.

TABLE 2-1   What's on the Help Menu

MICROSOFT ACCESS HELP	Is an assistant that comes from Microsoft Office. Find out more in the following section.
CONTENTS AND INDEX	Which is the traditional help system that's been part of Windows for years. You can use it to look up helpful information much as you would look in the index of a book.
WHAT'S THIS?	Is what you use to find about things you see on the screen and want to know more about. You can find out an on-screen item's name, its purpose, and, often, a hint about how you can use it.
MICROSOFT ON THE WEB	Is a collection of sites on the Internet that contain helpful information for Access users. You can download free software and get the latest and greatest information on Access.
ABOUT MICROSOFT ACCESS	Is a treasure trove of information about your particular computer: how it's set up, what helper software is running, and what instructions your initialization files contain. This really comes in handy when you need to call Microsoft for help.

May I Be of Assistance?

Do you remember what I said earlier about never having to feel like you're alone with Access?

Follow these steps, and I'll prove it to you:

1. Move your mouse cursor to the **Help** menu and click. Access displays its Help menu.

2. Move your mouse cursor down one item to **Microsoft Access Help** and click again. Access calls up an Assistant such as the one you see in Figure 2-3.

The Assistant is the animated cartoon moving around in a little window in your screen. Though you see it here in Access, the Assistant actually comes from Microsoft Office, the suite of software of which Access is a part. For that reason, you also see the same Assistant in other Office '97 applications.

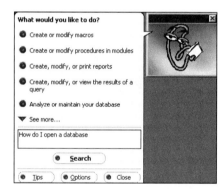

Figure 2-3 You always have an assistant ready to help you.

Next to the Assistant's window, you see a word bubble. It's the bubble that really holds the key to your finding out the information you need.

Notice that there are three parts to the bubble. First, at its top you find a question about what Access thinks you would like to do at this point. The question you see depends on where you are in Access. Second, just below the question is a bulleted list of tasks that appears to be Access attempting to answer its own question — and that's what it is. For example, if you're working with tables, then table-related tasks would be suggested. If you're working with queries or reports, then query- or report-related tasks would be suggested. Click one of the suggested tasks, and Access displays a help topic.

Hmm... What if none of the tasks Access suggests fit the bill? Well then, on to Plan B, where you move to the third part of the bubble and type a normal English question into the text box you find just below the words "See more..." Using its understanding of grammar, Access parses your question and then sees if it has the answer to your question. More often than not, it will. If it does, Access displays its new suggestions in bullets above the text box.

FEATURE FOCUS The Microsoft Office Assistant is a new feature with Access 97. It's like a little friend whose only purpose is to provide you with answers to your questions.

Our programme d'artiste

Hiding in your copy of Microsoft Office and Access is an entire cast of characters waiting to assist you. Each one has a different personality. You pick the one you like best, and then every time you need help, that'll be the one to do it. See Table 2-2 for a description of each assistant available to you.

TABLE 2-2 Office Assistants

Graphic Assistant	Description
	Clippit is a little guy who tries to help you keep it together as you do your Access work. "Keep it together" — get it?
	Dot is a changeling who gives you enthusiastic pointers to help. I wonder if he's from the same planet as that guy on Star Trek: Deep Space Nine?
	The Genius bears a striking resemblance in intellect and visage to your humble author; always even-tempered, always helpful. Allegations to the contrary by vengeful editors are false! FALSE, I SAY!
	Hoverbot is an intelligent robot who glides above your desktop, offering solutions as it thinks you need them.
	Office Logo claims not to be a distraction as it lets you take care of business. I don't know... sometimes you just have to shake your head at marketing hype.
	Mother Nature is an environmentalist changeling, gentle and supportive.

Graphic Assistant	Description
	Power Pup is a frisky little helper.
	Scribble is a cat who, unlike its real-life counterparts, is always ready to come to your aid.
	Will is my favorite scribe and helper. He always knows what's right, and he says it so well...

Changing assistants

What happens if you get bored with one assistant and want to use another? *Très easy* as the French say.

Here's how to do it:

1. With the Office Assistant bubble visible, click the [Options] button. Access displays its Office Assistant dialog box, as shown in Figure 2-4.

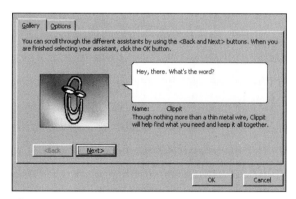

Figure 2-4   There is a gallery of options to make the Assistant your own.

2. With the Gallery tab active (which it is by default), click the [Next] button to audition another assistant. As you move through the list of assistants, you can also click [Back] to see previously auditioned assistants.

3. When you see an Assistant you like, click [OK]. Access (Microsoft Office, actually) notes your choice and implements it.

By the way, after you decide on a particular Assistant, it will appear whenever you need help in any Microsoft Office '97 product.

Help, Topically Speaking

Although you call it up from within Access, the help system is actually a facility of Windows itself. As a matter of fact, all Windows-based programs have almost exactly the same kind of help system.

No matter how you call up Access help, the bottom line is that you will eventually be presented with a small window that's full of information: a window we call "a help topic." You get the answer to your question from the information within a help topic.

"Although you call it up from within Access, the help system is actually a facility of Windows itself."

Now seems a good time to take a close look at Access help topics, so let's do so. The first thing to do is call one up. Oops — we may be getting a bit ahead of ourselves...

* If you can see your Assistant and a bubble, fine. Skip the next two bulleted items and go to the following numbered steps.

* If you can see your Assistant without a bubble, click on the Assistant's window. Access calls up a bubble. If you see it, you can skip the next bulleted item and continue with the following numbered steps.

* If you can't see your Assistant because it's dormant, press F1. Access displays your Assistant with its bubble.

Whew... Okay, here we go.

Follow these steps to quickly see a help topic:

1. Move your mouse cursor into the text box within the bubble, the one just under the words, "See more..." Type **Show me how to create a table** in the text box and press Enter, just as I've done in Figure 2-5. After you've done this, either press Enter or click Search. Access displays a list of topics it thinks will answer your question.

2. Click the first bulleted item, Tables: What they are and how they work. Access displays an overview help topic such as the one in Figure 2-6. This is how you start getting information about tables from the Help system.

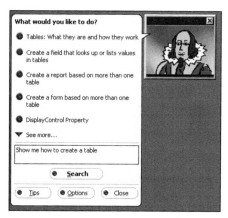

Figure 2-5 Let's see how to create a table.

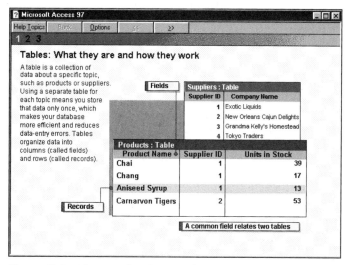

Figure 2-6 The overview is a good place to start getting help.

I'm looking it over

Let's pause for a moment and look at the overview help topic. When you think about tables, you know that they contain records and fields. You may also know that you can associate two tables — something called *joining* tables — through common fields that can be used to relate them. Notice that there, right on the help topic, are little yellow callouts pointing to parts of the picture. When you click any one of them, you see a popup window that goes into more detail about the subject.

By the way, I'm using "overview help topic" generically here. There are a number of overview topics. Each one is like a graphical index to its particular subject.

Notice the series of buttons along the top of the topic's window. Although they look much alike, there are really two kinds of buttons: ones that let you manipulate the help system and ones that let you move among help topics.

* **Help Topics and Options** are the buttons you use to manipulate the help system.

* **Back, <<, and >>** are buttons that let you move among help topics.

We'll look at all the Help Topics and Options buttons in the next section. For now, just click the >> button to move to the next overview topic. You can see an example of this in Figure 2-7. Notice how the 1 in the window's upper left corner has now become a 2. This tells you that you're now looking at number 2 of 3 related windows. And, as with the preceding window, you can click a yellow call-out to see more information about its subject.

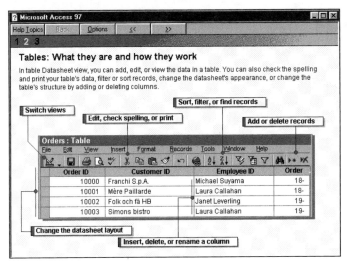

Figure 2-7   Even more details about tables.

It's optional

As you work with Help topics, you'll eventually find the need to do some house-keeping. I'm talking about the kinds of things you don't need to do all the time but are handy to be able to do when you need to. That's where the Options button comes in. When you click it, you see a menu such as the one in Figure 2-8.

Table 2-3 presents a rundown of what each one does.

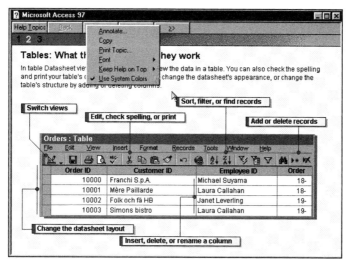

Figure 2-8 Options are for housekeeping.

TABLE 2-3 Help Options

Option	What It Does
ANNOTATE	This is where you keep notes to yourself. For example, as you're learning a new subject from a book like this, it may be that you'll think of something you know will be useful later. You can select Annotate, and Access displays a notes window. You can then type in your reminder and save it. Access places a picture of a paper clip next to the help topic's title to remind you that you left a note there. When you revisit this help subject, you can then retrieve the note.
COPY	This option lets you grab some text from the help topic so you can paste it into another document. I've found this to be useful when I need to pass along help information to my coworkers. Simply copy and paste a help topic or two into a memo — and *voilà!* It's impersonal, I know. But sometimes you just can't be everywhere at once.
PRINT TOPIC	This is one of the handiest help options. It lets you do just that: print a hard copy of the topic. I find this very useful when learning a new way of doing something with Access. I can read the steps I need to follow with the paper right next to my computer. And with my brain being such a sieve, this is a *big* help.
FONT	This option gives you a limited way of changing the help topic's appearance. You have a choice of small, normal, and large type.

(continued)

TABLE 2-3 Help Options (*continued*)

Option	What It Does
KEEP HELP ON TOP	This option gives you control over how the help topic is placed on your computer screen. As you know by now from working with Windows, the window you're working with typically is the one you can see most easily — the one that's "on top." Using this option, you can change this behavior so that the help window is *always* the one on top. I've found this to be very handy when I'm at a computer that has a high-resolution display, something like 800 x 600 pixels or 1024 x 768 pixels (pixels are simply a unit of measurement for the screen). At the more usual 600 x 480 pixels, you'll probably find that there's simply not enough screen real estate to take advantage of Keep Help on Top.
USE SYSTEM COLORS	This is an off/on toggle. You won't be using it very much unless you have some kind of wacky screen display and can't easily read the help topic because of the colors in which it's displayed.

Looking at Some Contents

Let's say that the worst has happened — what Access offers you hasn't satisfied your craving for information. After all, it's part of a stupid computer, and you're an intelligent human being. What you need to do is search out the information "by hand" as it were. The best place to start, I'd say, is with the Contents tab, which shows you a table of Help contents.

Follow these steps, and you're on your way:

1. From the Help menu, select Contents and Index . (It's the second item, right next to the book icon.) Access displays a new dialog box containing three tabs: Contents, Index, and Find.

2. If it's not the active one, click the Contents tab. Access displays its Help table of contents, such as the one in Figure 2-9.

3. Notice that the Table of Contents is much like a book's table of contents in outline form. Click one of the book icons, and Access shows you what topics are covered in that, um, chapter with an open book icon. The question mark icons you see represent individual help topics; click one and Access displays it. The book icons, on the other hand, tell you that there are one or more categories of help topics available there.

You can scroll up and down through the Table of Contents to find the information you're looking for. Once you find the right topic, click it, and Access opens the topic for you to read.

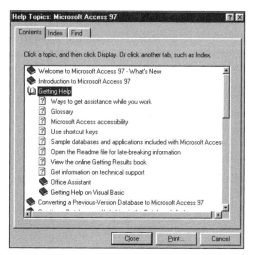

Figure 2-9 The Contents tab is another good place to start.

Using the Index

So, what happens if you can't find what you're looking for in the Contents? Well, just as with a book, you can turn to the index. The big difference here, though, is that this is a *very* intelligent index.

Follow these steps so I can show you:

1. With the Help Topics dialog visible, click the Index tab to make it active. Access displays an index such as the one shown in Figure 2-10.

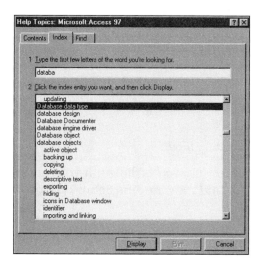

Figure 2-10 An intelligent index searches as you type.

2. Notice that there is a blank text box at the top of the dialog box. This is where you type a key word or phrase to let Access know what you're looking for. As you type the word(s), Access searches through its built-in list of keywords, trying to make a match between what you're typing and what it has stored.

3. When you see a keyword that looks promising, double click it. Access does one of two things in response:

   a. If it can, Access displays the help topic associated with that keyword.

   b. Occasionally, there will be more than one topic associated with a keyword. In that case, Access displays a Topics Found dialog box that lists possible help topics. An example of this is shown in Figure 2-11: Click one of the topic titles to display it.

Figure 2-11 One of these is sure to work!

Finding specific words

Okay. Let's say you aren't able to find the information you need from either the Contents or the Index. You're still not out of luck. Access has one last ace up its sleeve: the Find facility.

Perform these steps, and you can try it out:

1. Click the Find tab of the Help Topics dialog. If you haven't used Find before, Access calls up and runs the Find Setup Wizard, as shown in Figure 2-12.

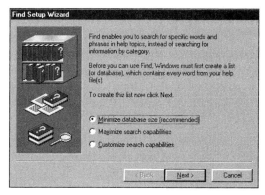

Figure 2-12 After you set up Find, you can find almost any word in the Help system.

2. In the Find Setup Wizard, select <u>M</u>inimize database size (recommended) and then click <u>Next</u> and then click <u>Finish</u>. Access cooks for a while, indexing all the words available in all the help documents it contains. When it's done, Access displays the Help Topics dialog again, this time with the Find tab facilities fully available. You can see an example in Figure 2-13.

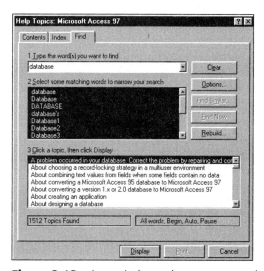

Figure 2-13 Access indexes almost every word.

3. To find a word, type it in the first text box you see at the top of the Help Topics dialog box. Access looks through its newly constructed index and calls up every — and I mean *every* — form of that word as well as the title of every help topic containing any forms of the word.

As you can see from the illustration, when I typed in the word "database," Access found well over a thousand topics that contain some form of that word. That's a lot, friend. And if you can't find the information you need from all of that, well, then it's probably just not there!

Understanding topics, jumps, and popups

As you've seen so far, you *can* get to the information you need for guidance. There's one more aspect of using help topics that I want you to understand, however. It has to do with what you see in a help topic.

Take a look for a moment please at Figure 2-14. It's a help topic having to do with the `InputMask` property, which itself isn't germane to our present discussion. I chose this topic because it happens to be a good example of some neat things contained by many Access help topics.

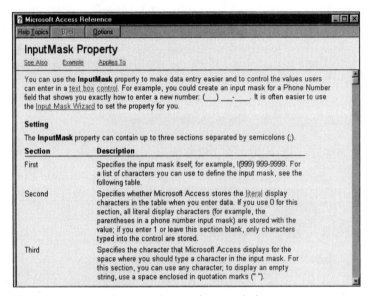

Figure 2-14 A help topic about to be revealed.

First, I want you to look at the body of the text in the help topic. Occasionally, you'll see some words that are set in green type and with a dashed underline; for example, the words "text box control" as you see in Figure 2-14. That kind of underlined text is called a *hotspot*. Hotspots often contain words that are particularly technical or stand out in some other way. The dashed underline tells you that if you click the hotspot, Access will display a popup that contains a note explaining or defining the underlined words. Figure 2-15 shows an example of what I mean.

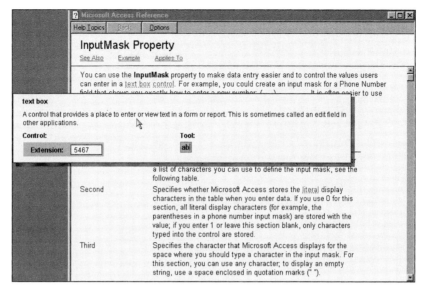

Figure 2-15 Popups often contain definitions.

Now look a bit farther down in Figure 2-14. Notice the words "Input Mask Wizard," which are also set in green type but are underlined with a solid line. Words displayed this way are connected to an entirely different help topic. When you click them, Access displays the new help topic in place of the current one.

SIDE TRIP

JUMPY, VERY JUMPY

When you work with Access help topics, you're working with text that's electronically stored and presented to you. Sure, it strongly resembles its printed cousin. But electronic text doesn't share one of a book's weak points. When you try to quickly obtain specific information in a printed book, you pretty much have to work linearly. Even if you start with an index that gives you a specific page number, you still have to turn to that page and read sequentially until you see the information you're looking for. The reason for this is obvious: That's simply the way books are made.

Well, electronic "books" such as Access help don't have that limitation. Because they store text electronically, you get to any particular tidbit of information nonsequentially. You can jump to the information, as it were. And that's exactly what people in the biz call this process: jumping. We've even made a noun out of the thing we use to do the jumping. We call it a *jump*.

A trio of notes

Now turn your attention to the top part of the help topic shown in Figure 2-14. Notice the help topic's title, InputMask Property, near the top of the screen. Just below that are three jumps: See Also, Example, and Applies To. To use any of these jumps, you simply click it. If you're curious, here's what they do:

See Also shows you a list of other help topics that are directly related to this one, kind of like a cross reference. Figure 2-16 shows you some topics related to the `InputMask` property.

Example gives you some specific ideas about how to implement the information contained in the current help topic. Figure 2-17 will give you a better idea of what I mean.

Applies To displays a list of topics that show where you can use the subject of the current help topic. Figure 2-18 shows that you can use the `InputMask` property with certain fields and controls. To get more specific information, click one of the topics in the Topics Found dialog box, and Access displays it for you.

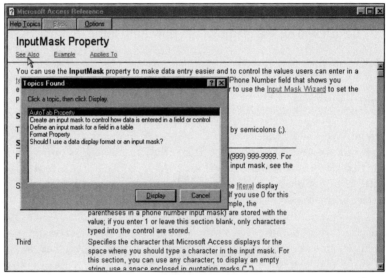

Figure 2-16   See Also's are cross references to the current topic.

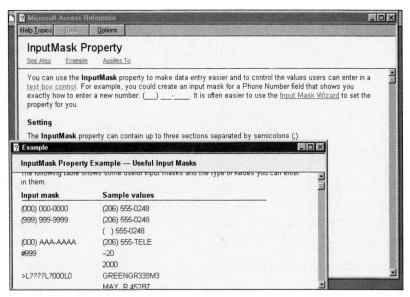

Figure 2-17 An Example of how you can use this information.

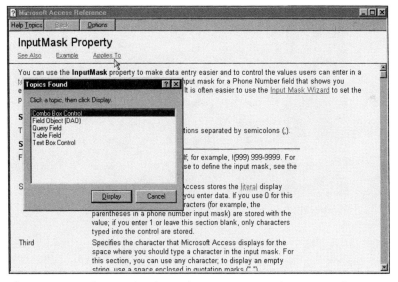

Figure 2-18 These topics show where you can use the InputMask property.

BONUS

Help on the Web

It seems these days that you can't escape the all-encompassing World Wide Web. Like most things, that can be bad or good. I'd call it bad when you have to work your way through all kinds of drivel to find useful information. I'd call it good when I see the way Microsoft has made it easy for you to get information about Access. Not that I'm "rah, rah" for the monolith, but this is one of the places they've got it right.

Here's how to get, for the most part, automatic help from the Web:

1. From the main menu, click Help → Microsoft on the Web . Access displays a pop-up menu, as shown in Figure 2-19.

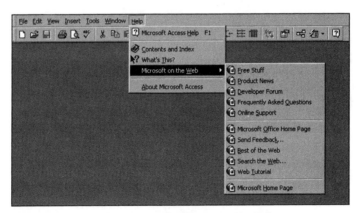

Figure 2-19 Click an item to go there on the Web.

2. Pick one of the items you see and click it. I thought Online Support looked interesting, so I clicked that one. Access called my browser, dialed my Internet service provider, and showed me a Web page such as the one shown in Figure 2-20.

Figure 2-20   Online support from the Web to my computer.

Giving 'Em the Big Call

ere's something extra: how you go to the source — the Microsoft Monolith itself. Actually, it's not all that big a deal. They offer anyone who buys Access free technical support except for the cost of the phone call — and your time, of course. The free technical support is there to help you get your Access installed and running. The free period lasts for 90 days after you first call them with a problem.

TIP   **You can pay for more extensive Microsoft technical support, of course. That support deals with more involved and time-consuming kinds of database and networking problems than simple installation questions. Instructions on how you do so are included in the online help topics.**

Before you make the call, arm yourself with some information that the person who helps you is likely to need. This includes:

* That you're using Access 97 (as opposed to Access version 7.0 or version 2.0)

* The make and model of computer you're using

* The operating system you're running on the computer

* The exact words you saw displayed by Access in any warning dialog boxes

* Your memory of what you were doing when the problem occurred
* What you did to try to, um, "fix" the problem

Some of the more technical information you need (particulars about your computer, for example) are kind of hidden away.

SIDE TRIP

DO YOU HAVE ANY QUESTIONS?

One thing is certain about using new software: You'll always have questions. And questions aren't the problem — it's getting answers that can be difficult. Turns out this is yet another problem that's been solved for you by software developers.

On the Internet, there's an often-found facility called an *FAQ*, which stands for "frequently asked questions." An FAQ is a collection of questions and answers usually compiled by whomever created the software in, well, question.

There are enough questions about Access that Microsoft has created an entire Web page devoted to its Access FAQ. You get to it by clicking <u>H</u>elp→Microsoft on the <u>W</u>eb→Frequently Asked <u>Q</u>uestions, and it looks like the page shown in the following figure.

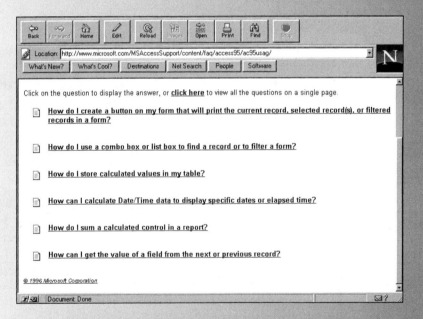

To get an answer, scroll down the Web page until you find your question. Click that question, and your browser displays the answer. If you can't find the question you want, I'm afraid you simply have to call Microsoft or speak to that geeky computer guru down the hall.

Here's how to get to that technical information:

1. From your main menu, click Help → About Microsoft Access . Access displays a dialog such as the one shown in Figure 2-21.

Figure 2-21 The Access Help About dialog is the key to your computer's software innards.

2. Move to the lower right corner of the dialog box and click System Info . Access displays a dialog box similar to the one you see in Figure 2-22.

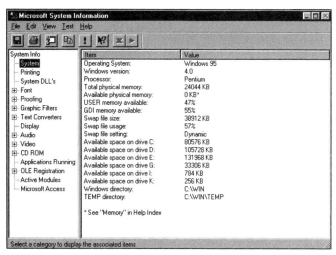

Figure 2-22 System Info shows you all kinds of information about your system.

As you can see, this dialog box and its subsidiaries show you all kinds of information about your system. Microsoft's tech support people use the information you find here and relay to them as clues to solving your particular problem.

Summary

Well, that about covers everything you need to know about getting help. I hope you understand now that you're not alone. It should be clear that if you have a problem, someone else has probably already faced it and that the answer is only as far away as a couple of keystrokes and a little reading.

In the next chapter, I show you how to jump in and create your very own database — lickety split! When you're done, you'll have your very own electronic address book.

By the way, the Christmas toys finally got put together. Turns out I had the instruction manual twisted upside down. The thing was much easier to read once I got *that* right. And the thirty bucks I gave to Joe the Handyman next door made it seem as though the toys — um — put themselves together. Of course! Fatherman the Fearless caused the toys to put *themselves* together. Me and Santa. Yeah! That's the ticket.

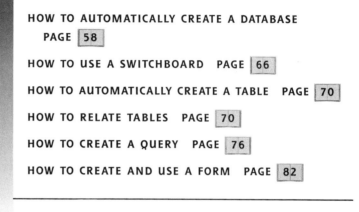

CHAPTER THREE

I'D LIKE TO JUMP IN AND GIVE IT A TRY

KEY GOALS OF THIS CHAPTER

HOW TO AUTOMATICALLY CREATE A DATABASE
PAGE `58`

HOW TO USE A SWITCHBOARD   PAGE `66`

HOW TO AUTOMATICALLY CREATE A TABLE   PAGE `70`

HOW TO RELATE TABLES   PAGE `70`

HOW TO CREATE A QUERY   PAGE `76`

HOW TO CREATE AND USE A FORM   PAGE `82`

W e were children, all gathered around the magician, waiting to be amazed. With a flourish, he brought out a small, red rubber ball. Showing it to us all, he placed the ball into my hands and closed my fingers around it. I clenched the ball in my fist.

I looked around at my friends. We all thought that we could figure out the trick, and each of us was eager to be the first one to do so. Barely listening to his magic words, I closely watched his other hand. If the magician was going to fool us, it would have to be with that. After all, I had the single, solitary rubber ball in my own hands — I knew that for a fact, and I certainly wasn't about to help him.

After a moment, the magician gave us a knowing look. Then, turning to me, he told me to open my hand. Confidently, I did so — and there were *two* small rubber balls! We'd all been fooled.

Turns out there's something of a magician called a "wizard" in your Access software. It can automatically create a database for you that includes a complete set of tables, forms, queries, and reports. In this chapter, I show you how to do just that. By the time you're done, you'll know how to use Access wizards to create all the parts for just about any database you'll ever need to use.

An Automatic Database

The first time you sit down to create your very own database can be very daunting. You have something of an idea of the data you want to store; but to do it all by yourself — knowing exactly how to get Access to do what you want — forget it! If only you had someone sitting next to you, giving you pointers, helping you along. Well, like the used-car salesman says, "Just look what I've got for you!"

> "Using Access's pre-built databases, you can automatically create everything from an address book to a workout tracker."

When you installed Access, you also installed without knowing it the framework for a number of already built-in databases, running the gamut of database types from A to Z. Using these pre-built databases, you can automatically create everything from an address book to a workout tracker. (I guess that's only A to W, but you get the idea.) For now, I show you how to create a simple address book.

Let's make sure we're on the same page

Our journey starts with opening an empty Access window, one that has no database active in it. But first, we need to be sure that we're both looking at the same thing:

✻ If you have Access running, close the database you have open but be sure you don't close Access itself.

✻ If you don't have Access running, then go ahead and open it up. When you see the initial dialog box, click Cancel.

If you've done this correctly, you should see a blank Access window such as the one in Figure 3-1.

Now that our ducks are all in a row, so to speak, I'll show you how Access automatically creates databases.

Here are the steps:

1. Move your mouse cursor to the upper left corner of the blank Access window and click ☐. Access displays the New dialog box, as shown in Figure 3-2.

   Notice that there are three tabs in this dialog: General, Databases, and Office 95 Templates. If you don't have Office 95, then you may only see two tabs. Not to worry — the Databases tab is the one that's important to you now.

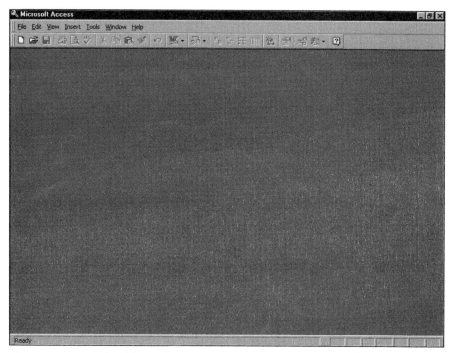

Figure 3-1 You should see a blank Access window at this point.

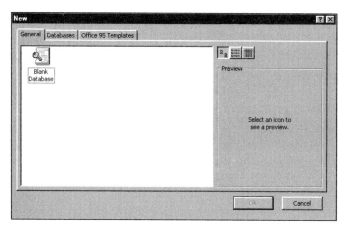

Figure 3-2 Create a new, blank database by clicking the New database button.

2. Click the Databases tab in the New dialog. The dialog display changes so that you can see all the database templates that were included when you installed Access, as shown in Figure 3-3.

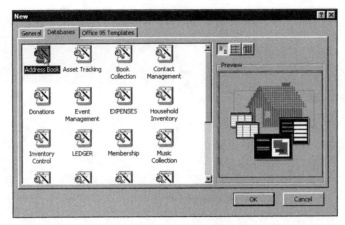

Figure 3-3 Here's a selection of database templates.

3. As you can see, there are icons displayed for all kinds of databases. (Remember what I said about "A to W?") You can scroll around to see what's available. When you're ready, however, click the one called Address Book and then click **OK**. Access displays the File New Database dialog box, as shown in Figure 3-4.

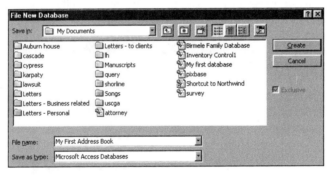

Figure 3-4 Every new database gets a name.

4. The File New Database dialog is the dialog box Access uses to create and save a database, and to do so using a specific filename. Access suggests the name Address Book 1 in the File name text box. You can accept that, of course, but I recommend that you use something more descriptive. In this case, type **My First Address Book** as the name of your database.

5. After you type the name for your database, click **Create**. Access cooks for a few moments, creating a container for your database. After it has done that, Access calls up the Database Wizard — the helper that asks you questions and then creates a database according to your answers. If you want to check what your screen should look like at this point, take a peek at Figure 3-5.

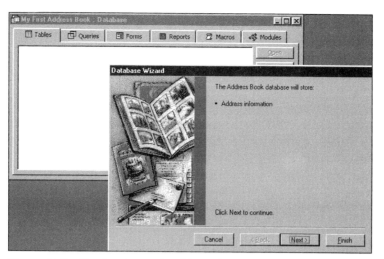

Figure 3-5 The Database Wizard is ready to help you.

FILL IN THE TEMPLATE

A *template* in computers is like an electronic framework for data. It's a description of what you want to create with your computer. In a database application such as Access, for example, a template is a description of a database. A template says to Access things such as: "the database should have such and such tables made up of this and that fields, and it should include these queries and those reports." In other words, everything a respectable Access database needs except for data!

Your servant, the Database Wizard

The Database Wizard, like all Microsoft Office wizards, is something of an electronic savant. It works by asking you a series of questions through dialog boxes. It then takes your answers and does its work, basing its efforts on what you tell it you want done.

There are two ways of working with Access wizards:

* You can let the wizard make all the decisions for you by clicking Finish in the first dialog you see. In this case, the wizard will create an address book that contains all the elements (fields, tables, queries, and reports) that the wizard offers as defaults.

* You can move from dialog to dialog, answering questions and making decisions as you go along. Then, at the last dialog you click Finish. The wizard creates an address book using only those elements you indicate that it should.

NOTE As you work with Access wizards, you never have to worry about the decisions they ask you to make. In each case, the wizard offers you options in the form of defaults. For example, in the Address book example the wizard offers to create fields for First Name, Last Name, and so on. Most often, in fact, you'll find that the default options the wizards offer will work fine for the task at hand. The neat thing is that you always enjoy a nice balance between assistance from Access and the control you retain over its operation.

As you answer the questions in each dialog, you typically click the Next button to continue. If you change your mind or simply want to review an earlier dialog box, click Back, and Access displays previous dialogs until you reach the one you want to see. You can then make any changes you like, clicking Next when you're ready again to move on. If you'd rather stop answering questions and have the wizard do the work, you can click Finish at any time. Access then automatically finishes the task, using the defaults if it needs to make any further decisions.

With all that in mind, try using the Access Database Wizard to automatically create your database.

To do so, follow these steps:

1. With the Database Wizard dialog active, click `Next`.

Access calls up the next wizard dialog box, which displays a list of all the fields it thinks you would want in the Address information table, as shown in Figure 3-6. Notice that Access knows for the most part the "correct" fields you need to store the kinds of data you would expect to track in an address book. This includes names and the parts of an address, of course. And, Access doesn't forget to make room for telephone numbers.

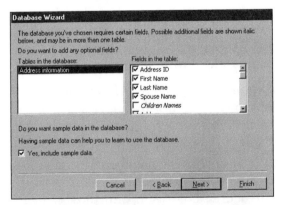

Figure 3-6 Here's where your decision-making starts.

2. Be sure to notice the list under the title Fields in the table on the right side of the dialog box. Scroll up and down that list, checking what fields Access thinks you want to track. Access also offers some optional fields in this list. The optional fields are displayed in italics. Check the fields, both optional and default, that you want for your database (or leave them checked, if Access has already done so for you). Uncheck the ones you don't want to include.

3. Before you finish with this dialog box, there's one more thing I want to bring to your attention. Down at the lower left corner of the dialog box is a checkbox labeled, Yes, include sample data. Check this box so that Access includes some sample data in your database.

   Doing this makes it easier for you to try out your database. Later, once you're ready to use the database, you can always delete the sample data even as you retain your database's structure.

4. After you choose the fields you want, click **Next** .

   Access displays the next screen in the Database Wizard, which enables you to choose a database style, as shown in Figure 3-7.

TIP **Remember that you can always change your mind. You can click Back to see the previous screen of the wizard.**

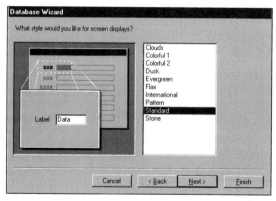

Figure 3-7 Choosing a style makes a database your very own.

As it implements your database template, Access creates forms for you to use in entering and viewing names and addresses. This screen of the wizard is where you indicate a "style" or "look" for your database. You do so by clicking one of the items listed at the right side of the dialog box. Access notes your choice and varies the look of the preview in the dialog box accordingly. If you like, you can "try on" different looks by clicking several different styles. As you do, Access displays a preview of your choice in the picture at the left side of the dialog box. You can see in Figure 3-7 that I went with the stodgy, old Standard style — but then, I'm often a stodgy, old kind of guy.

5. When you decide on the database style you want, click **Next**. Access calls the reports style dialog box, as shown in Figure 3-8.

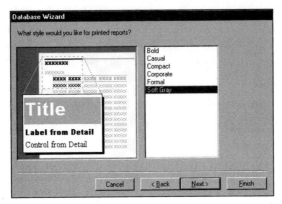

Figure 3-8   Even reports can have their own style.

Just as it creates forms, the Database Wizard also creates reports for you to print out your data. This dialog box works much the same as the forms style dialog box: You choose your style from the list at the right side of the dialog box and get an idea of what that style will look like in the sample at the left side of the dialog box.

6. Again, when you've made your choice, click **Next**. Access displays a title dialog box, as shown in Figure 3-9.

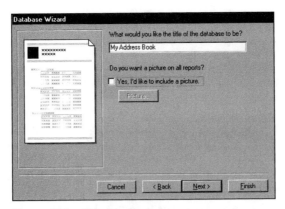

Figure 3-9   This title is what you see on your database forms.

Well, you're getting close now! About all that's left is for you to decide on a name for your database — this time, one that's displayed for you and other people to see. (Remember: The name you gave the database earlier is the name under which it was saved in Windows. It's the one used by Access, but not necessarily by you or other users.) Access offers Address Book as a title by default. I recommend that you type the word My before the Address Book to make this database truly yours.

7. Type **My** before the words Address Book in the title text box, and then click Next . Access displays the last Database Wizard dialog box, as shown in Figure 3-10.

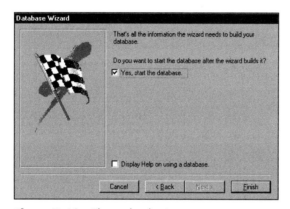

Figure 3-10   The end at last!

Well, you've almost got a database. This dialog is pretty much your last chance to change your mind — at least as far as the database wizard is concerned. You can change anything in the database once the wizard has done its work, of course; you just can't use the wizard to make the changes for you.

8. In any case, if you don't want to move backward through the database wizard dialog boxes (click Back) to make changes, then click Finish . Access cooks for a while and then displays your database's new Main Switchboard, as shown in Figure 3-11.

That's all there is to it, friend. To create any other database using a template, you do pretty much the same thing. The only possible differences would entail using different fields (which you'd expect if you were creating a different kind of database) or different styles for your on-screen display dialogs or your reports.

TIP   An Access *switchboard* is a kind of pushbutton menu.

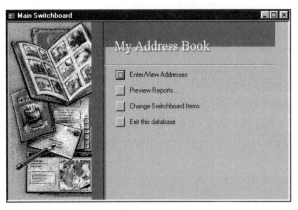

Figure 3-11   You're ready to go!

Switching, automatically

Well, you have before you your address book in the form of a special kind of Access dialog box: the switchboard. You can see it in Figure 3-11. The Database Wizard knew that you'd eventually work with your new database, and so it made things as easy as possible for you. To do so, it connected all the different objects in your database — forms, reports, and so on — to some buttons in the Main Switchboard. You click one and see your data entry forms; you click another and see your reports.

For example, here's what the buttons on this switchboard do:

* **Enter/View Addresses** opens a custom form that you use to enter, modify, and view your data.

* **Preview Reports** calls up another switchboard containing a number of reports created for you by the Database Wizard. (I discuss this in the next section.)

* **Change Switchboard Items** calls up a series of dialog boxes you use to modify the pushbutton options you find on your two switchboards (this opening one and the one you see when you click the Preview Reports button). This functionality is the result of some fairly sophisticated programming, more than we can go into in a book like this one.

* **Exit this database** does just what you'd expect: It closes this database, but it *doesn't* close Access.

NOTE   I want to draw your attention to the words "exiting the database" for a moment. Remember that your database and Access the database application are two different entities. So, when you "exit the database," most precisely it means that you are merely closing the database you are working with, not the tool (Access) that you're using to work with it.

Let's take a quick look around your new database. With the My Address Book switchboard on your screen, click the first button: Enter/View Addresses. You should see a screen similar to Figure 3-12.

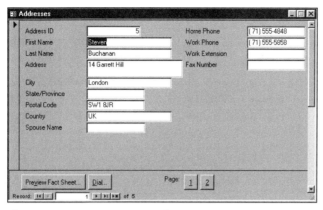

Figure 3-12 Enter and modify address data using this form.

This is the form that the Database Wizard created for you to use when you want to view or modify your data. As you can see from Figure 3-12, everything you need in an address book is right here. If you want to change anything, just put your mouse cursor in the appropriate field and start typing.

It's a two-part form (top and bottom), and you have two ways to move between the parts. The first way — and my favorite — is to grab the scroll bar handle at the right of the form and drag it up and down. Or, you can click either the Page 1 or 2 buttons to move up and down. You can see a picture of the bottom shown as page 2 of the form in Figure 3-13.

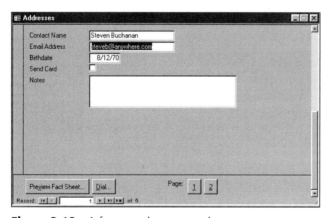

Figure 3-13 A form can have more than one page.

If you like, go ahead and add the names and phone numbers of a few dozen of your closest friends. To do so, just click the new record button at the bottom of the form and type your data into the blank fields Access displays.

Then, when you're done exploring, click the Close button at the very top left of the form. Access saves the data, closes the form, and displays the Main Switchboard dialog box.

 Warning! Warning! Warning! You're in danger, Will Robinson.

Access is very good at keeping data safe — as good as any unthinking software can be. It has to make certain assumptions to do its work. One of these is that if you move your mouse cursor into a field that's part of a record that already contains data, then you must want to modify the data in that field (and record).

If that's what you want to do, fine. If, on the other hand, what you want to do is to create a new record, then you need to be more explicit. You should click the New Record button, which is the rightmost of the navigation buttons you find at the bottom of the form. (The button is shown in the margin next to this paragraph.) Access creates a new record containing blank fields. When you type data into the fields, the data is saved as new data in a new record, not data that overwrites earlier data.

SIDE TRIP

NAVIGATING FORMSPACE

Moving from record to record in a form is as easy as pie — or at least as easy as clicking a button. By default, Access displays a row of navigation buttons at the bottom left corner of each form. These buttons are much like the buttons on your VCR (and you know how to run *that*, don't you?) and they work in much the same way.

Access Record Navigation Buttons

Button	Its Purpose
◄◄	Displays the first record in this database. Which one it displays as "first" depends on how your database is sorted. If it's unsorted, then the record displayed as "first" is the first one that was entered into the table or query.
◄	Displays the record that comes in order just before the current one.
►	Displays the record that comes in order just after the current one.

Button	Its Purpose
▶┃	Displays the "last" record in the table or query. Just as with the first record it displays, the last one is the one that comes at the end of the sorted table or query or the last one entered if the database is unsorted.
▶∗	Creates a new, blank record and places your mouse cursor in its first field, ready for you to enter data.

My Address Book on paper

When you're ready to look again at the Main Switchboard, how about taking a quick peek at the Reports Switchboard. This is where you find the canned reports created by the Database Wizard. To get there, click the Preview Reports button. Access calls up the Reports Switchboard as shown in Figure 3-14.

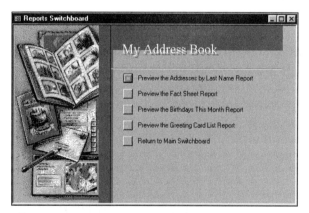

Figure 3-14 You can choose from a bunch of pre-built reports.

What you have here is a handy-dandy list of canned reports. The data for the reports comes from the names and addresses stored in your database. The first one, Preview the Address by Last Name Report, shows you a list of all the people's names waiting there in your database, sorted by — well — their last names. (This is why you should give descriptive names to the objects in your databases. It makes things easier for everyone.) Click the button next to the label and you see a preview version of the report, very much like the one in Figure 3-15.

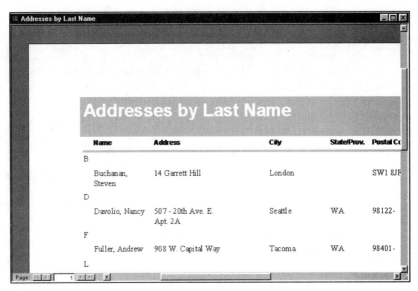

Figure 3-15 A close look at your friends.

The reason Access shows you a preview of your report rather than simply going ahead and printing it is so that you can change it at the last minute, if you'd like. Access assumes that you may not quite like the way it's laid out the report. Perhaps the spacing isn't quite acceptable. Maybe you'd rather have the report printed in portrait mode (long side up and down) rather than in landscape mode (short side up and down). The more you get into Access, the more you'll find that it is extremely flexible. If and when the report looks okay to you, click the Print button on the toolbar and, in a few moments, you'll see your report sliding out of your printer.

If you'd rather not print the report at this time, click the Close button on the toolbar. Access closes the report and displays the Reports Switchboard. When you see the switchboard again, you can preview other reports or you can click the Return to Main Switchboard button. Access closes this switchboard and opens the Main Switchboard.

Using the Table Wizard

Well, you've got something of an address book cooking here. But what if you wanted to expand it a bit? For example, what if your friends have children? I'd like to show you how to use the Table Wizard to create another table for your database, one that will track the little darlings.

 X-REF First, you have some design decisions to make. I haven't discussed database design much yet. That comes in the next chapter, Chapter 4, "It's All in the Design." For now, we the unknowing will simply have to use our common sense. ("Using our common sense" brings to mind a story I read in Reader's Digest once. Seems a guy was at work when his boss asked him to sweep the place. "But I'm a college graduate," the fellow complained. "Oh," answered the boss, "in that case, I'll show you how.")

There are two things all children have, two pieces of datum we can track. They have parents, and they have names. The former is necessary for them to exist; the latter is so their parents can be specific when they complain to each other about their little — um — darlings. Each of the people (parents, presumably) now in our Address Book also has a unique number associated with his or her name. Because one parent can have many children, we'll relate the two tables using that unique number. You'll understand what I'm talking about as you work through the exercise.

Preparing the wizard

Let's get started. First, I want you to make sure that My Address Book is the active database. It doesn't really matter whether or not you can see a switchboard; we just want it out of the way for now. If it's visible, I'd recommend you either put it away for the moment by clicking its minimize button or close it by clicking its close button.

Once it is, follow these steps as I show you how it's done:

1. Expand the My Address Book database container by clicking the Restore Window button at the upper right of the container. Access expands the database container.

2. Click the Tables tab to make it active, then click ☐ New ☐ to call up the New Table dialog box, as shown in Figure 3-16.

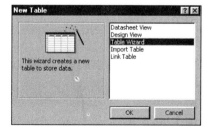

Figure 3-16 The Table Wizard helps you create a table to store your data.

3. On the right side of the dialog box, you see a list of table-related tools. Highlight the one called Table Wizard and click ☐ OK ☐. Access calls up the Table Wizard dialog box, as shown in Figure 3-17.

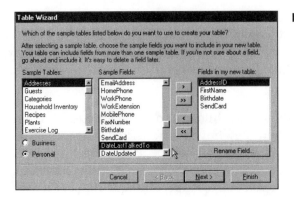

Figure 3-17 You can automatically create tables to store business and personal data.

As you can see, the Table Wizard has the capability to create all kinds of tables, including business and personal. Because you're working with a more personal database, it's more likely that you'll find the kind of table you need among the personal types.

4. Move your mouse cursor to the lower left of the dialog box and click the Personal radio button. Access changes the display to include personal kinds of data tables.

5. Our friend, Addresses, is right at the top of the list, so select it.

6. Move over to the next list, labeled Sample Fields. This is the list where you choose fields to be included in the new table. Scroll up and down the list, highlighting field names and then clicking the single right arrow to the right of the list. Access moves the field you chose from the sample fields to the list of fields to be included in your new table. I included four fields in my children's table: AddressID (which will be renamed), FirstName, Birthdate, and SendCard.

TIP The four arrow buttons are pretty common in Windows. They're always used in the same way as within the Table Wizard dialog box: to help you move fields or whatever you choose from a list of items to another list that shows what items you've chosen. In this case, you move sample field names to the fields that will be included in your new table. From top to bottom the buttons do the following:

> Move a single item from the sample list to the list of items to be included

>> Move all of the items in the sample list to the list of items to be included

< Move a single item from the list of items to be included back to the list of sample items

<< Move all of the items to be included back to the list of sample items

7. You'll want to rename the AddressID field ParentID. That way you won't get confused by two tables containing fields of the same name. With AddressID highlighted, click [**Rename Field**]. Access displays the Rename Field dialog box as shown in Figure 3-18.

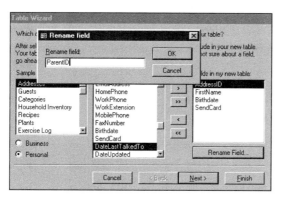

Figure 3-18   You can rename any field — even before it's made!

8. Type **ParentID** in the Rename Field dialog and click [**OK**]. Access renames the field and shows you the new name in the list of fields to be included in your table in the Table Wizard dialog box. After the name change, your Table Wizard should look like the one in Figure 3-19.

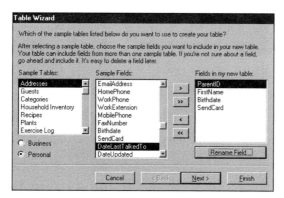

Figure 3-19   The Table Wizard should look like this after you select the fields you want.

She's off and running

Now that you've made most of the important decisions, you're ready to have the wizard create the new Children's table.

To do so, follow these steps:

1. Make sure that the fields you've selected match the ones in Figure 3-20. After you've done that, click **Next** . Access calls up the next dialog box, where you're asked for a name for your table.

2. The dialog offers you the name Address for your new table by default. You already have a table by that name (silly Access), so type **Children** in its place (see Figure 3-20).

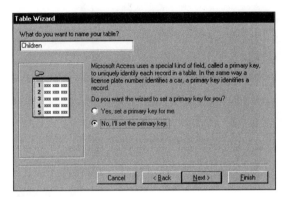

Figure 3-20 You have to name your new table.

3. Also in this dialog box are two radio buttons having to do with a primary key. We don't want Access to set the primary key — actually you don't need one for this table — so click the No, I'll set the primary key radio button and then click **Next** . Access displays the next dialog box, as shown in Figure 3-21.

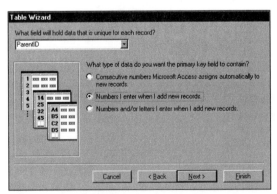

Figure 3-21 Access wants each record to be unique.

4. Access wants to make sure that each record in a table is unique in some way. In this dialog box, it offers you the ParentID field for that purpose. That's okay as far as it goes. We don't want Access to automatically

enter a number for that field in each record. To keep it from doing so, click the Numbers I enter when I add new records radio button and then click `Next`. Access displays the next Table Wizard dialog box, as shown in Figure 3-22.

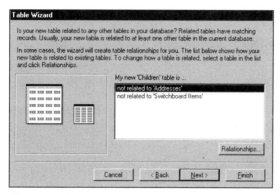

Figure 3-22   Relationships among tables, like those among people, are important.

5. Access is one of a family of more capable database applications called *relational databases*. That's because Access can connect its database tables to each other, something I teach you about in Chapter 7, "Relationships Are Important." Because it is a relational database application, Access needs to know how tables are related. The way it wants to relate tables doesn't work for your address book, so for right now you don't want the tables to be related. Just click `Next` at this point. Access calls up the last Table Wizard dialog box, as shown in Figure 3-23.

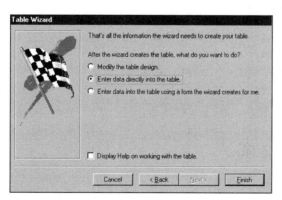

Figure 3-23   Finally, the end!

6. While you will soon be able to do so, you're not yet at the point where you can jump in and modify a table's design. So, click the Enter data directly into the table radio button and then click `Finish`. Access creates

your table and displays it, ready for you to enter data, as shown in
Figure 3-24.

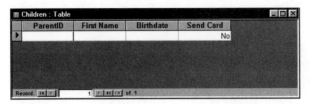

Figure 3-24 Your new table is ready for its data.

This table sure doesn't look very useful, does it? I mean, you can enter data
into it, but it's not very elegant. There must be a better way, and that's what's
coming next.

Running the Simple Query Wizard

In most database applications, a query is merely a way of interrogating your
database. You can use queries for that same purpose in Access, of course, but
I'm going to show you how you can use a query to manipulate your database as you enter data and get useful information at the same time. What I
have in mind is the following: What if at the same time you enter children's
names into your database, you have Access look up and display their parents'
names? In a moment, you'll do exactly that with the Access Query Wizard. First,
however, we need to take a short side track.

Do you remember including a field called ParentID in our Children database? And do you also remember that you included an AddressID field in the
Addresses table? Those two fields — in different tables — hold similar kinds of
data. They're close enough, in fact, that you can use whatever number happens
to be in an AddressID field as shorthand for the name of the person in that
record. You can then store only that number (and not the entire name) in the
Children table. Pretty efficient, don't you think?

For Access to be able to work this magic, you need to make sure it knows
exactly how you want the Addresses and Children tables to be related to each
other.

Here's how you go about it:

1. From the Tools menu, choose Relationships, as shown in Figure 3-25.
   Access displays the Relationships window with the Show Table dialog
   box on top of it. Double click the Addresses table and double click the
   Children table, then close the Show Table dialog box.

Figure 3-25 You get to Access relationships through this menu item.

2. In the Relationships window, you can see our two tables: Addresses on the left and Children on the right. Click the AddressID field in the Addresses table and drag the field to the ParentID field in the Children table. As you do the dragging, Access changes your cursor so that it looks like the one in Figure 3-26.

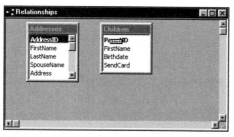

Figure 3-26 You click and drag fields to indicate relationships.

After you drag the AddressID field to the ParentID field in the Children table, Access displays a Relationships dialog box, as shown in Figure 3-27. This is where you specify exactly what kind of relationship Access should make between these two tables. Because the two tables are joined logically, we also call the relationship between them a *join*.

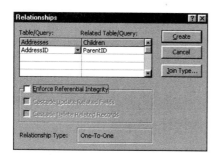

Figure 3-27 Relationships are joins.

3. Click ⟨Join Type⟩ to see more of what I mean. When you do, Access displays its Join Properties dialog, as shown in Figure 3-28.

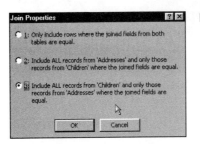

Figure 3-28 We want a family relationship: few parents and many children.

4. There are three choices for the kind of join/relationship the two tables can have. Because a single parent can have many children, use the third option, the one where all the records that match a particular parent are joined. To do that, click option 3 then click ⟨OK⟩, and finally click ⟨Create⟩.

And that's all there is to it!

Going with the Query Wizard

What I'm about to show you has to do with what I find most fascinating about Access. This is where we mix data and information in such a way that our work becomes easier — and more interesting, actually. I'm going to walk you through the process by which you take data from your Addresses table and use it to make entering data into your Children table easier and more accurate.

Now, if you'll follow along, here we go:

1. With the database container active and visible, click the Queries tab. There are no queries in your database at this point, so all you see is an empty container. (That, by the way, is also why the Open and Design buttons are "grayed out" and unavailable.)

2. Click ⟨New⟩ and Access calls up its New Query dialog, as shown in Figure 3-29.

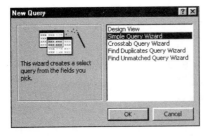

Figure 3-29 All new queries start here.

3. You're creating a simple query, so move your mouse cursor to Simple Query Wizard in the list of query types at the right side of the dialog box. Highlight it by clicking it and then click **OK**. Access calls up the first dialog box in the Simple Query wizard, as shown in Figure 3-30.

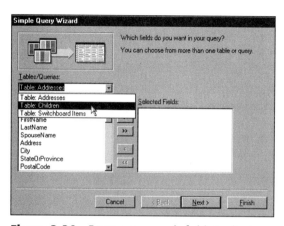

Figure 3-30 Every query needs fields to display.

4. There are three parts to this dialog box: the list of Tables/Queries, the list of Available Fields in each table or query, and the list of Selected Fields. For your current purposes, the Children table is most important, so choose it from the list of Tables/Queries. Access displays all its fields in the list of Available Fields. Move all of the Children table's fields over to the list of Selected Fields.

5. With the same dialog box still open, choose the Addresses table from the list of Tables/Queries. All you need from the Addresses table are the AddressID, FirstName, and LastName fields, so move these over to the list of Selected Fields. When you're done, your Simple Query Wizard dialog box should look like the one in Figure 3-31.

NOTE I wonder if you noticed that Access added the names of the tables to the FirstName fields in your list of Selected fields? Access did so to avoid confusion about which FirstName should be referred to. It's kind of like the way our mothers would call us by our full name when they were mad and wanted us to behave *right now!*

6. Click **Next** and Access displays a dialog box where you indicate whether you want a detailed or summary view of the data. The dialog box is shown in Figure 3-32. In this case, you want to see every record, so leave the Detail radio button clicked.

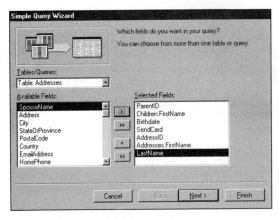

Figure 3-31 Your fields are all chosen.

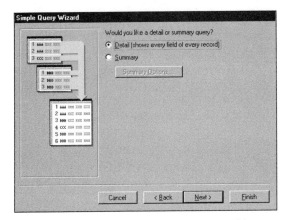

Figure 3-32 Detail shows you every record in this query.

7. With that taken care of, click **Next**. Access shows you the last Simple Query Wizard dialog box. This one's certainly "last but not least" because it's where you give the query a name. If you look for a moment at Figure 3-33, you'll notice that I've named the query "Children Query." The reason I've been very precise in naming the query is so that later, when I've forgotten the details or reasons behind some of my decisions regarding this database's design, I won't be confused by the names I've given its parts. Type **Children Query** as the name for your query and then click **Finish**. Access cooks for a moment, creates the query, and then opens it for you to enter data.

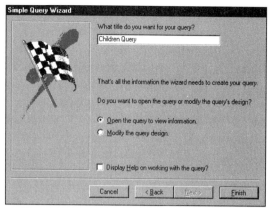

Figure 3-33 Each query should have a complete name.

Using Your New Query

So you've done it! You have a new query. Now comes the neat part I was telling you about.

Look for a moment at Figure 3-34. It's a datasheet view of the new query with some data I've entered. Here's what I find so fascinating: When I enter a number into the ParentID field, Access looks up the first and last names of the person in the Addresses database who has that same number in their AddressID field. Access then takes those names and automatically displays them in my Children Query. This makes it *much easier* for me to keep straight the names of which child goes with which parent. In this case, Janet seems to have two boys, while Nancy has one girl.

	ParentID	First Name	Birthdate	Send Card	Address ID	First Name	Last Name
	1	Bev	6/30/53	Yes	1	Nancy	Davolio
	3	Chris	6/30/80	Yes	3	Janet	Leverling
	3	Michael	12/18/81	Yes	3	Janet	Leverling
*					(AutoNumber)		

Figure 3-34 Our first query!

One last thing before we move on: Although the query shows me the parents' names as I enter children's names, the parents' names aren't stored again with the children's data. Remember, all you're storing in the Children table is an ID number, the child's name, the child's birthday, and whether you should send a card. You've created this query for entering data into the Children table. In other words: the parents' names are merely being displayed to make it easier for you to add data. The actual parents' names are each stored once in their own table, the one we called Addresses.

Yes, I find this kind of thing to be cool — and yes, I lead a sedentary, unexciting life.

BONUS

Creating with the Form Wizard

The last thing I want to show you in this chapter is how easy it is for you to have Access automatically create a form for you to use for viewing and arranging your data. What you're going to do is have Access use your new query in datasheet view to create a form.

Follow along, and you'll see what I mean:

1. With your new query open in datasheet view, click 🖼️ on the toolbar.

   When you click the button, Access cooks for a moment, and then *voilà!* You see before you a form containing your query's information. It should look much like the one in Figure 3-35.

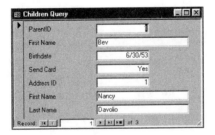

Figure 3-35 A form derived from a query looks just like a form derived from a table.

2. Save your form by clicking on the toolbar. I gave my version of the form the name Children Form. I recommend that you do so too.

While I have your attention, take a second look at the new form. Notice that at its bottom, Access has automatically placed navigation buttons. I told you earlier that Access did that, and now you know that I can be trusted to always tell you the truth.

Summary

Well, it's been something of a long road, this chapter. I trust you've learned that you really don't have to know much about database theory or about how Access works to be able to automatically create a database — and to begin using it. In chapters to come, we get into more of the nitty gritty of Access. For now, however, why not try to create your own database? If you're using this at home, a database to track videos you own might be useful. If you're at work, you'll blow away your bosses if you show them how well you can track assets with Access. (Note: People working in yuppie offices can create a wine list database instead.)

By the way, remember the magician? Turns out that what I thought was a single ball he'd placed into my hand was actually two foam rubber balls he had cleverly squeezed together. But please don't tell my kids — I showed it to them, and they still haven't figured *that* one out!

GETTING MORE THAN OUR TOES WET

THIS PART CONTAINS THE FOLLOWING CHAPTERS:

This part of *Discover Access 97* delves a little deeper into the nitty gritty of working with Access. As you know by now, Access is more than just a simple database program. Forms, reports, datasheets, tables, queries — they're all parts of Access that contribute to creating useful databases. In Part One, you received a healthy introduction to these elements. Here, you'll fine-tune your Access skills with more detailed examples and explanations of Access's various components, as well as learn the essentials of planning and creating good databases and the power of creating relationships between Access tables. By the end of this part, you will be well prepared to create a database from scratch, to create easy-to-use forms for data entry, to create queries that turn the data into information, and to create reports that let you share that information with others.

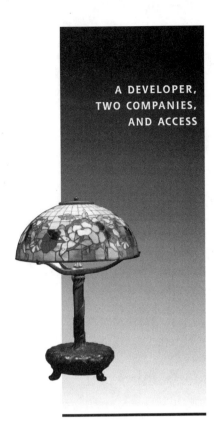

If Stan Leszynski had to use one word to describe how Access is used in his two companies, it would be "versatile." Both of his companies have worked with Access even before version 1.0 was released to the public, and Leszynski is the first person outside of Microsoft to create an end-user solution.

In 1982, Leszynski started his first company, called Leszynski Company, Inc. (www.lciinfo.com), a consulting firm. Using Access, the firm creates very powerful and cost-effective solutions for hundreds of companies that range in size from the mom-and-pop Quick Stop Shop all the way to AT&T. For workgroup-sized applications (1 to 30 users), Leszynski says there's almost nothing that Access can't do; the reason is versatility.

For smaller solutions, Access can be used to create a quick data-entry application in as little as 50 to 100 hours of development time. Even such simple applications can radically alter the way a company functions, perhaps saving hundreds of employee hours per month, says Leszyinski. Access's capability to let you quickly build data tables, validation rules, forms, and reports and to pull them together with a switchboard menu means that you don't have to be "super geek programmer" to make Access work effectively.

For larger solutions, Leszynski uses Access as one tool in a multi-faceted solution, sharing the workload with Excel, Word, and other products. High-end Access applications provide forms that link beyond Jet data to server-based records on micros, minis, or even mainframes. Such robust applications usually include Visual Basic for Applications (VBA) code to automate complex processes or to assist users with specific tasks.

Leszynski's second company, Kwery Corporation (www.kwery.com), which creates tools and utilities for developers, shipped the first retail Access add-on product, called "Access To Word." Access code itself was used to create a wizard that allowed users to select records from Access and merge them seamlessly into Word. (Unfortunately for Kwery Corp., Microsoft liked the idea so much it added these capabilities into Access 2.0 and put the product out of a job!) More recently, Kwery has been able to create advanced wizards that do things such as building databases automatically from a specification document and write code or audit VBA code.

Leszynski, who has written a book on Access and contributed to 12 other Access or Visual Basic books in addition to writing the Developer's View column for *Access/Visual Basic Advisor* magazine, says that the sky is the limit with Access; almost any task can be coded into Access as a wizard, builder, or menu add-in using its own forms and language.

IT'S ALL IN
THE DESIGN

KEY GOALS OF THIS CHAPTER

4

Outside the conference room the weather was warm and sunny; inside it was hot and tense. The design committee had been given an assignment by the High Poobah of the startup genetics company: to create a carbon-based, fuel-efficient, load-bearing animal. What started as cordial discussion and planning among colleagues had deteriorated. Scheduled for three days, the staff had been at their "discussions" for six weeks now.

Eighteen designs had been submitted. The ground rules required unanimity. With each design some member of the committee had found fault, and so none could be agreed to. Careers were being wrecked, families broken, suicide and homicide were actively contemplated. The scent of sweat and fear leaked under the door and into the hallway.

Aren't you glad you weren't there?

As you've seen so far, you can get up and running with a simple database very quickly using Access wizards. They're helpful, it's true, but using wizards won't give you an understanding of the concepts underlying the design of a database. If a situation comes up that's not well handled by a wizard, what would you do?

Well, actually, you're in pretty good shape already. By now you've got the beginnings of a practical background in databases and how they operate. With that, you're at the point where I can give you something of a more theoretical foundation.

In this chapter, I show you how to go about planning a new database. You start by looking at the nature of data and how it compares with information. I give you a list of the things you want to think about as you get started with a database. You then see how to decide what objects to create within Access that turn the abstract into something real. I finish by showing you a couple of wizards Access has that will help you fine-tune your new database.

Is It Data or Is It Information?

One of the most important distinctions in the database world is the one between data and information. You might be surprised to learn that they're not the same things. Data — the plural form of "datum" — describes attributes that a thing possesses. Information, on the other hand, is what you get when you meaningfully combine data. Let me give you an example.

Here are attributes — data points — possessed by some animals.

* Has two eyes
* Bears live children
* Has vertebrae
* Has two ears

So far, this data could fit an awful lot of animals, human or otherwise. If you try now to put the data together to get information, you might be fairly baffled. Let's add some more data to the mix.

* Has four legs
* Has whiskers
* Can growl

I can see your mind working, combining these data with data from your life experience. By making simple comparisons, you've already come up with the information that, when put together, this data don't describe human animals — well, not sober human animals anyway. Let's add one more datum.

* Can meow

Putting all this data together, we can reasonably figure that it best fits the animal sitting on my lap as I type this: *felis domesticus*, the common house cat. *Eureka!* We have achieved information!

"One of the most important distinctions in the database world is the one between data and information."

The point I'm trying to make is that a datum by itself is not information — it's a simple attribute: the simpler the better, as far as databases go. And even many datums — excuse me, data — simply shaken together don't equal information. No, to derive information, you have to put together your database's data in some meaningful way.

First, Stop and Think

Creating a new database is, well, a creative process — more cerebral than immediately practical. As a matter of fact, the first thing you need to do when creating a database is to turn away from your computer. I recommend that you turn it off, even. That's because every efficient database begins in your mind, not in your computer. It begins with a plan in which you look at the database question as a whole, refining that plan down to its details before you actually create the database. The central question you want to be able to answer is: What information will I need to obtain from this database?

There are two ways you can go about designing your database:

* **Top-down,** in which you look at the tasks you need to accomplish and decide what tables, queries, and reports you need in your database to get the tasks done.

* **Bottom-up,** in which you look at the information you need to provide and decide what tables, queries, and reports will let you do so.

I'm a "bottom-up" kind of guy as far as database design goes. I figure that the information needed is a function of the tasks that need to be accomplished. And so, if I can get a handle on the information, then the rest will automatically fall into place.

A Mental Checklist

I've found it helpful to use a checklist when I sit down to design a database. Basically, I look at the tools available in Access and then decide which of them I'll need to use — or rather, which of them my users will need to use — in order to get the information they require.

What will people want to know?

This is the most basic question you want your database to answer. In the case of our Address book, the types of information that people will want include "what is so-and-so's address?" and "what is so-and-so's telephone number?" If they will want to know more related information (about the children of the people listed in the database, for example), then you know that you're probably going to need more than one table.

What data is available?

This is where you look at the preceding question, and begin to decide what data you need to answer the question. In the case of your Address book, you know the full name, address, and phone number of each person listed. That kind of data is intuitive. What's less intuitive is the kind of data that results from decisions we make about people. For example, if you want to track your decision about whether you're going to send someone in your database a birthday card, then you also need to include that fact as data to be stored in its own field.

Tables are necessary

You can't have a building without building blocks, and you can't have an Access database without tables. And because Access is a relational database program, you can end up with a large number of tables.

To get this process started, I usually take a small tablet of paper and first create my tables on paper, one sheet per table. I want to arrive at the point where each table is small and pretty much self-contained. If I see that I need to combine data from two or more tables, I make sure that each of the tables has a single field I can use to make the connection.

This process is called *normalization*, and I'll give you a more concrete example of it in a moment. For now, here are the guidelines I follow:

* Each field in each record may contain only one particular value: a single datum, in other words.
* Each table should not contain fields that contain the same kind of data. In other words, you shouldn't include two "city" or "first name" fields in a single address record.
* The value of each field must be directly related to the key field for a particular table so that the values the fields contain make sense together. For example, it wouldn't be rational to have fields containing the titles of library books as well as fields containing people's names and addresses in the same table. It would make sense, however, to relate a smaller table of names and addresses with another table containing the library book titles.
* The values of non-key fields must be independent of each other.

I know this sounds too obvious for words, and I don't mean to be overly pedantic. It's just that this is a concept that's central to the design of efficient databases, ones we call normalized. And it's upon such a simple basis as this that all the best databases are created.

NORMALIZATION

Normalization is a process in which each table in a database is checked to make sure that it is as small as possible, easy to understand and change, and each field in its records contains a unique and non-repeating type of data. In practice, this means that if fields in a record are found to be common, then the table is divided until all its records contain unique data. When the tables cannot be further divided, the database is said to be fully normalized.

In the case of the address book example you created, you know by looking at your list of data to be tracked that you will probably want to have at least two tables. One table will store the normal kinds of name and address data found in any phone book. The other table will be related to it, and it will contain the data having to do with the children of the people you listed in the name and address table.

Different types of data

There's one last bit of knowledge I've found helpful when creating tables: knowing exactly what kind of data can be held by each field in a database. The type of data you choose to store in a field has a direct bearing on how efficiently your database operates.

Table 4-1 contains a list of data types supported by Access. I've included a short description of how much space is taken up by each type of data. Remember: Smaller is better. If you can store a datum in 50 bytes, then you never want to take up more room than that.

FEATURE FOCUS The Hyperlink data type is new in Access 97. It lets you jump right to another Access object, to a document, and even to a page on the Internet!

Forms for inputting and browsing

Once you know what tables your database will contain, it's time to think about the forms that you want to include. If you've done your normalization well, you'll likely find that each table lends itself to an individual form. Each of these entry forms provides you or your user a view of a bite-sized chunk of your database.

TABLE 4-1 Types of Data

Data Type	What It Stores	How Much Space It Needs
TEXT	This type of data includes any characters you can type. In the case of numbers, they should be numbers you don't use in any calculations.	By default, Access makes room in the table for 50 characters (50 bytes) of data for this field in each record. You can have up to 255 characters, however. Also, Access only stores as many bytes as you actually type in. That way, for example, if you type 30 characters in a field you've defined as 50 characters, Access only uses 30 bytes worth of disk space.
MEMO	Long textual data.	Up to 64,000 characters, normally. This might sound like a lot, but it's really not that much. A memo field actually takes up 10 bytes in your table. The actual memos themselves are stored in another table that is automatically linked to the one containing the memo field. Each record (memo) in the linked memo table grows just big enough to hold whatever you type in it — up to the approximately 64,000 character limit, of course.
NUMBER	Number values you use in calculations.	Each number value can use 1, 2, 4, or 8 bytes of memory, depending on how large is the number you store in the field.
DATE/TIME	Dates and/or times. The value of the dates can run from the year 100 through a post-Star Trek 9999.	Dates always run 8 bytes.
CURRENCY	Money values or numbers that need to be calculated with up to 15 characters of precision to the left of the decimal and 4 characters to the right of the decimal.	8 bytes.

Data Type	What It Stores	How Much Space It Needs
AUTONUMBER	A number automatically created and inserted by Access that's unique for each record. It can be serial (1 through *n*) or random.	4 bytes.
YES/NO	An either/or number. For example, it can be a Yes or a No, a True or a False, or an On or an Off.	1 bit. (This is the smallest type of data Access can store.)
OLE OBJECT	A discrete object such as a picture, a spreadsheet, or a document that's linked or embedded in your Access table.	Up to a gigabyte (1,000 megabytes) or the size of your computer's hard disk, whichever is smaller.
HYPERLINK	Text or numbers configured as an address of information located somewhere on your computer, on your computer network, or in cyberspace.	A hyperlink is made up of three parts, each of which can use up to 2048 bytes of memory.
LOOKUP WIZARD	A special field that lets you choose a value from a list of values contained in another table.	This will be the same size as that of the primary key field used to do the lookup.

 X-REF **I take a closer look at forms in Chapter 9, "Formally Yours," but I think it's appropriate here to give you a couple of pointers.**

✳ Lay out your form so that similar types of data are found near each other. For example, first names go well right next to last names; addresses are most easily found right under those names.

✳ Neatness counts. Instead of scattering your data entry fields hilter kilter around a form, neatly align their left margins. Use lines to logically separate disparate fields. You'll find that the more orderly your forms are, the more quickly other people will be able to understand and use your database.

Querying questions

If getting information from a database is your main purpose, then queries are the main tools you use to achieve that purpose. They're like a bridge from your data to the reports you print to share the information in your database. They also let you work with subsets of your data, subsets that are often easier to work with and informative in their own right.

Here are some things to think about when contemplating queries:

* What data is available that would have a bearing on the information users may seek?

* How are the tables that contain that data related to each other?

* Do I need to have Access make any calculations on that data? This is very useful in that you don't have to store in your database numbers that are solely dependent on other numbers in your database.

* Will I have to collect my data into logical groups in order to create the information? A good example of this would be in a company of sales reps, where you group the activities of sales personnel by department. Another example has to do with your address book, where you'd want to group the names of children with the names of their parent.

Reports

Reports are the other side of the data-to-information bridge. They are your basic tool in sharing your database's information. When I decide what reports I need, I start thinking about my audience — the people for whom I will prepare the reports.

For my boss, I know I'll need a report that presents information in a general way, a kind of executive summary. She doesn't have the time to be looking at details minions like me are here to handle. My coworkers, on the other hand, will most likely need a report that they can use like a quickie reference work, a report that I can print out every so often for them to keep at their desks and leaf through as they need the information. As for myself — well, I've got the database and I can query it at any time, so I don't need a report.

The bottom line, and something I'd like you to understand, is: The information you want to get out of your database — and its audience of users — is what basically drives its design.

Determining Input by Understanding Output

By now you know that a database collects data related to a more or less specific subject. Let's use as an example your Address Database from the previous chapter. If you were going to set up a people database — which is what an address database is, after all — what kinds of information would you want to get from it? I can think of several simple kinds of information right off the bat:

* Where does this person live?
* What number do I have to dial to call him on the telephone?
* Which spouse goes with which, um, other spouse?

To answer these questions in a general sense, all you need is a single table wherein each record contains the fields necessary to hold these data. And in this case, you want to make sure that each record contains a field for the person's name, address, telephone number, and so on.

Information from a single record

To refresh your memory, the My First Address Book database contains a table called Addresses. Its fields hold the names, addresses, phone numbers, and such of the individuals in the database. It's a well laid-out — a normalized — table from which you can derive information, and it lends itself very well to a form.

For example, if you look at Figure 4-1, you'll notice that Nancy Devolio lives in Seattle, her phone number is found in area code 504, and that Paul is her (presumably) loving spouse. To get all this information, you had only to look at a single record in the table.

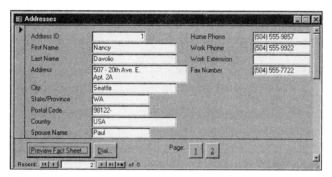

Figure 4-1 A single well-conceived record can answer a lot of questions.

Information from a whole table

Let's move on to answer a more involved question: Which people in your database live in Washington state? Theoretically speaking, this question requires you to look at the entire table and not just a single record. In practical terms, however, to get the answer you need to create a query in which Access leafs through all the records in the table, noting the ones in which the State/Province field equals WA, and lists the contents of the First Name and Last Name fields for each of the appropriate records. I've done just this in Figure 4-2.

Figure 4-2 The denizens of Washington.

As you can see, there are four individuals in the database who live in Washington. Our friend Nancy from the previous example leads the list, one that's neatly alphabetized by Access for your convenience. This is what I meant when I said that queries are the key to getting information from your Access database.

The Table Analyzer Wizard

In the last chapter, I showed you how you can create a table and have Access wizards do most of the work. What I'm going to show you now is a continuation of that idea. The difference is that this example should give you complete confidence in your ability to create an efficient database. That's because even if you create a database without the benefit of wizards, Access can check the database for you and fix as many of your mistakes as it can given the limits of its programming — it's not a human, after all.

The Table Analyzer Wizard looks at a single table at a time and tries to determine if any fields contain duplicate data. If so, it separates the table into two or more smaller tables. As a result, your database becomes more efficient. The database operates faster as you enter and update your data, and it's total size also becomes smaller.

Doing it the right way

To show you what I mean, take another look at the Addresses table of the My Address Book database, but this time through the eyes of the Access Table Analyzer Wizard.

TIP We're only looking at one table in this example, and that's all we need. Once you've gone through the process with one table, you can do the same thing with any of them. One thing to remember, however: The Table Analyzer Wizard looks only at one table at a time — the one you highlight. Obviously, then, if you want your database to be as efficient as possible, you need to have it look at each table in the database individually.

The first thing I want you to do is open the My Address Book database. Once it's running, close the main switchboard and open the database container.

In case you need it, here's a quick reminder of how to do so:

1. If Access isn't running, start it. Click the File menu and then select the My Address Book database from the numbered list of databases. If My Address Book isn't there, you can open it from the My Documents folder on your desktop.

2. When My First Address Book opens, it automatically displays its Main Switchboard. Close that and display the My First Address Book database container instead.

3. Click the Tables tab so that it's active. After you've done this, you should see the same thing on your Access window as shown in Figure 4-3.

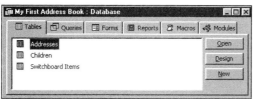

Figure 4-3 Your database container is ready for its tables to be analyzed.

With that bit of preparation, you're ready to run the Table Analyzer Wizard.

To do so, follow these steps:

1. From the Tools menu, select Analyze → Table (see Figure 4-4). If you haven't yet used the Table Analyzer Wizard, Access displays the first of two introductory pages, as shown in Figure 4-5. The introductory pages explain a bit of what I've been telling you — how duplicate information stored in a single table is something you want to avoid.

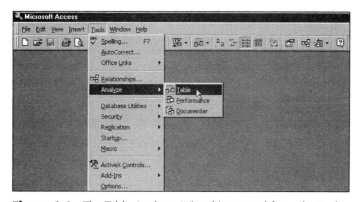

Figure 4-4 The Table Analyzer Wizard is opened from the Tools menu.

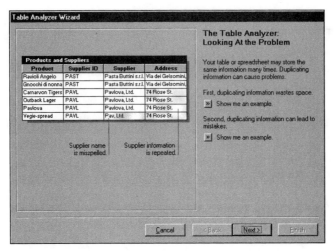

Figure 4-5 Access introduces and explains the Table Analyzer Wizard.

2. To see the explanations, click on one or both of the buttons next to Show me an example. Access pops up a dialog box that provides more explanation of what the Table Analyzer is about to do. Close the window by clicking on the close button at the window's upper right corner.

3. Click ⎡Next⎤ and Access displays the second introductory page, as shown in Figure 4-6. This page explains how the Table Analyzer attempts to solve the problem. It too has Show me an example buttons that you can click to pop up some additional explanatory text.

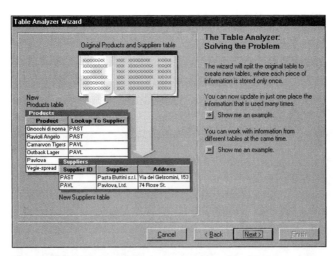

Figure 4-6 You can find out more about how Access solves the problem of inefficient tables.

4. As soon as you're ready, click ⎡Next⎤. Access displays the Table Analyzer Wizard dialog box, as shown in Figure 4-7. This is the first "for real" Table

Analyzer Wizard dialog box, and it's where you indicate which table you want analyzed by highlighting the table name in the list of tables.

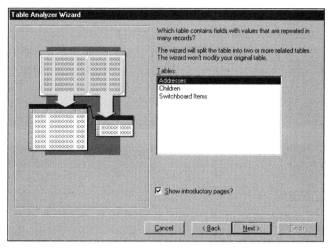

Figure 4-7   You can analyze a single table at a time.

TIP   **If you don't want to see the two introductory windows each time you start the Table Analyzer Wizard, click the Show Introductory pages? checkbox so the check mark disappears.**

5. With the name of the table you want to analyze highlighted, click   Next . Access displays the next Table Analyzer Wizard dialog box, as shown in Figure 4-8. This is where you need to make a decision: Do you want to tell Access in which tables duplicate fields should go or do you want Access to decide where the duplicate fields should go by itself?

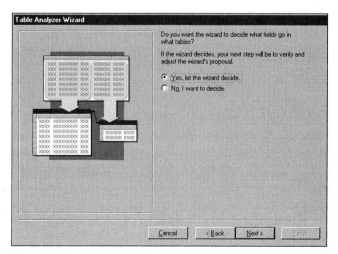

Figure 4-8   You have control, even if Access does most of the analyzing work.

6. When you've indicated your decision by clicking one of the two radio buttons, click ▐ **Next** ▌. Access looks at the Address table, finds no problems, and pops up the final Table Analyzer Wizard dialog box, as shown in Figure 4-9.

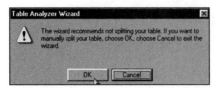

Figure 4-9   Looks like everything is okay with our table.

7. Click ▐ **OK** ▌ and you're done analyzing the Addresses table, confident that you've made it as efficient as possible.

Doing it the wrong way

You've seen it done the correct way. What would happen if the table weren't designed correctly? What if you designed the database so that instead of having two tables, one for addresses and another for children, you more or less combined the two? What I have in mind is a structure such as the one shown in Figure 4-10.

Field Name	Data Type	Description
AddressID	AutoNumber	ID number automatically generated by Access
FirstName	Text	First name
LastName	Text	Surname
SpouseName	Text	Spouse name
Address	Text	Street address
City	Text	City of residence
StateOrProvince	Text	State or Province
PostalCode	Text	Postal or Zip code
Country	Text	Country of residence
EmailAddress	Text	Email address
HomePhone	Text	Home telephone number
WorkPhone	Text	Work telephon number
WorkExtension	Text	Work telephone extension
FaxNumber	Text	Fax telephone number
Birthdate	Date/Time	Date of Birth
SendCard	Yes/No	Should we send this person a card?
Notes	Memo	Notes about the person
Child	Text	Their child
Child_DOB	Date/Time	The child's date of birth
Send_Child_Card	Yes/No	Should we spoil the little tyke?

Figure 4-10   An inefficient structure for the address table.

As you may well guess, with a structure like this there's only room for a single child's name for each person in the My Addresses database. If one of your acquaintances has more than one child, you'd be forced to either create several records for that person, or you'd have to ignore the other children. Come to think of some people I know, that may not be such a bad idea after all. But I digress.

Let's see what would happen if you asked Access to analyze this poorly designed table. Rather than having you create a new (inefficient) table, I'll simply describe the process to you, beginning with Figure 4-11.

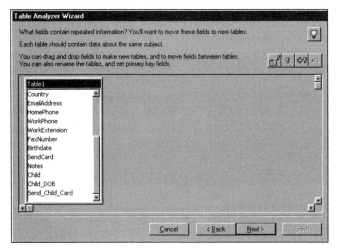

Figure 4-11 Here's looking at the inefficient table.

If you'll take a quick look at Figure 4-11, you'll see a copy of the inefficient table's structure. I got to this point by calling up the Table Analyzer Wizard and telling it that I wanted to analyze the Addresses table. Now I need to click and drag the fields having to do with children into a new table.

Figure 4-12 shows you what happens when I do just that. For the first field, Access creates a new table, one that includes an index field containing an automatically generated number. Because this is the first field I'm putting into the new table, to Access this means I'm changing the original (inefficient) table. Are we straight so far? Good.

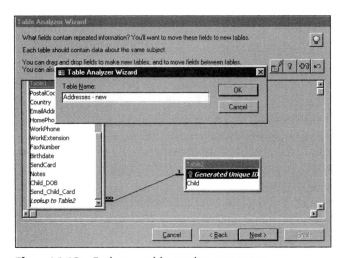

Figure 4-12 Each new table needs a new name.

Because the old table is being changed and because Access keeps an unchanged copy of it just in case I change my mind, Access asks me to name this new table. I don't have much of an imagination, so I called it Addresses — new.

There are two more fields to be dragged over to my new children's table. You can see in Figure 4-13 the results when I did just that. At that point I was pretty satisfied, so I clicked Next. Access called up its last Table Analyzer Wizard dialog box, where it asks if I want to create a query. You can see what I mean in Figure 4-14.

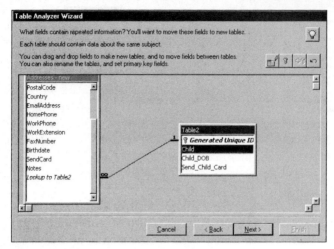

Figure 4-13 A new children's table comes from the Addresses — new table.

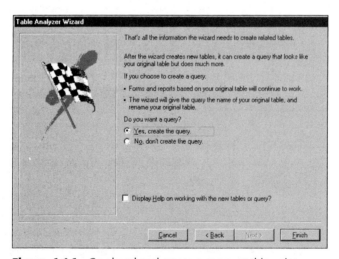

Figure 4-14 Go ahead and create a query at this point.

Do you remember that I told you a couple of chapters ago that queries look and work much the same way tables do? Here's the proof. Access is asking me if I want it to create a query, because if I do then all my reports and forms will work just as they did before I split the Addresses table. I won't have to change them, and yet all the underlying data will be kept straight by Access. Well, that works for me. I left the Yes, create the query radio button selected, and I clicked Finish. Access cooked for a moment and then displayed the new query along with a friendly little dialog box. You can see it in Figure 4-15.

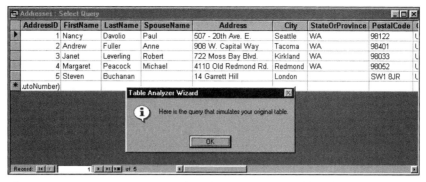

Figure 4-15 My new query, ready to impersonate the old Addresses table.

BONUS

The Performance Analyzer Wizard

The last thing I'd like to show you here is the Performance Analyzer Wizard. Unlike the Table Analyzer Wizard, which looks at only a single table at a time, this wizard works by taking a close look at your entire database, including tables, queries, forms, and reports.

After it has given your database the once over, if it finds a problem with your creation the Performance Analyzer Wizard shows you a recommendation, a suggestion, or an idea about the problem it has found. Which of the three it offers depends on how "serious" Access considers the problem or problems it finds.

Here's a quick primer on how to run the Performance Analyzer Wizard:

1. From the ☐ Tools ☐ menu, select ☐ Analyze ☐ → ☐ Performance ☐. Access pops up the Performance Analyzer Wizard dialog box, as shown in Figure 4-16.

   You can check almost any part of your database. The dialog box has tabs you can click to call up each kind of object (table, query, form, and so on). It also has another tab labeled All. That's the one I clicked for the illustration.

2. Click the checkbox next to the object or objects whose performance you want to analyze. You can select the whole lot by clicking Select <u>A</u>ll.

3. After you make your selections, click ☐ OK ☐. Access cooks for a moment and then displays the second Performance Analyzer dialog box, as shown in Figure 4-17.

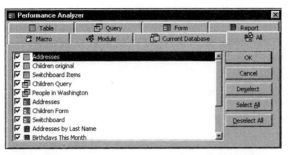

Figure 4-16 You can check the performance of almost any part of your Access database.

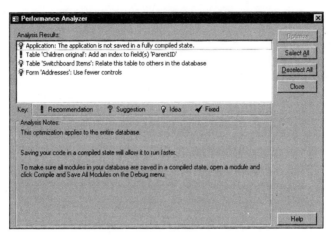

Figure 4-17 Access offers you its recommendations, suggestions, and ideas.

Access shows you a list of analysis results. Below the list you'll find a few comments in the area labeled Analysis Notes. Depending on what it finds, for each result Access offers the following:

a. Recommendations often have to do with the structure of your database or with adding some object Access finds missing. It's usually best to go along with Access recommendations.

b. Suggestions are not as imperative to follow as recommendations. If Access has a suggestion, it often offers tradeoffs to consider before you accept or reject what it proposes.

c. Ideas are simply comments about what Access finds during its optimization.

4. Highlight an analysis result to see its associated comments in the Analysis notes area of the dialog box. Then, if you want to go along with the recommendation or suggestion, click Optimize . Access performs the optimization with no further input from you.

Summary

Well, there you have it: a sound understanding of the art of database design. As you create your databases, remember that it's information you're after and it's data that helps you get there. Also remember that you're never on your own, even if you create your own database without help from the database wizard.

I wish our biotech committee from the beginning of the chapter had remembered that. What could have been a fine American Quarter Horse turned out to be a camel. But then, you already knew *that*, didn't you?

In the next chapter, I tell you about the datasheet, something that gives you a direct view of all the data in any of your database's tables. With this tool, you can sort your records in any order and even filter out extraneous data. Good stuff... let's turn the page and have at it.

THE DATA'S ON THE SHEET

5

Ol' Mac was a Thane. That was a good thing to be, if you, like he, were stuck in a place as medieval as Codor. Better, for example, than being a Varlet or some such. Thanes ate higher on the hog and slept on softer beds. All wasn't roses and perfume for our friend Mac, however. Seems he had a problem with the nearby forest. The old fellow could see it, but not its trees. And he'd been told he would be in deep trouble if the forest ever moved. Well, *that* at least didn't bother him; Mac knew that trees just don't move.

Mac, who (like most of us) couldn't see the forest for the trees, was born, lived, bred, and died before databases were invented. Talk about history repeating itself, though. There are an awful lot of us modern types who have a similar problem with our data, as though it were a metaphorical forest for us. We can see the whole thing and still not know what to do about the details.

In this chapter, we take a look at those fine points. While we're at it, I want to do three things. First, I want to give you an overview of Access datasheets so that you become very familiar with all their ins and outs. Then, I tell you some neat ways you can manipulate your datasheets. Finally, I show you a quick and sneaky way to sieve information from your datasheet.

The datasheets with which we're working in this chapter are the Products and Employees tables from the Northwind database. Northwind is one of the example databases that you received with Access. If you know how to call it up, please do so. If not, here's how:

1. From the | File | menu, select | Open Database |. Access displays its Open dialog box.

2. Look for the Office97\Office\Samples directory.

3. Highlight the Northwind database and click | Open |. Access opens the Northwind database, and displays its database container.

4. Click the Tables tab to make it active, then double click on either the Products or Employees table — I'll let you know which one when the time comes. Access opens the table in datasheet view.

FEATURE FOCUS You can find out what's going on "behind the scenes" with the Northwind database by clicking Show Me on the menu bar.

Another Look at Columns and Rows

If I may, I'd like to introduce you to a new friend, the datasheet. You can see a bunch of them in Figure 5-1. As you read the next couple of paragraphs, please refer to this figure. As you work your way through this section, you'll look at the datasheets from their insides out.

Datasheets are grids

The first thing I want you to notice is the fact that every datasheet is pretty much the same. Each one is a grid made up of columns and rows and filled with words and numbers. Looking a bit more closely, you can probably tell that each row is a complete record. You can usually read a record in a datasheet fairly easily by going from left to right — just like a sentence or paragraph. As a matter of fact, that's for the most part why datasheet records are laid out in rows instead of columns.

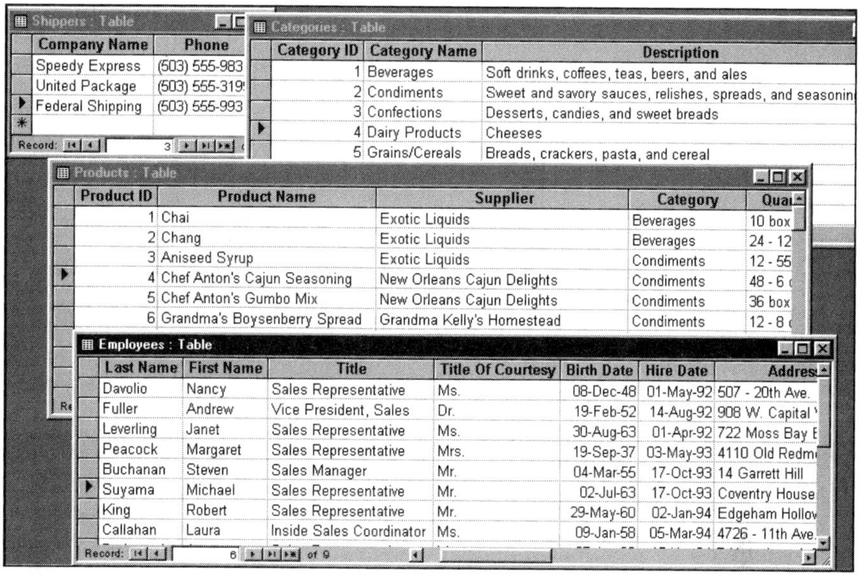

Figure 5-1 Every datasheet looks pretty much the same.

Knowing that rows are records, I'll bet you've guessed that each datasheet column is a field. That's correct. Each little grid square within a column (field) contains the same kind of data as the ones above and below it. (Notice that I said it contains the same *kind* of data — *not* the same data.) You use that bit of knowledge to turn this data into information in just a bit. Also, I follow datasheet convention and in this context use the words "field" and "column" interchangeably.

Before we continue, however, I want you to look for a moment at the first row of each datasheet. Can you see that each of the first rows is a bit different from the other rows? The first row of an Access datasheet always contains a caption for the fields below it. The caption comes from one of two places. If, as you're designing the table, you explicitly include a caption, that's what will appear at the top of each column. If you don't, then Access simply uses the field name you gave the field. Each of the captioned buttons in the first row is called a *field selector*, because when you click one, you select the entire field in that table.

"You can usually read a record in a datasheet fairly easily by going from left to right."

Now take a look at the column of gray squares at the extreme left of each row. These are called *record selectors*. Just as you click a field selector to select an entire field, you click a record selector to select an entire record. They are also a smart indicator that lets you know which record Access thinks you're working with. I say that they're "smart" because they change according to what Access thinks you're doing with the records.

If you're not working with a record, then the record selector stays blank. Otherwise, the record selector has a little picture in it, as shown in Table 5-1.

TABLE 5-1 What the Record Selector Means

Record Selector Picture	Its Meaning
▶	You've selected this record. You may be just looking at it, or you may be ready to modify its data.
✳	This is a brand new record that you're entering. It's so new that it hasn't even been saved yet.
✐	You are modifying the data that was earlier saved in this record.
⊘	This record has been locked by someone else on your network using this same table. You can read the data in this record, but because it's locked you can't modify it.

TIP You move from record to record in your datasheet using the same navigation tools as with any other kind of Access window: You use the navigation buttons at the bottom left of the datasheet window.

Just as a reminder, from left to right the navigation buttons are:

* Move to the first record
* Move to the previous record
* Move to the next record
* Move to the last record
* Create a new record

Granting a Ph.D.

What you're about to do next is an academic cheater's dream: You're going to grant a doctorate to a Northwind Traders employee. At the same time, you're going to find out how extremely easy it is to modify data in a datasheet. The first thing to do is for you to open the Employees table from the Northwind database. (I told you how to do it in the sidebar titled "If You Want to Follow Along," so if you need a reminder, please look there.) When you're ready, you should see a table like the one in Figure 5-2.

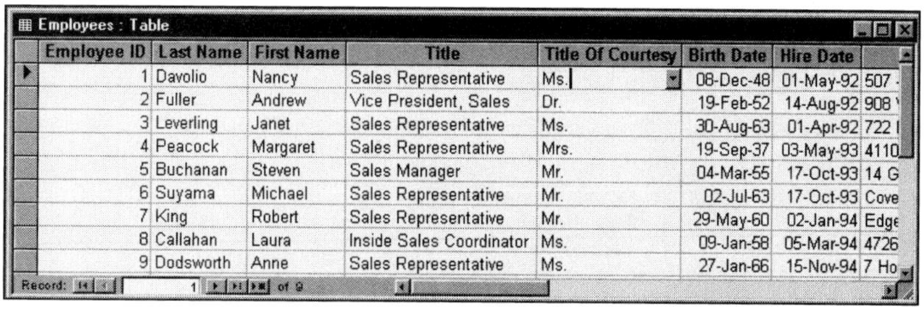

Figure 5-2 Here are all the employees of Northwind Traders.

To change data in a datasheet, all you have to do is move your mouse cursor into the field you want to change and start typing. Access treats any text that might be data in that field just like text in a dialog box text box you want to change. You can highlight the text and start typing, and Access automatically erases the "old" text and replaces it with what you type. Or, you can place your mouse cursor at any point in the field and start typing. Access moves as necessary the text that's already in the field.

> **"To change data in a datasheet, all you have to do is move your mouse cursor into the field you want to change and start typing."**

Access saves your newly changed record when you move out of that record, or when you select another record. In this example, you work with the first record in the Employees table, the one storing data on our friend from a couple of chapters ago, Nancy Davolio.

Follow these steps:

1. Move your mouse cursor to the field in Nancy Davolio's record named Title Of Courtesy.

2. Click on the field. Access displays a drop-down pointer at the right side of the field. That drop-down pointer tells you that instead of having to type data into this field, you can make a choice from a drop-down list. Notice also that that field's record selector changes to a triangle, denoting that Nancy Davolio's record is the one you're working with (see Figure 5-3).

3. In the drop-down list, click on the title Dr. Access changes Nancy's title from Ms. to Dr. and changes the record selector to a picture of a pen. (Of course, you can simply type Dr. in the field yourself, if you'd rather do that.)

4. Press [**Down Arrow**]. Access saves the newly changed record. Nancy's parents hear about her good fortune and congratulate each other on bringing up such a fine young lady. You can see the result in Figure 5-4.

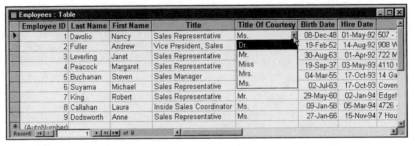

Figure 5-3 You don't always have to type data into a field to change it.

Employee ID	Last Name	First Name	Title	Title Of Courtesy	Birth Date	Hire Date	
1	Davolio	Nancy	Sales Representative	Dr.	08-Dec-48	01-May-92	507 - :
2	Fuller	Andrew	Vice President, Sales	Dr.	19-Feb-52	14-Aug-92	908 W
3	Leverling	Janet	Sales Representative	Ms.	30-Aug-63	01-Apr-92	722 N
4	Peacock	Margaret	Sales Representative	Mrs.	19-Sep-37	03-May-93	4110
5	Buchanan	Steven	Sales Manager	Mr.	04-Mar-55	17-Oct-93	14 Ga
6	Suyama	Michael	Sales Representative	Mr.	02-Jul-63	17-Oct-93	Coven
7	King	Robert	Sales Representative	Mr.	29-May-60	02-Jan-94	Edgel
8	Callahan	Laura	Inside Sales Coordinator	Ms.	09-Jan-58	05-Mar-94	4726 -
9	Dodsworth	Anne	Sales Representative	Ms.	27-Jan-66	15-Nov-94	7 Hou

Figure 5-4 Our Nancy is now a Doctor!

And that, friend, is all there is to changing the data in a record. Pretty simple, huh?

Adding a New Record

For my next trick, I'd like to show you how to add a new record to your table. Pretend you have a new employee for Northwind Traders and you need to add his name to the Employees table.

To do so, leave open the Employees table from the preceding example and follow these steps:

1. Move your mouse cursor to the bottom of the employees table, to the blank record you'll find there.

2. Because the first field in this new record is an autonumber field, you can't type data into it. So, ignore it for now and place your mouse cursor in the second column, the one labeled Last Name.

3. With your cursor in the Last Name field, type **Lee**, the last name of your new employee. Access knows that you are adding a new record to the table and so automatically places a number in the new record's Employee ID field. It also changes the new record's selector to a picture of a pen and adds yet another blank record under the current one.

4. When you're done typing in the first field, press Tab or Enter to move to the next field, labeled First Name. Type the name **Christian** in this field, a traditional name for your fictional employee.

5. After you finish typing data in the First Name field, continue entering data in the same way, tabbing over to the next field as you go. I won't put an intelligent person such as yourself through the tedium of having to type in exactly what I say here, so simply type in "bogus" data as you see fit for the rest of the record. If you want to see what I've done, it's shown in Figure 5-5.

Employee ID	Last Name	First Name	Title	Title Of Courtesy	Birth Date	Hire Date	
1	Davolio	Nancy	Sales Representative	Dr.	08-Dec-48	01-May-92	507 - 20t
2	Fuller	Andrew	Vice President, Sales	Dr.	19-Feb-52	14-Aug-92	908 W. C
3	Leverling	Janet	Sales Representative	Ms.	30-Aug-63	01-Apr-92	722 Mos
4	Peacock	Margaret	Sales Representative	Mrs.	19-Sep-37	03-May-93	4110 Old
5	Buchanan	Steven	Sales Manager	Mr.	04-Mar-55	17-Oct-93	14 Garre
6	Suyama	Michael	Sales Representative	Mr.	02-Jul-63	17-Oct-93	Coventry
7	King	Robert	Sales Representative	Mr.	29-May-60	02-Jan-94	Edgehan
8	Callahan	Laura	Inside Sales Coordinator	Ms.	09-Jan-58	05-Mar-94	4726 - 11
9	Dodsworth	Anne	Sales Representative	Ms.	27-Jan-66	15-Nov-94	7 Hounds
11	Lee	Christian	Photographer	Mr.	30-Jun-80	12-Jan-97	8306 22
(AutoNumber)							

Figure 5-5 My (bogus) data added to the Employees table.

It's not kindergarten, but you'll learn all you need to know about entering data after typing data into three or four fields.

TIP As you type dates into date fields in Access, it doesn't really matter what format you use. In other words, you can employ slashes (/) or dashes (-) to separate the months, days, and years. After you're done entering the date into a field, Access looks at the date format set for that field when the database was created and changes what you type to conform to the original format.

SIDE TRIP

MOVING AROUND MADE EASY

Moving around an Access datasheet is easiness itself. You can move your mouse cursor around clicking as you get to your destination, of course, but more often you'll find it more convenient to use keyboard shortcuts. Table 5-2 shows you which keys I've found to be most helpful as I navigate datasheets.

TABLE 5-2 Navigating Keyboard Shortcuts

Press This Key	To Do This
`Tab` , `Enter` , `→`	Move to the next field (to the right)
`Shift + Tab` , `←`	Move to the previous field (to the left)
`End`	Move to the last field in the record (all the way to the right)
`Home`	Move to the first field in the record (all the way to the left)
`↓`	Move to the same field, but in the next record (the one just below this one)
`↑`	Move to the same field, but in the previous record (the one just above this one)
`Ctrl + End`	Move to the very last field in the very last record in the table
`Ctrl + Home`	Move to the very first field in the very first record in the table

Hiding What You Don't Need to See

I don't know about you, but I find autonumber fields to be something of a pain. I mean, you often need them to make sure that each record is unique — but you don't have to let them get in the way. As a matter of fact, Access lets you easily hide them from view. When you do so, the field is still there, and Access continues to automatically add a number to it whenever you add a new record. You just can't see it.

If you want to hide the autonumber field, follow these steps:

1. With the Employees datasheet in view, move to the Employee ID column selector and click on it. (It's at the top of the column and contains the words, Employee ID.) Access highlights the entire column.

2. With the column highlighted, click your right mouse button. Access pops up a menu as shown in Figure 5-6

3. Click `Hide Columns` . Access hides the column from view, as shown in Figure 5-7.

Although you happened to hide an autonumber field in this example, you can hide any column in any Access table using this same method.

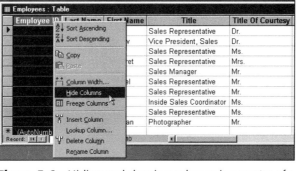

Figure 5-6 Hiding and showing columns is a matter of a mouse click.

Last Name	First Name	Title	Title Of Courtesy	Birth Date	Hire Date	Address
Davolio	Nancy	Sales Representative	Dr.	08-Dec-48	01-May-92	507 - 20th Ave. E.
Fuller	Andrew	Vice President, Sales	Dr.	19-Feb-52	14-Aug-92	908 W. Capital Way
Leverling	Janet	Sales Representative	Ms.	30-Aug-63	01-Apr-92	722 Moss Bay Blvd.
Peacock	Margaret	Sales Representative	Mrs.	19-Sep-37	03-May-93	4110 Old Redmond Rd
Buchanan	Steven	Sales Manager	Mr.	04-Mar-55	17-Oct-93	14 Garrett Hill
Suyama	Michael	Sales Representative	Mr.	02-Jul-63	17-Oct-93	Coventry House
King	Robert	Sales Representative	Mr.	29-May-60	02-Jan-94	Edgeham Hollow
Callahan	Laura	Inside Sales Coordinator	Ms.	09-Jan-58	05-Mar-94	4726 - 11th Ave. N.E.
Dodsworth	Anne	Sales Representative	Ms.	27-Jan-66	15-Nov-94	7 Houndstooth Rd.
Lee	Christian	Photographer	Mr.	30-Jun-80	12-Jan-97	13306 222 Ave Ct. E.

Figure 5-7 Here's the slimmed-down datasheet.

Showing a Hidden Column

Once a field is hidden, there may come a time when you want to see it again. Fortunately, doing so isn't a treasure hunt.

Here's how:

1. Move your mouse cursor somewhere on your datasheet's title bar and click your right mouse button. (The title bar is the very top part of the datasheet window and contains the datasheet's name along with the word Table.) Access pops up a utility menu, as shown in Figure 5-8.

Figure 5-8 The utility menu lets you control your datasheet.

2. Click ❙ **Unhide Columns** ❙, the last option on the utility menu. Access displays the Unhide Columns dialog box, as shown in Figure 5-9.

Figure 5-9 You can hide and unhide any column in your datasheet.

3. As you can see from the dialog box, columns that are hidden don't have a check mark in their checkboxes. So, to unhide a column, simply check its box. At the same time, if you want to hide any other columns, you can uncheck their checkboxes.

4. Click ❙ **Close** ❙ when you're done selecting the columns you want to hide or unhide. Access closes the Unhide Columns dialog box, makes visible the columns that you checked, and hides any columns you unchecked.

Freeze It and Leave It There

One of the problems with datasheets is the sheer volume of data they contain. With no trouble at all, you can create a datasheet that has so many columns you can't see all of them at once on your screen. If you have a photographic memory or if you are *really* into detail, this might not present a difficulty for you. My mind, however, isn't like that. It's a sieve — "out of sight, out of mind" as it were.

To solve this little dilemma, I freeze certain columns so they remain in view while I scroll through their siblings. This is especially useful with a table containing personnel data like Employees in the Northwind database.

Follow along, and I'll show you how it works:

1. With the Employees table open in datasheet view (and with the Employee ID field hidden), move your mouse cursor to the Last Name column selector.

2. Highlight both the Last Name and First Name column selectors by clicking the first column selector, and then holding down the Shift key and clicking on the second column selector.

3. With both columns highlighted, click your right mouse button while continuing to hold down the Shift key. Access pops up a utility menu, as shown in Figure 5-10.

Figure 5-10 Freezing columns makes it easier to understand extensive datasheets.

4. Select [**Freeze columns**] from the utility menu. Access moves the highlighted columns to the extreme left side of your datasheet and draws a vertical line at their right side. That vertical line is your visual cue that the fields to its left have been "frozen."

Here's something to keep in mind when you freeze columns. Whenever you highlight a column and freeze it, Access always moves it to the extreme left side of your datasheet. Access never leaves a column you freeze between unfrozen columns.

5. With the employee names columns frozen, try scrolling the Employee datasheet to the right. Notice that the people's names stay in place while the rest of the data appears to scroll under them. I bet it will take you all of three seconds to realize how handy this little feature can be.

Thawing Out Your Frozen Columns

After you've frozen a column or two, there might come a time when you want those puppies thawed.

Thawing out columns is the opposite of freezing them, and here's how you do it:

1. Click [**Format**] on the Access main menu bar. Access pops up the Format menu, as shown in Figure 5-11.

Figure 5-11 The Format menu lets you unfreeze your columns.

2. Select [**Unfreeze All Columns**]. Access unfreezes the frozen columns. Polar bears hear of the thaw and think spring has come.

Oh, yes — Access *doesn't* move the newly unfrozen columns. So, if you froze a column in the middle of your datasheet that Access moved over to the left, it will stay at the left until you move it.

Slippery, Sliding Columns

Speaking of columns lying there, what if you want to move one or two of them to a different order? After all, there's nothing sacred about the order your columns are in. Every now and then it makes informational sense to have different fields be next to each other.

Let me show you how to move a column:

1. Click the column selector of the field you want moved. Access highlights the column.

2. Drag the column selector to where you want the field to be. When you release the mouse button, Access moves your column, making room for it as necessary.

I Need Another Field

I wish I could anticipate every eventuality — especially things like exactly which stocks are about to go through the roof, or which horse is going to win at Belmont, or all the fields I'll ever need for this database. Regarding the former two, I'm out of luck. But as for the latter, it's no problem.

Access lets you add and delete columns from your table pretty much at will. You can add a field just about any time. And, as long as the fields aren't in a relationship with fields in another table, you can pretty much delete a field at any time. If you do, of course, you will lose any data you might have stored in that field. (Sorry to belabor the obvious, but, as they say, "there's always one in the audience.")

For this example, I use the Products table from the Northwind database, so if you want to follow along, you need to open that table. By the way, I've hidden its pesky Product ID field. (You remember how to do *that*, don't you?)

Here are the steps to follow:

1. Click the column selector of the field that is just to the right of where you want the new column inserted. Access highlights that column. In this case, I've decided to make my new column the second one on the datasheet. You can see the "before" view in Figure 5-12.

Product Name	Supplier	Category	Quantity Per Unit
Chang	Exotic Liquids	Beverages	24 - 12 oz bottles
Aniseed Syrup	Exotic Liquids	Condiments	12 - 550 ml bottles
Chef Anton's Cajun Seasoning	New Orleans Cajun Delights	Condiments	48 - 6 oz jars
Chef Anton's Gumbo Mix	New Orleans Cajun Delights	Condiments	36 boxes
Grandma's Boysenberry Spread	Grandma Kelly's Homestead	Condiments	12 - 8 oz jars
Uncle Bob's Organic Dried Pears	Grandma Kelly's Homestead	Produce	12 - 1 lb pkgs.
Northwoods Cranberry Sauce	Grandma Kelly's Homestead	Condiments	12 - 12 oz jars
Mishi Kobe Niku	Tokyo Traders	Meat/Poultry	18 - 500 g pkgs.
Ikura	Tokyo Traders	Seafood	12 - 200 ml jars
Queso Cabrales	Cooperativa de Quesos 'Las Cabras'	Dairy Products	1 kg pkg.
Queso Manchego La Pastora	Cooperativa de Quesos 'Las Cabras'	Dairy Products	10 - 500 g pkgs.
Konbu	Mayumi's	Seafood	2 kg box
Tofu	Mayumi's	Produce	40 - 100 g pkgs.
Genen Shouyu	Mayumi's	Condiments	24 - 250 ml bottles
Pavlova	Pavlova, Ltd.	Confections	32 - 500 g boxes
Alice Mutton	Pavlova, Ltd.	Meat/Poultry	20 - 1 kg tins

Figure 5-12   The datasheet looks like this just before you insert a new field.

2. With the Supplier column selected, right click and then select `Insert Column` from the utility menu that appears. Access slides the highlighted column and all its fellows to the right and inserts your new field, giving it the name Field1, as shown in Figure 5-13.

Product Name	Field1	Supplier	Category	Qua
Chai		Exotic Liquids	Beverages	10 box
Chang		Exotic Liquids	Beverages	24 - 12
Aniseed Syrup		Exotic Liquids	Condiments	12 - 55
Chef Anton's Cajun Seasoning		New Orleans Cajun Delights	Condiments	48 - 6
Chef Anton's Gumbo Mix		New Orleans Cajun Delights	Condiments	36 box
Grandma's Boysenberry Spread		Grandma Kelly's Homestead	Condiments	12 - 8
Uncle Bob's Organic Dried Pears		Grandma Kelly's Homestead	Produce	12 - 1
Northwoods Cranberry Sauce		Grandma Kelly's Homestead	Condiments	12 - 12
Mishi Kobe Niku		Tokyo Traders	Meat/Poultry	18 - 50
Ikura		Tokyo Traders	Seafood	12 - 20
Queso Cabrales		Cooperativa de Quesos 'Las Cabras'	Dairy Products	1 kg p
Queso Manchego La Pastora		Cooperativa de Quesos 'Las Cabras'	Dairy Products	10 - 50
Konbu		Mayumi's	Seafood	2 kg b
Tofu		Mayumi's	Produce	40 - 10
Genen Shouyu		Mayumi's	Condiments	24 - 25
Pavlova		Pavlova, Ltd.	Confections	32 - 50

Figure 5-13   Here's your brand new field, ready for data.

After a column has been inserted in a datasheet, it's ready for data. By default, Access gives it a data type of Text, 50 characters. You can change that, of course, but to do so you need to change from datasheet view to table design view.

Deleting My New Column

Getting rid of an unwanted column is easier than filling a recycling bin.

The steps are as follows:

1. Highlight the column you want to delete and right click. Access displays the now familiar utility menu.

2. Select `Delete Column` from the utility menu. Access displays a warning dialog box in which you click `Yes`. Access deletes the column and the column's data from your table.

My Column Gets a New Name

Having a column in your table by the name of Field1 is about as useful as — well, I'll let you imagine your own metaphor. For my part, I don't regard Field1 as being a very useful moniker.

Accordingly, here's how to go about renaming a field:

1. Right click the Field1 column selector. Access displays the utility menu.

2. Select `Rename Column` from the utility menu. Access highlights the name of the column, ready for you to rename the field.

3. Type a new name for your field. In this case, I've decided to call the new field, Cuisine, as shown in Figure 5-14.

You can rename any field in your table; it makes absolutely no difference to Access. The only obvious caveat is that you should name your columns something that makes sense for the data it holds.

Putting Your Data into Useful Order

There's one database kind of question I find myself having to answer quite often: "Who did the most of this or that?" And even more often, I find myself having to quickly scan a table to find one particular item of data: For example, "How many hours does Joe have in?"

Product Name	Cuisine	Supplier	Category	Qua⌃
Chai	Oriental	Exotic Liquids	Beverages	10 box
Chang	Oriental	Exotic Liquids	Beverages	24 - 12
Aniseed Syrup	Middle Eastern	Exotic Liquids	Condiments	12 - 55
Chef Anton's Cajun Seasoning	Creole	New Orleans Cajun Delights	Condiments	48 - 6 (
Chef Anton's Gumbo Mix	Creole	New Orleans Cajun Delights	Condiments	36 box
Grandma's Boysenberry Spread	American	Grandma Kelly's Homestead	Condiments	12 - 8 (
Uncle Bob's Organic Dried Pears	New Age	Grandma Kelly's Homestead	Produce	12 - 1 l
Northwoods Cranberry Sauce	American	Grandma Kelly's Homestead	Condiments	12 - 12
Mishi Kobe Niku	Japanese	Tokyo Traders	Meat/Poultry	18 - 50
Ikura	Japanese	Tokyo Traders	Seafood	12 - 20
Queso Cabrales	Mexican	Cooperativa de Quesos 'Las Cabras'	Dairy Products	1 kg pk
Queso Manchego La Pastora		Cooperativa de Quesos 'Las Cabras'	Dairy Products	10 - 50
Konbu		Mayumi's	Seafood	2 kg bc
Tofu		Mayumi's	Produce	40 - 10
Genen Shouyu		Mayumi's	Condiments	24 - 25
Pavlova		Pavlova, Ltd.	Confections	32 - 50

Record: |◄| ◄ | 12 | ► | ►| |►*| of 77

Figure 5-14 The newly renamed field is being put to use.

These questions are different, but they have one important thing in common. To answer them, it's usually faster to give my table a quick eyeball scan than to go through the process of writing a query or filtering the data. And there's nothing that makes an eyeball scan easier than sorting a table. Here, I'll show you what I mean.

Let's say you're working for Northwind Traders, and your boss suddenly becomes curious about which product costs the most per unit item. This kind of question is tailor-made for a sorting solution.

If you want to see, follow along with these steps:

1. With the Northwind database active, open the Products table.

2. Click the Unit Price column selector. Access highlights the entire column.

3. Right click your mouse button. Access pops up the utility menu as shown in Figure 5-15.

Figure 5-15 You can perform ascending and descending sorts.

4. Select Sort Descending from the utility menu. Access rearranges the records in the entire table based on the values it finds in the Unit Price column. Because you chose a descending sort, Access puts the largest number first (which is the highest price), and follows it in order by the second largest number, then by the third largest number, and so on all the way to the last record in the table. You can see the result in Figure 5-16.

Product Name	Supplier	Category	Unit Price	Units
Côte de Blaye	Aux joyeux ecclésiastiques	Beverages	$263.50	
Thüringer Rostbratwurst	Plutzer Lebensmittelgroßmärkte AG	Meat/Poultry	$123.79	
Mishi Kobe Niku	Tokyo Traders	Meat/Poultry	$97.00	
Carnarvon Tigers	Pavlova, Ltd.	Seafood	$62.50	
Raclette Courdavault	Gai pâturage	Dairy Products	$55.00	
Ipoh Coffee	Leka Trading	Beverages	$46.00	
Vegie-spread	Pavlova, Ltd.	Condiments	$43.90	
Northwoods Cranberry Sauce	Grandma Kelly's Homestead	Condiments	$40.00	
Alice Mutton	Pavlova, Ltd.	Meat/Poultry	$39.00	
Gnocchi di nonna Alice	Pasta Buttini s.r.l.	Grains/Cereals	$38.00	
Queso Manchego La Pastora	Cooperativa de Quesos 'Las Cabras'	Dairy Products	$38.00	
Gudbrandsdalsost	Norske Meierier	Dairy Products	$36.00	
Mozzarella di Giovanni	Formaggi Fortini s.r.l.	Dairy Products	$34.80	
Camembert Pierrot	Gai pâturage	Dairy Products	$34.00	
Wimmers gute Semmelknödel	Plutzer Lebensmittelgroßmärkte AG	Grains/Cereals	$33.25	
Perth Pasties	G'day, Mate	Meat/Poultry	$32.80	
Mascarpone Fabioli	Formaggi Fortini s.r.l.	Dairy Products	$32.00	
Ikura	Tokyo Traders	Seafood	$31.00	
Sirop d'érable	Forêts d'érables	Condiments	$28.50	
Gravad lax	Svensk Sjöföda AB	Seafood	$26.00	

Record: 1 of 59 (Filtered)

Figure 5-16 The table has been sorted according to Unit Price.

Well, what do you know? Looks like the wine with the fancy name made by joyful monks wins the prize! And another quick peek at the data lets you know that if you use it to wash down the sausage that's product number two, that meal would set you back a pretty penny. Several pretty pennies, in fact, and some ugly ones too.

The point I want to make is that sorting your data is quick, easy, and useful. It can often enable you to quickly provide information that can get your work team moving.

TIP When you need to look up a name in a table, you'll often find it faster by simply alphabetically sorting all the names in the table and then quickly scanning the names for the one you want.

BONUS

A Filter for Information

Do you remember at the beginning of this chapter, where I said I'd show you a sneaky way of quickly getting information from your datasheet? Well, that's exactly what I'm about to do. But first, a little background. Information is what we get when we thresh a large amount of chaff data down to something meaningful. With computers, this usually means a kind of brute force method where we throw out everything we don't need, leaving us finally with the meaningful germ. Because we don't want to actually throw out the data — we only want the extraneous stuff not to be visible and distracting to us — we use a logical filtering facility that's built into Access.

This logical filter works in very much the same was as a physical filter. It lets you kind of pour your data through it, allowing unneeded data to pass while holding back only the kinds of data that can become information for you.

You make a filter work by telling it what is meaningful data. It remembers this and looks at each record to see if the record contains any meaningful data. If so, the filter keeps the record visible; if not, the filter hides the record.

Filtering by Selection

N ow, for our example. Imagine that you want to know which products out of all the products offered by Northwind traders are beverages. I bet you're thinking that all you have to do is select records that contain the word beverages, and that would be that.

Well, follow these steps to find out:

1. Open the Products table from the Northwind database. Then move your mouse cursor to a Category field that contains the data, Beverages.

2. Highlight the word Beverages and right click. Access displays the records pop-up menu, as shown in Figure 5-17.

Figure 5-17 The records pop-up menu lets you sort and filter your records.

3. Select ⬛ **Filter by Selection** ⬛ from the pop-up menu. Access hides every record where the Category field does not contain the word Beverages, as shown in Figure 5-18.

So there you have information from your database. And to keep you from being confused — this does look pretty much like any other datasheet, after all — Access notes for you that this is a filtered datasheet (in the status bar at the bottom of the window labeled, Products: Table).

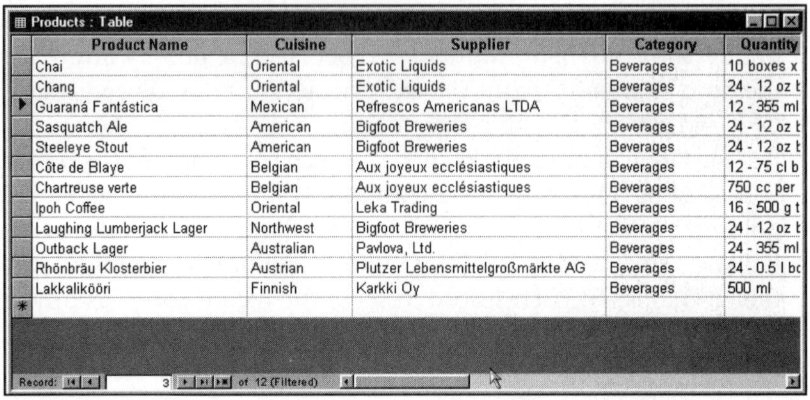
Products : Table

	Product Name	Cuisine	Supplier	Category	Quantity
	Chai	Oriental	Exotic Liquids	Beverages	10 boxes x
	Chang	Oriental	Exotic Liquids	Beverages	24 - 12 oz b
▶	Guaraná Fantástica	Mexican	Refrescos Americanas LTDA	Beverages	12 - 355 ml
	Sasquatch Ale	American	Bigfoot Breweries	Beverages	24 - 12 oz b
	Steeleye Stout	American	Bigfoot Breweries	Beverages	24 - 12 oz b
	Côte de Blaye	Belgian	Aux joyeux ecclésiastiques	Beverages	12 - 75 cl b
	Chartreuse verte	Belgian	Aux joyeux ecclésiastiques	Beverages	750 cc per
	Ipoh Coffee	Oriental	Leka Trading	Beverages	16 - 500 g t
	Laughing Lumberjack Lager	Northwest	Bigfoot Breweries	Beverages	24 - 12 oz b
	Outback Lager	Australian	Pavlova, Ltd.	Beverages	24 - 355 ml
	Rhönbräu Klosterbier	Austrian	Plutzer Lebensmittelgroßmärkte AG	Beverages	24 - 0.5 l bo
	Lakkalikööri	Finnish	Karkki Oy	Beverages	500 ml
*					

Record: 3 of 12 (Filtered)

Figure 5-18 Now this is information!

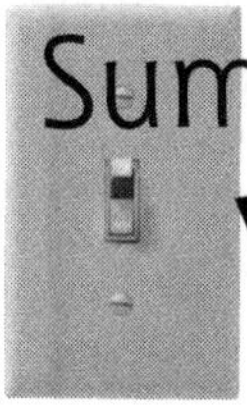

Summary

Well, now you know your way around an Access datasheet. You've learned how to add records and change data. You have to admit that filtering your data to get information is a pretty neat deal — all to help you see the trees in the forest.

Speaking of which, turns out our friend from the beginning of this chapter, old Mac, was wrong — dead wrong, in fact — about trees not moving. He got blood on his hands, the trees moved, and the next thing you know, Mac was done in by Duncan. Kind of poetic, isn't it?

Coming up in the next chapter, I show you how to pick and choose among all the data in your tables. While it's all important, not all the data in a table is important all the time. The next chapter is where you learn to make the best use of that fact. A quick flip of the wrist and a turn of the page, and you'll see what I mean.

I'LL TAKE ONE OF THESE AND TWO OF THOSE

KEY GOALS OF THIS CHAPTER:

The other day our family went to dinner. My kids have outgrown — fortunately — that place with yellow half-round things growing out of its roof. Now I like to take them to steak houses. So after a family vote, which I lost, we decided to eat at a smorgasbord. My younger son loves the buffet at such restaurants. (*Buffet*, Fr., go get it yourself.) Out of all the fare available, he invariably and specifically chooses two things: chicken and dessert. Not quite a balanced meal, but done once in a while it can't be too harmful.

Access tables are a lot like smorgasbords. You have all that data sitting there like so many pieces of wilting lettuce and curling fish. When you need information, it will usually be so you can answer a specific question. You pick out a little of this data and a few of that from your tables, and the next thing you know you have exactly what you need.

In this chapter, I show you how to use Access queries to sift through your data for you. We look at the Access Query by Example (QBE) interface and learn how it works. Then we look at how you can get data from more than one table at a time. When you're done, you'll have an excellent grasp of exactly how to gather information from your data smorgasbord.

What's a Query, Mister?

'm glad you asked that question. A query is a systematic way of extracting information from the data stored in an Access database.

When you create a query, you do two things: First, you tell Access what tables you want it to look through; second, you show Access which fields in those tables hold the data you want to see. Access then shows you the contents of those fields in something that looks like another table, but it's not. It's called a *dynaset*, a new word thought up at Microsoft by our own esteemed Technical Editor, Robert Wazeka, Ph.D.

Of course, Access is sophisticated enough to make it even easier for you to derive information than simply showing you stored data, even if the data you need for information doesn't actually exist in your database. Once you've shown Access which fields to use, for example, you can at the same time have Access count how many times a certain datum occurs. That's new data that didn't previously exist in your database. Or you can have Access sum all the data in a number field and then display the total for you. You can even have Access sort the query results for you.

X-REF Access is capable of performing a number of different kinds of queries. In this book, we look for the most part at what are called *Select queries* (in this chapter) and a bit at what are called *Action queries* (in Chapter 8, "Let's Make Some Changes"). Even so, I think it's important for you to know a little about each kind of query Access can perform. Table 6-1 puts it all together for you.

SIDE TRIP

Dynasets

The word dynaset connotes the fact that the results of a query are a temporary, dynamic, subset of the data contained within the table(s) queried. Although a dynaset looks like a regular table datasheet, it actually exists only in your computer's RAM memory and not on your computer's hard disk. When you close a dynaset, it's gone. To get it back, you need to rerun the query, thus re-creating the dynaset.

TABLE 6-1 Access Query Types

Access Query Type	What It Does
SELECT	Displays the data from a selection of fields according to criteria you supply. This is Access's straightforward answer to a question you pose. Select queries don't change the data in your tables.
ACTION	Lets you have Access look through each record in your data and copy or modify the contents of certain fields. For example, you could update the data in those fields or delete the data. You'll notice that the essential difference between Action queries and Select queries is that the former changes your data, while the latter doesn't.
CROSSTAB	Lets you compare the contents of some fields against the contents of others. This is especially helpful when you want to see the relationship among fields holding numerical data.
FIND UNMATCHED/ DUPLICATES	These are specialized queries you most easily create using built-in wizards. They let you find records that are duplicated in a table or compare records from two tables to find those that are unmatched.
PARAMETER	Each time you run this type of query, Access shows you a dialog box for you to indicate what criteria to use for that run.
SQL	(Which stands for *Structured Query Language*.) Enables you to have full control over any part of an Access database by your writing a software program. You can combine matching data from more than one table into another table, pass instructions to another database, or even define new tables and indexes.

I Query by Example

I've found that it's often easier to show someone what I want than it is to tell him or her what I want. It's the same thing with Access and me. I must not be the only one, because the people who wrote Access built into it a way of getting information called Query By Example. You show Access what you're looking for, and it goes to your tables and finds it for you.

Here's an example. Let's say you want a simple phone list of everyone working at Northwind Traders. Common sense would tell you that the Employees table probably holds that information. So to get at it, you'd want to obtain a list of the contents of the FirstName, LastName, and HomePhone fields in that table.

This is the table you need

The first thing you need to do is let Access know which table(s) to use to find your information.

Follow these steps to do so:

1. With the Northwind database open and its database container visible, click the Queries tab. Access displays the database container with the Queries tab active.

2. Click New . Access displays the New Query dialog box, as shown in Figure 6-1.

Figure 6-1 Queries start with the New Query dialog box.

3. Select the first option, Design View, and then click OK . Access displays its QBE window (labeled, Query1: Select Query) and its Show Table dialog box. The QBE window is where you show Access in which fields to find the information you need, and the Show Table dialog box is what you use to select the table(s) that contain those fields.

4. The Show Table dialog box has three tabs: Tables, Queries, and Both. With the Tables tab active, highlight Employees and click Add . Access places a list of fields in the Employees table in the top half of the QBE window, as shown in Figure 6-2.

5. After you've selected the Employees table, click Close .

With that, you're done with the first part of creating your query. Before we move on, however, I want to point something out to you. Access will do its best to find the information you need, whether it exists in a table or in the results of another query. That's why you can use the Show Table dialog box to add field lists from tables, queries, or both to your query.

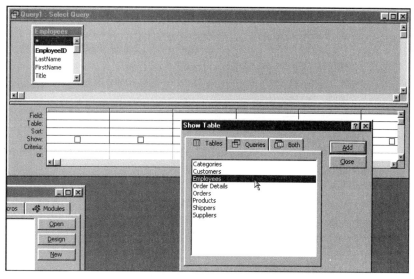

Figure 6-2 You can use tables and other queries in a new query.

If you want to add another table or query to the query you're creating and you've already closed the Show Table dialog box, you're not out of luck. Simply click the Show Table icon on the toolbar to open the dialog again. You can then add whatever tables or queries you want.

"Access will do its best to find the information you need, whether it exists in a table or in the results of another query."

Giving Access your example

Now that Access "knows" which tables to use, the next thing is to show it which fields to use from those tables.

I'm sure you'll agree that this is simplicity itself as you follow these steps:

1. With the QBE window visible, highlight and then drag the FirstName field from the field list down to the first column of the query design grid at the bottom of the window. Your mouse cursor changes into a small rectangle that you can place there in the first column. Access automatically places the field in the Field row regardless of what row you happen to place it in.

2. Do the same thing with the LastName and HomePhone fields. When you're done, the QBE window should look much like Figure 6-3.

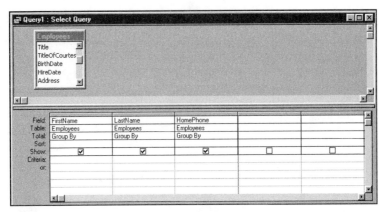

Figure 6-3 The QBE window, almost ready for you to run your new query.

3. Before you do anything else, *SAVE YOUR NEW QUERY!* Click  on the toolbar at the top of your Access window. Access displays the (now familiar) Save As dialog box, as shown in Figure 6-4.

Figure 6-4 Always include the object type (such as, table or query) in your object names.

4. Type **Phone List Query** in the Query Name text box to give your new query a name. Notice that when you do, the QBE window title bar changes to include the new name.

A NAMING QUESTION

You may be wondering why I suggest that you add the word Query to the name of your new query. The reason has to do with ambiguity.

Access is an object-oriented program. It treats similar objects in similar ways. For example, when you chose the Employees table from the Show Table dialog box, you could have also chosen a query named Employees if such a query existed. The ambiguity is obvious: which Employees are you choosing, the table or the query? But if you add the word Table or Query to the name of the object you create, you'll never be confused as to which one you're working with.

I only wish that the people at Microsoft who created the Northwind sample database felt the same way. In that database, there are two things called Employees (one is a table and the other is a form) and there are *three* things called Customers (a table, a form, and a macro). The only way you know which one you're working with at any given time is by context, and that's not good enough, in my humble opinion.

My point is this: When you create and name your own objects, *always* make it clear to your user (or yourself) what kind of object it is.

5. Now you're ready to actually run your new query. (Is your pulse quickening?) Click ❗. Access goes to the Employees tables, reads all the FirstName, LastName, and HomePhone fields, and copies them to a dynaset, which it then displays, as shown in Figure 6-5.

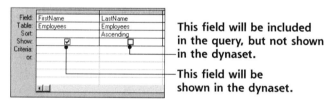

First Name	Last Name	Home Phone
Nancy	Davolio	(206) 555-9857
Andrew	Fuller	(206) 555-9482
Janet	Leverling	(206) 555-3412
Margaret	Peacock	(206) 555-8122
Steven	Buchanan	(71) 555-4848
Michael	Suyama	(71) 555-7773
Robert	King	(71) 555-5598
Laura	Callahan	(206) 555-1189
Anne	Dodsworth	(71) 555-4444
Christian	Lee	

Figure 6-5 A query dynaset looks just like a table datasheet.

TIP If you take a look at your QBE grid, you'll notice that there's one row labeled Show (see Figure 6-6). This row contains a small square box in each of its columns. You use the boxes to show (with the box checked) the contents of the field in the dynaset or to hide (with the box unchecked) the contents of the field in the dynaset. Whether a field is shown in the dynaset or not, it's still used by Access in the query.

Field:	FirstName	LastName
Table:	Employees	Employees
Sort:		Ascending
Show:	☑	☐
Criteria:		
or:		

This field will be included in the query, but not shown in the dynaset.

This field will be shown in the dynaset.

Figure 6-6 You can show or hide fields in a dynaset.

It really should be sorted

Now that you have a phone list, you should easily be able to find anyone's home phone number. It's a good thing, however, that there are so few people working at Northwind Traders. With such a disorganized list of names, you'd be in big trouble if this were a list of, say, government employees. What you need to do is sort the list, and the most logical sort is by the employees' last names.

Follow these steps to do so:

1. Click 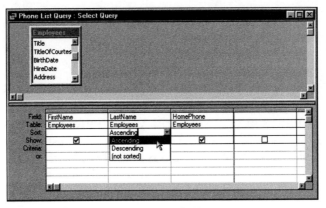 on your toolbar. Access displays again the QBE window.

2. Move your mouse cursor to the third row in the second column of the QBE grid, the one for the LastName field. The third row is the one where you indicate sort order. Click your mouse cursor on the arrow there at the left side of the cell, and Access displays a sort order list, as shown in Figure 6-7.

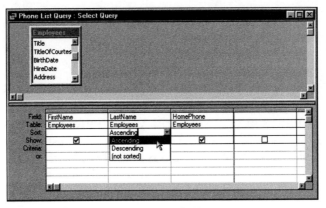

Figure 6-7 You can sort on any field in a query.

3. Select Ascending (from A to Z) sort order from the list. Access places the word Ascending in the sort order cell in the QBE grid.

4. Click ▌ on your toolbar. Access reruns the query, this time sorting it as shown in Figure 6-8.

Figure 6-8 Looking through a sorted list is more efficient than looking through an unsorted list.

As you can well imagine, it's a lot easier to find a particular name in a sorted list than it is in an unsorted, unorganized list.

A SLIGHTLY CLOSER LOOK AT SORTING

You can sort on any number of query fields, and those sorts can be nested. What you need to remember, however, is that Access reads fields in the QBE grid from left to right. That means it sorts the first field it comes to, continues reading fields to the right and sorting them — within the previous sort — until it has gone through all your query fields. This kind of sort-within-a-sort is called a *nested sort*.

For example, if you want to sort by zip code and last name, you place the zip code field to the left of the last name field. Then you sort on both by including a sort order (Ascending or Descending) for each field. Access keeps things straight by collecting in groups all the records from each zip code together, looking at and sorting the last names in each zip code group, and then setting each group one after the other.

I hope I'm not confusing you here. You may be wondering what the resulting mailing labels would look like if you put the zip code field "in front of" the last name field. Well, you can set your mind at ease. The order of your query fields actually doesn't matter to Access. Access automatically straightens everything out when it lays out your mailing labels, so they print out just as you would expect them to — but in sorted order.

New Data from a Query to a Table

In the last example, you might have noticed that you're missing one employee's home telephone number. At first you might think that you have to open the table to add that data. Well, Access is a step ahead of you. You can change the data right in your dynaset, and Access automatically makes the corresponding change to the underlying Employees table. Follow along, and you'll see what I mean:

1. With the dynaset in datasheet view, move your mouse cursor to the empty phone number field.

2. Type **(206) 555-0351** as a telephone number in that field and press Enter. Access saves the new number in the dynaset and in the underlying table, as shown in Figure 6-9.

And I want this, too

Often, you'll find that a single criterion won't get you the information you need. For example, to find Northwind's American employees who were hired in 1992, you need at least two criteria: their country and their hire date.

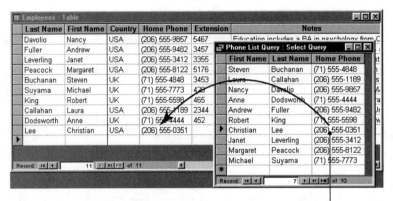

You've changed the phone number in the query.

Figure 6-9 Changes you make in dynaset data is immediately reflected in the underlying table's data.

To help you solve this common problem, Access allows you to include several criteria at once in your query. As a matter of fact, that's why there are so many empty cells in the QBE window. Each one can hold a criterion. There's something you need to keep in mind, however:

✳ Use OR when you place criteria one under the other in the same column; you are telling Access to find records that contain either of the criteria in that field.

✳ Use AND when you place criteria in the same row (in different columns); you are telling Access to find records that contain *both* criteria.

TIP **You need to watch out when you AND & OR your criteria. Access reads *all* the filled-in columns in your query. Consequently, you might be saying "and" or "or" about things you don't mean to.**

Follow these steps to add multiple criteria to a query:

1. Open the Phone List Query again in design view.

2. Drag the name of the HireDate field to the QBE grid. (The Country field should already be there if you've been following the steps in this chapter. If not, you need to drag the Country field to the QBE grid as well.)

3. In the Country column, type **USA**.

4. In the HireDate column, type **between 1/1/92 and 12/31/92**. Access adds pound signs (#) to each date. (This is the way Access notes that these are dates and not some other kind of numeric data.) When you're done, the query should look like Figure 6-10. By the way, if you can't see

all of your criteria because the column is too narrow, you can expand the column in this query just as you'd expand a column anywhere else in Microsoft Office: Click and drag the line between two columns to one side or the other.

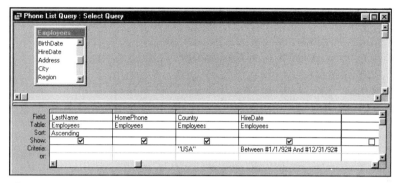

Figure 6-10 This multicriteria query is ready to be run.

5. Click ▮ to execute the query. Access displays a dynaset such as the one shown in Figure 6-11.

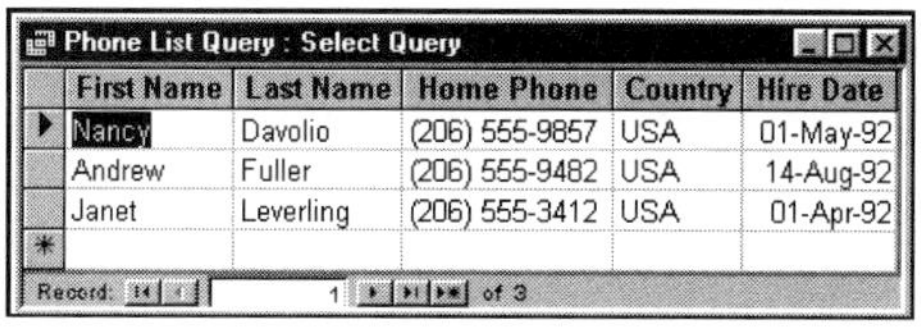

Figure 6-11 Three people in Northwind America were hired in 1992.

But I'm not sure

I don't know about you, but I simply can't remember names. On occasion, I have even forgotten my own. You may occasionally be faced with a similar problem. For example, what if you need to call up an employee's name, but can remember only that it starts with the letter *m*?

To help in this kind of situation, Access lets you use wildcard characters as query criteria. Wildcards, much like their poker game counterparts, are characters that can stand in place of any other character. Table 6-2 shows you the wildcard characters you can use.

TIP If you remember DOS wildcards, then Access query wildcards will be a cinch — they're the same thing, and they act the same.

TABLE 6-2 Query Criteria Wildcard Characters

Wildcard	What It Means	How to Use It
* (ASTERISK)	Any character(s) from here on.	* (alone) finds any characters at all. (Ironically, it's the same thing as using nothing.) *ra** finds the characters *ra* and any others following — for example, *ray, rain,* or *rapid.*
?	Any character occupying this place.	*f?ll* finds *fell, fill,* or *fall,* for example.
[] (SQUARE BRACKETS)	Find any of these characters that occupy this space.	*f[ea]ll* finds *fell* and *fall,* but it won't find *fill.*
- (USED WITH [&])	Find any of the characters in this alphabetic range.	*f[a-h]ll* finds *fall* or *fell,* but not *fill.*
! (USED WITH [&])	Not whatever characters are within the brackets.	*f[!ie]ll* finds *fall* but not *fill* or *fell.*
#	Find any numeric character that occupies this space.	*2#3* finds *213, 223, 233,* and so on.

With that bit of background, what do you say we give it a try? The scenario is this: You need some guy's name, but all you can remember is that it begins with the letter *m*.

Follow these steps to find the name:

1. Open the Phone List Query in design view.

2. If they're still there, erase the criteria you used in the preceding example.

3. In the criteria row for the FirstName field, type **m***. (You don't even need to make it a capital M, if you don't want to.) Notice that Access adds the word Like to what you typed. That sure makes the criteria easier to read, doesn't it? Nice touch, if I do say so myself. Your query should look like the one in Figure 6-12 at this point.

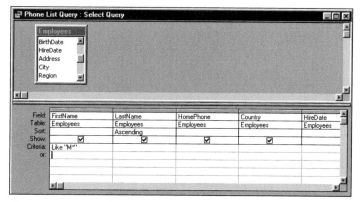

Figure 6-12 A wildcard makes for a flexible query.

4. Run the query by clicking ▮ on the toolbar. Access finds two names: Margaret's and Michael's. As you can see in Figure 6-13, he lives in England. Looks like it's going to be a long-distance call.

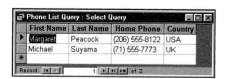

Figure 6-13 There are two Northwind employees whose names begin with the letter *m*.

BONUS

Here's a Sample Example

Now that you know how to get Access to snatch individual fields in your database tables, what if that's too much? What if only some records contain the data you need? How can you be more selective in your queries?

So many questions! It's a good thing I'm here to give the answer: examples as easy as one-two-three!

One: You give Access an example of the criteria for which you're looking.

Two: Access looks for something like your example in only those fields you specify in the query.

Three: Access shows you the records that match in a dynaset.

Let's say you want to know the names of only those Northwind employees who work in the United Kingdom (of Great Britain and Northern Ireland). To get that information, you first need to add the Country field to your query. Then you have to show Access that you want to see only those records that have "UK" stored in their Country field.

Follow along as I give you an example of what I mean:

1. Open the Phone List Query from our last example in design view.

2. From the field list, drag the Country field to the QBE grid at the bottom of the QBE window.

3. Move your mouse cursor to the cell in the criteria row for the Country field. Type **UK** there. This is your example to Access of what you're looking for. Notice that Access automatically adds quotation marks to UK. Once you've typed this, your query should look like Figure 6-14.

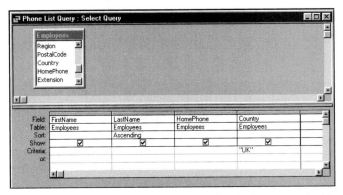

Figure 6-14   You give Access an example of what you're looking for.

4. Click ■ on the toolbar to execute your query. Access displays a new dynaset that includes only those people who are from the UK, as shown in Figure 6-15.

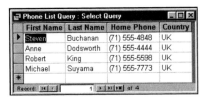

Figure 6-15   Northwind employees, over the pond.

GIVE THIS A TRY

What if you need to know more particulars about Northwind employees in the UK? For example, you might want to know their title and to whom they report. All you have to do is go to your Phone List Query (in design view) and add the Title and Reports To fields to your query. Run the query and *voilà!* You have the additional information you seek.

Summary

Well, we bit off quite a mouthful with this first chapter on queries. I'll expand on it after you get a bit more background in the next chapter on relationships. For now, though, you can extract some useful information from your Access databases — almost as easily as my son extracts a delicious meal from a smorgasbord.

CHAPTER SEVEN

RELATIONSHIPS ARE IMPORTANT

KEY GOALS OF THIS CHAPTER

When I'm not turning out best-selling computer books and living the glamorous life of an author, I spend some of my free time playing a double bass. Apropos of which, I recently heard a story about a double bass player and a couple with a troubled marriage.

It seems the husband and wife went to a counselor in an attempt to save their marriage. The meeting went poorly, with both of them bickering the entire time. Finally, the marriage counselor decided to take a break, so he got up and started playing his instrument. As he did so, the couple started speaking to each other, resolving issue after issue as if by magic. The obvious moral to the story is this: Everyone always talks during the bass solo.

You won't hear me playing much today — standing up and clapping at the news is unnecessary — but you will hear me talking about relationships.

This chapter is about relationships of the database kind. Unlike most of the others in this book, it's of necessity more theoretical than hands on. I want to give you a good understanding of the kinds of relationships you can create — and break — among Access tables. You'll find that relationships among database tables, while not as complicated as those between "significant others," are as useful and as necessary. First, for some background.

Databases: Flat and Full

There are basically two kinds of databases in the computer world: ones we in the biz call *flat file*, and all the rest, which we call *relational*. Flat file databases comprise a single table wherein you have to store all the database's data. If there's some additional data that you want to track, you either have to add a new field to the table or you have to create an entirely new table (re-entering into it any duplicate data).

A good example of a flat file is your checkbook and its register. They are actually two tables: One is a table of records that you give out (the checks), and the other is a table of records you keep for yourself (the register). The two tables are flat files in that you have to re-enter into your register the exact same information you entered onto a check — assuming you don't have duplicate checks, of course.

SIDE TRIP

A WORD ABOUT FLAT FILES

Reading about flat files here, they may seem to you like an awfully inefficient way of doing things — and they are. You may be wondering why anyone would want to use flat files. You may not realize that a business's entire paper record system held in filing cabinets is a collection of flat files. In the days before computers, that was the model we all used.

Just imagine how things in your company would have been then. Down in the accounting department there would have been a file of customers' names and addresses, another for employees, another for vendors, and so forth. Each of those files could be represented in a single flat ledger — the old-fashioned analog for a database table.

Continuing, every invoice lying in the orders filing cabinet would have had on it a freshly typed copy of the customer's address, a new copy of the company's address, as well as additional lines for retyped inventory items. They each had such repeatedly-entered data because there was no way short of cutting and pasting to get it onto each new record, um, invoice.

Finally, the reason businesses keep their filed papers in alphabetical order is because that way it is easier to leaf through all of them until their people get to the one they need.

The limitations inherent in flat files are completely done away with in a relational database like Access. With it, you never have to enter the same data more than once.

NOTE When we talk about databases in this chapter, we're only talking about the parts of them where you actually store data — their tables, in other words. We're leaving the extra stuff like queries out of the first part of this chapter's discussion.

> "A good example of a flat file is your checkbook and its register. They are actually two tables: One is a table of records that you give out (the checks), and the other is a table of records you keep for yourself (the register)."

A relational database, on the other hand, is one where each table can be logically connected with other tables. This connection is called a *join*. All it takes to join two tables is for both of them to contain a common field; an ID number, for example. Once two tables are joined and data is entered into them, you never have to re-enter data again. All you need to enter is the ID number. Access automatically goes and looks up the associated data it's already storing.

NOTE A *relational database is* a database comprising two or more tables that are linked together through common fields. Each of the tables in a relational database can be joined with more than one other table.

Not to belabor my checkbook example, but if you use duplicate checks, then you've got the beginnings of a relational database. You enter the data once, and it's automatically copied to the other record (your register). You relate the canceled checks the bank returns to you each month to the records in the register by the checks' numbers — the field they have in common.

Here's an example of how a relational database works with computers and real life. The company you work for probably has an accounting department. Let's take a risk and assume for the moment that the company is using Access. On its computers, the accounting department keeps only a single copy of each employee's, customer's, and vendor's name and address, each in its own Access table. Each employee, customer, and vendor record includes its own ID number (or some other distinguishing element).

When an order comes in, instead of retyping the customer's and vendor's full particulars, all the data entry person has to type is an ID number with which it's associated. When someone at your company needs to print an invoice, Access uses the customer's ID number to look up the customer's name and address and then types it on the order form. Then Access uses a product ID number to find out what the customer bought, how much it costs, how many your company has in inventory (do you need to reorder more?), and so on — all from a single ID number.

If you're becoming concerned or confused, please don't fret. This all sounds much more complicated than it is to use.

Dissecting the Relationship Dialog

With the preceding example in mind, how about actually relating a couple of tables in a database. I'm thinking our best bet would be with the My First Address Book database you created in an earlier chapter.

SIDE TRIP

OPENING THE MY FIRST ADDRESS BOOK DATABASE, REPRISED

Follow these steps to open the My First Address Book database:

1. With Windows running, click My Computer to call up the explorer.

2. Click your way to the My Documents folder. In it, look for a file called My First Address Book. It will have an Access application icon — the one with a yellow key on it — and it will look like the one shown in the following figure.

3. When you find the My First Address Book icon, double click it to open the database. Access starts running and automatically loads the My First Address Book database.

That's all you need to do here, and it doesn't matter for now that the switchboard is displayed. You can continue with the example by returning to the main body of text.

Your basic tool for creating relationships is the Relationships dialog box. With it, you tell Access which tables you want to be related and how you want them to be related. Access then uses that information to logically connect your data as you create queries. Using the queries you create, you can easily create forms and reports that automatically take advantage of the connected data.

Creating a relationship between tables is basically a one-two-three step process.

* One: You tell Access which tables are to be joined in the relationship.
* Two: You indicate which fields in those tables should be linked.
* Three: You indicate what kind of join you want to have between the tables.

I go into each of these steps in detail as I guide you through the rest of this chapter.

Choosing tables to join

Let's take a look at the Relationships dialog box. To get to it, you have to have the My First Address Book database open. If you need a refresher on how to do that, please see the sidebar.

If not — and with the database open — you can follow these steps:

1. Select **Relationships** from the **Tools** menu, as shown in Figure 7-1. Access displays the Relationships dialog box. If you haven't yet set any relationships in this database, then Access also calls up the Show Table dialog box.

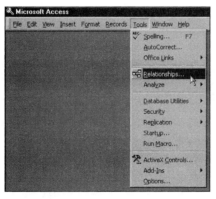

Figure 7-1 Relationships are one of the data manipulation tools available to you.

2. If necessary, drag the two tables Addresses and Children from the Show Table dialog box to the Relationships dialog box. Access places the lists of the tables and their fields into the Relationships dialog box, much as is shown in Figure 7-2.

3. Click **Close** when you're done. Access closes the show Table dialog box and leaves open the Relationships dialog box.

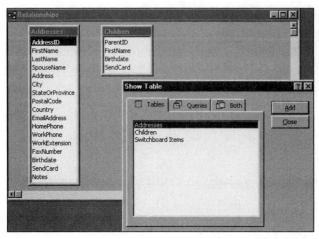

Figure 7-2 Use the Show Table dialog box to add tables to relationships and to queries.

That's all there is to the first step — that of telling Access which tables to logically join. The next thing to do is relate the tables.

Making the relationship

You can relate about as many of your database's tables as you care to have joined together. Each table, as a matter of fact, can be related to several other tables, even using the same field. But when you get right down to details, each individual relationship — each join — is that of one table to a single other table.

TIP   **When you want to relate two tables, there's something you need to keep in mind. While the tables can have different names and sizes, each of the fields you use in a join must at least be of the same data type. That means, for example, you can link two character, number, or date fields, but you can't join a number field to a character field or to a date field.**

Follow these steps, and I'll show you how the whole process of joining tables works:

1. Highlight the AddressID field in the Addresses table and drag the highlighted field to the ParentID field in the Children table. Access displays the detail Relationships dialog box, as you can see in Figure 7-3.

   Notice that Access has filled in for you both the names of the tables as well as the names of the ID fields.

2. Click **Create** . Access creates the relationship and closes the detail Relationships dialog box. When it's done, the Relationships dialog box displays a new line drawn between the two tables. It runs from the AddressID field in the Addresses table to the ParentID field in the Children table, as shown in Figure 7-4.

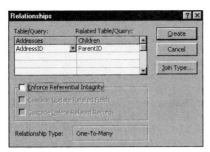

Figure 7-3 Access allows you to create many kinds of joins.

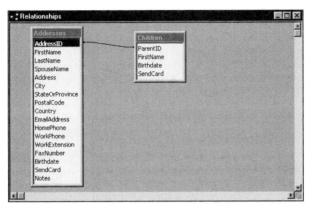

Figure 7-4 A join is indicated by a line between two tables.

That's it! You have a relationship between these two tables. From now on, whenever you create a query involving one table — or anything based on a query (such as a form or report) — with no further effort on your part, you automatically include the other table almost as if they were one.

Decisions, decisions

When you join two tables, you need to make some decisions about the nature of the relationship. Almost sounds like getting married, doesn't it? Fortunately, joining decisions aren't as complicated as all that. Now seems like a good time to talk about these decisions in some detail and so... you need to decide:

* The type of join to create between the tables; in other words, which records in each table to include.

* Whether or not to enforce referential integrity when you manipulate the records in those tables.

* How you want to handle adding or deleting records, for example, as into the Children table when there isn't a matching linked record in the Addresses table. This is called *cascading* updates and deletions.

Follow these steps, if you please:

1. With the Relationships dialog box open, double click the join line between the two tables. Access displays again the detail Relationships dialog box.

2. Click the [Join Type] button. Access displays the Join Properties dialog box, as shown in Figure 7-5. This is where it gets interesting.

Figure 7-5   Which kind of join do you want to use?

3. Click the third option, the one that includes all the records from the Children table and only those from the Addresses table for which the joined fields are of the same value.

4. Click [OK]. Access closes the Join Properties dialog box and again displays the detail Relationships dialog box.

5. Check the box labeled Enforce Referential Integrity. Access enables the two Cascade checkboxes below it.

6. Check the boxes labeled Cascade Update Related Fields and Cascade Delete Related Fields. (I'll tell you why in a moment.) When you're done, your detail Relationships dialog box should look like the one in Figure 7-6. Notice that Access announces at the bottom of the dialog box that this is now a one-to-many relationship.

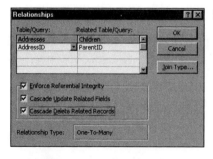

Figure 7-6   Referential Integrity keeps your database from becoming confused.

7. Click [OK]. Access closes the detail Relationship dialog box, modifies the earlier one-to-one relationship, and redraws the join line between the two tables in the Relationships dialog box, as shown in Figure 7-7.

Notice that on the many side of the join, Access displays an infinity symbol (∞). Notice also, that on the one side of the join, Access displays a one (1). That's its shorthand message to you that this is a one-to-many relationship and which side is which.

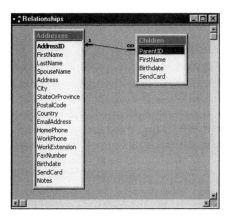

Figure 7-7 You can graphically see the one-to-many relationship.

SIDE TRIP

A WORD OR TWO ON JOIN PROPERTIES

The Join Properties dialog box offers you three choices. Let's look at each one in turn.

1. Only include rows where the joined fields from both tables are equal.

This is the famous one-to-one relationship. It's what Access offers as a default, probably because it's the "safest" one. Actually, the one-to-one is the relationship you'll use least often in real life. It's effect is to create a join in which the two tables behave as if they are actually one table. I'm trying to think where this would be useful, and I can think of only three situations:

- Access allows you to have up to 255 fields in a single table. If, for some reason, you need more than that, I suppose you could simulate this gargantuan table using one-to-one relationships. If so, however, I strongly recommend you take another look at your database design.

- Sometimes you want to keep things secret. For example, you might have a couple of personnel tables: one holding general name, address, and phone number data, and the other holding more sensitive data such as birth dates and Social Security numbers. Using a one-to-one relationship between the two tables gives you a bit of freedom. You can create forms and reports that incorporate only the general data to be used by anyone, and other forms and reports that incorporate both tables and are used by only those "in the know."

(continued)

A WORD OR TWO ON JOIN PROPERTIES *(continued)*

- You have a huge database where you don't really need to use every field to hold data for every record. You can place your less-used fields in the second table of the one-to-one relationship and then incorporate these fields only when you need to use their space.

By the way, the technical term for the link in this one-to-one relationship is *inner join* or *equi-join*. It's called "inner" because of the way relational algebra works. In this case, both sides of the join incorporate records that aren't empty, and that are to be included; hence, inner. If one side or the other of the join needs to incorporate empty records, then we'd call it an *outer join*. The term equi-join is just a fancy way of saying one-to-one.

2. Include ALL records from Addresses and only those records from Children where the joined fields are equal.

This is called a one-to-many relationship. It's the one most often used, and your common sense tells you why. Each parent's record in the Addresses table can be linked to many children records in the Children table. Unfortunately, this particular join doesn't work for our example. It's kind of backward, given our current situation. We really should call it a many-to-one relationship.

In the biz, the technical term for this particular relationship is a *left inner join*. It's a lefty because the many side of the one-to-many is on the left side of the relational algebra expression.

3. Include ALL records from Children and only those records from Addresses where the joined fields are equal.

This is another one-to-many relationship, one that exactly fits the bill for our example. With it, Access recognizes that we can have many children for each parent record. This is particularly convenient in this case because the general term for the table on the one side in any one-to-many relationship is a *parent table*, while the table on the many side is generally called a *child table*. Clever, huh?

Oh yes. If I might again get a bit technical, the link in this relationship is — you guessed it — a *right inner join*.

BONUS

Integrity and Cascade Foothills

The last thing I want to cover in this chapter has to do with two new concepts for you: *referential integrity cascading updates* and *cascading deletes*. We'll take them one at a time.

Referring with integrity

Built into the Jet database engine that underlies Access is a series of rules that Access uses to make sure your data doesn't become inadvertently corrupted. Access can't know if you're entering "garbage" data, of course. But it can do what it can to see to it that once your data is in there, it doesn't get mangled.

Absent your computer going on the fritz and blowing smoke, the only way already-stored data gets mangled is when it gets modified. With a single table database, this isn't much of a problem. After all, the only way single-table data gets modified is for you to look at it and modify it. Joined tables, on the other hand, because Access does a lot of their handling automatically and "behind the scenes," don't always work that way.

"Built into the Jet database engine that underlies Access are a series of rules that Access uses to make sure your data doesn't become inadvertently corrupted."

Look at our My First Address Book database. Because the tables are related, you could have a logical connection among, say, three records: one parent and two children. What do you suppose would happen to those children records if you deleted their associated parent record? Just like in real life, those two darlings would become orphans, even if you didn't really mean to kill off the parent record. In database terms, the orphaned child records would have no parent record to which to refer.

With Access checking referential integrity for you, if you try to delete a parent record that has associated with it any children records, you get an error message. Access would prevent the tragedy.

Before you have Access enforce referential integrity, you first need to make sure of a couple of things.

* Both of the tables you've linked must be from within the same Access database. They can't be linked to another kind of database or even linked to another Access database on your computer or on your network.

* Your parent record — the one side of a one-to-many relationship — must either have a unique index or it must be a Primary Key field.

* The fields you use to link the two tables must be of the same data type. Also, if they're not text fields, then they both must also be of the same size.

Cascading those references

With referential integrity active, each time you work with a record on one side or the other of a join, Access automatically keeps track of its relationship behind the scenes. That means Access will do things on its own that keep your data automatically intact — according to built-in rules, of course. One of these things (or two things, I suppose) Access does has to do with how Access coordinates data within parent and child records.

In the Children table of the My First Address Book database, you know which children belong to which parents by keeping a copy of the parent's number in the children's records. What would happen if you decided to arbitrarily change a parent's number?

If you tell Access to cascade update related fields, then Access automatically finds each of the parent's children records and changes the ID numbers there for you. If there were another table of child records linked to the child records — grandchild records? — then Access would change those as well. You can see how the name cascading updates was chosen.

The same kind of thing happens when you have Access automatically cascade delete related files. If you were to delete a parent record, then Access would automatically kill off the related children records as well. Sounds kind of draconian, doesn't it?

TIP **You don't always want to make both cascade update and cascade delete active. The classic example of this situation is in a database where you're tracking customers and their orders. If you deleted a customer from your database, you probably wouldn't also want to delete all the order records too.**

Summary

Well, so much for this theory chapter. You now have a pretty good understanding of what goes into an Access relationship. You know about referential integrity and cascading updates and deletes. All in all a pretty good day's work, I'd say.

It's Miller time, and I feel like jammin'. What shall it be? Dark glasses, a fedora, and cool jazz? Or blue jeans, a tee shirt, and bluegrass? Dum, da dum dum dum. Smokin'.

LET'S MAKE SOME CHANGES

KEY GOALS OF THIS CHAPTER:

HOW TO CREATE A QUERY USING TWO TABLES
    PAGE 154

HOW TO USE FUNCTIONS SUCH AS AVG AND SUM
    PAGE 159

HOW TO MAKE A NEW TABLE USING A QUERY
    PAGE 164

HOW TO UPDATE DATA AUTOMATICALLY   PAGE 166

I've been told that the average working stiff in North America is employed at an average of 20 jobs during his or her lifetime. If that's true, then I'm way above average. I've been thrown out of *many* more than 20 jobs, some of them a whole lot nicer than what I'm doing now. I have my standards, after all.

Going hither and yon like this, I've seen a lot of changes. Important things like human beings walking on the moon, grownups driving 70 miles per hour on the freeway again (legally!), and latte technology brought almost to its peak. But the best thing of all — it says here — I now know the mystery behind Access automatically making changes to my databases. Hey, color me nerd.

Now that you've gotten this far in this book and you have a good understanding of queries and relationships, I think it's about time I reveal to you the answer to that same mystery. As you've probably guessed, it involves queries — slightly more advanced queries to be sure, but the same friendly and familiar Access queries nonetheless.

In this chapter, the first thing you learn is how to create a table using more than one field. Then you create a couple of *action queries*. These are a special kind of queries that act on the data — hence their name. The action queries you create will average a group of data items and sum a few. You're also going to see how to use an action query to automatically update data and to create a table out of thin air!

Tea for Two

Although I mentioned earlier the fact that you can use more than one table in your queries, I haven't really explained this concept. What I want to do now is revisit the My First Address Book database and create a query that gets information from both the Addresses and Children tables. We're going to look for a list of the grownups and children in the database.

Creating a query that retrieves data from more than one table or query is much the same as getting the data from a single table or query: Put the table's or query's field list(s) at the top of the QBE window, drag the field names to the QBE grid, and then run your query. If you want to use criteria, that's the same too.

Including your tables

The first thing you need to do is to start Access and to open the My First Address Book database.

After it's running, follow these steps:

1. Close the switchboard and open the database container.

2. Click the Queries tab to make it active. Access displays all the queries you've created so far for this database. Not many there yet, huh? Well, we'll change that in a minute.

3. Click New . Access displays the New Query dialog box.

4. Because this is where you're going to design a simple Select Query, leave Design View highlighted and click OK . Access shows us our friend, the QBE window, along with its sibling, the Show Table dialog box.

TIP When you create a query, you put field lists from the tables and/or queries you want to use into the top of the QBE window. You can click and drag them, of course. But sometimes it's faster to simply Ctrl+Click (hold down your Control key while clicking your left mouse button) each table or query name you want to highlight them all at once and then click Add. Access then does the dragging for you, and the field lists automatically appear at the top of your QBE window.

5. Highlight and move the names of the Addresses and Children tables from the Show Tables dialog box to the top of the QBE window. Access creates two field lists at the top of the QBE window. Because you've already created a relationship between them in Chapter 7, "Relationships Are Important," Access draws a join line between the two field lists.

After you've performed these five steps, your QBE window should look like the one in Figure 8-1. When you close the Show Table dialog box, you've done the first part of creating your new query.

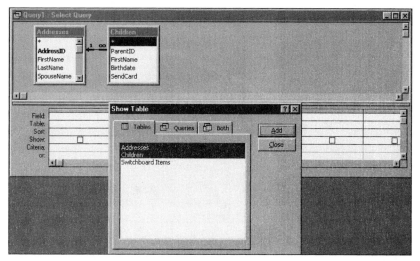

Figure 8-1 All existing relationships between tables remain unchanged when those tables are used in queries.

A small but helpful detail

Your databases may often contain one or more tables that include fields with the same name. They're probably different fields holding different data, but they still have the same name. For example, in the My First Address Book database, both the Addresses and Children tables have a field called FirstName. Things can easily get confusing in this situation.

Access keeps field names straight internally by noting which table each field comes from. It even lets you see the tables' names in your QBE window. As a matter of regular practice, I like to always have that row visible.

Just in case it isn't visible in your version of Access, here's how to make it so:

1. Close the Show Tables dialog box, and then, with your QBE window visible, move your mouse cursor to the ⌞ **View** ⌟ menu.

2. In the ⌞ **View** ⌟ menu, make sure that the ⌞ **Table Names** ⌟ option is checked, as shown in Figure 8-2.

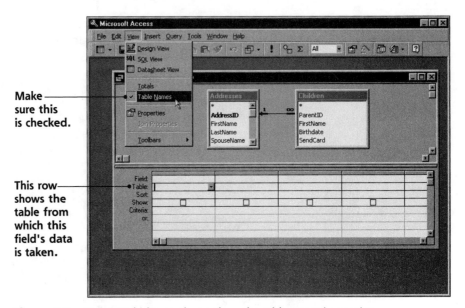

Make sure this is checked.

This row shows the table from which this field's data is taken.

Figure 8-2   It's a good idea to always show the table name in queries.

Choosing your fields

The next thing you need to do is to select the fields you'll use for the names of the parents and children.

To do so, follow these steps:

1. Because all you're looking for is a list of names, drag the LastName field name from the Addresses table to the Field row in the first column in the QBE grid. Notice that when you do, Access places the table name right under the field name.

2. Do the same thing with the FirstName fields from each of the Addresses and Children tables. When you're done, the query should look like the one in Figure 8-3.

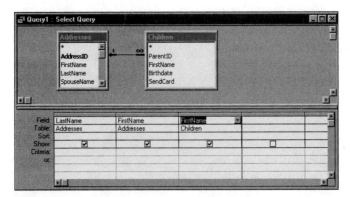

Figure 8-3   Your query is almost ready to run.

3. Save the Query as List of Names query. If you need a quickie refresher on how to do that, here 'tis: Move your mouse cursor to the [**File**] menu and select [**Save**] from it. Access displays the Save As dialog box in which you type **List of Names query** and click [**OK**].

4. The only thing left to do now is to run your new query. Click [!] on the Access toolbar. Access looks at the two tables in your database and shows you the result in a dynaset that looks like the one in Figure 8-4.

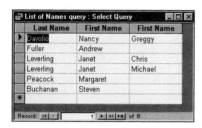

Figure 8-4 The dynaset shows information from two tables.

From Figure 8-4, you can see that two families, the Davolios and the Leverlings, have children. But that's not all the people in the database, and we want a list of all the names. Hmmmm. What's wrong?

Turning an inie into an outie

Actually, there's nothing "wrong" with our query *per se*. It's just that the inner join we arranged in the last chapter has done its work. (Remember, when you create a relationship between tables, it persists when those tables are used again.) What you need to do is have Access include in the Addresses table the records of those people who don't also have children in the Children table.

> **"Remember, when you create a relationship between tables, it persists when those tables are used again."**

Sounds hard, doesn't it? Well friend, you're gonna laugh when you see how easy *this* is!

Just follow along:

1. With the dynaset active, click [▧▾] on the toolbar. Like Cinderella running from the ball, the query changes the dynaset back to its QBE version.

Notice the arrow that joins the two field lists. See how it is pointing from right to left on your screen and in Figure 8-5.

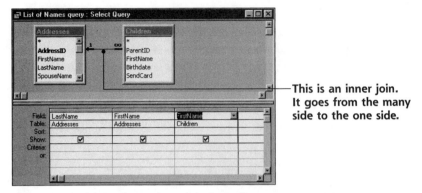

This is an inner join. It goes from the many side to the one side.

Figure 8-5 This is what an inner join looks like.

The way this join works is like this "recipe:"

  a. Access looks first in the Children table to see if a FirstName contains a value.

  b. If so, it then looks at the Addresses table and snatches out the contents of the corresponding FirstName and LastName fields.

  c. If not, Access looks for the next filled FirstName field, and repeats until done.

2. Double click anywhere on the join line. Access displays the Join Properties dialog box.

3. Notice that the third option button is selected in the Join Properties dialog box. Click the second option instead, as shown in Figure 8-6.

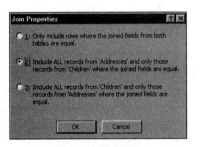

Figure 8-6 Turning an inner join into an outer join.

4. Click **OK**. Access closes the Join Properties dialog box and changes the direction of the join line arrow in the QBE window. If you look at Figure 8-7, you'll see what I mean.

5. Finally, click ▣ on the toolbar. Access reruns the query and displays the dynaset shown in Figure 8-8. Notice that now you have a list that includes everyone in the database.

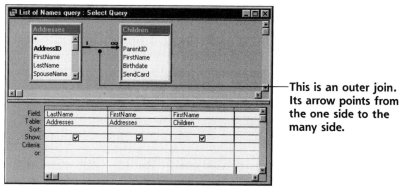

Figure 8-7 This is what an outer join looks like.

This is an outer join. Its arrow points from the one side to the many side.

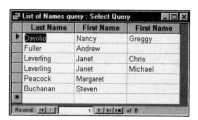

Figure 8-8 Our list of names is complete.

Functionally Speaking

Every now and then, the information you need isn't hidden in the data itself, but rather in the way the data all goes together. That would be good, for example, if you wanted to know how many records of a certain thing are stored in your database or if you needed to know how much they were worth all together.

Access has built into it a number of functions that help you get the answers to questions like these. You can look for them in the Access Help facilities, of course. To make things easier for the moment, however, Table 8-1 contains a list of the more commonly used functions.

TABLE 8-1 Access Functions

Function	What It Does	Cogent Comments
FIRST	Displays the first value in this field.	Like, no kidding, Dude!
AVG	Calculates arithmetic mean of the values stored in this field.	Works only with number or currency data. If the field stores a Null, then it's ignored, but if a field has the value of 0 it is included.
COUNT	Displays the number fields that contain a value.	Ignores fields that don't contain a value. You can use Count(*) and it will count all the fields for you, regardless of whether they contain anything.
MAX	Displays the largest value stored in this field.	If the field stores a number, then you see the biggest one. If it stores text, then you see the one with the highest ASCII number, *Z* for instance, regardless of whether it's upper or lower case. Empty fields are ignored.
MIN	Displays the smallest value stored in this field.	If the field stores a number, then you see the smallest one. If it stores text, then you see the one with the lowest ASCII number, *A* for instance, regardless of whether it's upper or lower case. Empty fields are ignored.
STDEV	Displays the standard deviation for all the values stored in this field.	Only works with number and currency data. If fewer than two fields contain a value, then it displays nothing.
SUM	Adds all the values stored in this field.	Works with only number and currency data.
VAR	Displays the statistical variance of all the values in this field.	Works with only number and currency data. If fewer than two fields contain a value, then it displays nothing.
LAST	Displays the last value in this field.	No way! Yes way! Most excellent!

Totally, Dude

arlier in this chapter, I told you about the Table row in the QBE grid. Well, Access has another useful row, this one for holding the functions we just discussed. Access uses the function you put in that row to manipulate the values of your data. Just as with the Table row, as a matter of regular practice I like to have the Total row visible too.

If it's not visible in your version of Access, here's how to make it so:

1. With the QBE window visible, move your mouse cursor to the View menu.

2. From the View menu, make sure that the Totals option is checked, as shown in Figure 8-9.

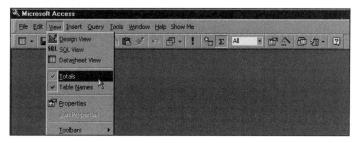

Figure 8-9   It's a good idea to always show the Total name in queries.

You might notice that Group By is the default value for each column in the Total row. Unfortunately, its meaning might be a bit misleading at this point. Here's a quick and dirty explanation.

X-REF   You might remember that underlying each Access query is the Structured Query Language, or SQL for short. (I cover SQL in more detail in Chapter 13, "A Sequel Can Come First.") In a short while, you'll get an intuitive idea of how Group By works. Suffice it to say for now that you can have what are called *SQL aggregate functions* on the Total row. These functions operate on groups of data, rather than on the contents of individual fields. For now, you can think of Group By as being in this case a kind of place holder. It's there until and unless you put another aggregate function in its place.

"SQL aggregate functions operate on groups of data, rather than on the contents of individual fields."

Doing the Math

Well now, don't you feel like it's time to try out some of this information? So do I. Let's pretend that you've come to work for Northwind Traders and that you have to learn some general facts about the company's product line.

As you know by now, Northwind Traders sells a wide variety of foodstuffs. In its database, the company holds product data in a Products table. The kinds of data they track for each product include such things as what the product is, how much it costs, and how many of them they have in stock. Normal stuff, in other words. Oh yes, the company also tracks in a Yes/No field whether the product has been discontinued.

What you're interested in — according to this scenario — is the average price of the various categories of products and how many of each product remain to be sold.

So, with the Northwind database up and running and the Queries tab active, follow along with these steps:

1. Click the New button to call up the QBE window. From the Show Tables dialog box, drag the Products and Categories field lists into the upper part of the QBE window. Access automatically draws the join line between them.

2. I've always found it wise to save my work early and often, so now would be a good time to do that with your new query. Save your work as Product Numbers Query.

3. You'll need to use the data from three fields to get the information you seek. From the Categories table, drag the CategoryName field to the first column in the QBE grid. Then from the Products table, drag the UnitPrice and UnitsInStock fields to the next two columns in the QBE grid. When you've done so, your query should look like the one shown in Figure 8-10.

   If you were to run the query now, all you'd get is a list of 77 products grouped together by category. Oh, go ahead; you won't hurt anything. But even though you might find it interesting, it's not really useful for the purposes of this example.

Putting in Sums and Such

The next thing to do is add the aggregate functions you need to have in your query's Total row.

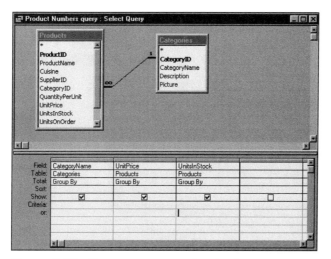

Figure 8-10   The query now contains the three necessary fields.

Here's how to do that:

1. Move your mouse cursor to the Total row in the UnitPrice column and click. Access displays a list box arrow in that cell.

2. Click the list box arrow. Access displays the list box. Move your mouse cursor down to Avg and click. You can see the result in Figure 8-11.

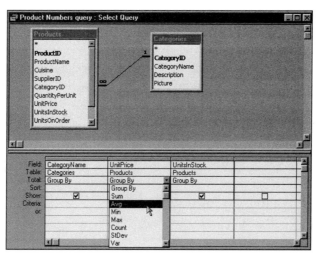

Figure 8-11   You can select any of the aggregate functions from the list box.

3. Move to the UnitsInStock column. Doing much the same thing as you just did in the UnitPrice column, add the Sum function to the UnitsInStock Total row.

With all that done, you can go ahead and run the query. You can see the result I got when I ran it in Figure 8-12. Notice that the query gives you exactly the information you're looking for, the average and total costs for each type of product Northwest Traders sells.

Product Numbers query : Select Query

Category Name	AvgOfUnitPrice	SumOfUnitsInStock
Beverages	$37.98	559
Condiments	$23.06	507
Confections	$25.16	386
Dairy Products	$28.73	393
Grains/Cereals	$20.25	308
Meat/Poultry	$54.01	165
Produce	$32.37	100
Seafood	$20.68	701

Record: 1 of 8

Figure 8-12 Now you know what's what.

Making Something New out of Nothing

At the beginning of this chapter, I told you that we'd use a query to create a table out of thin air. Bet you thought I was fooling! Not me — no sir-ee-bob.

The process is quite simple. You create a query that looks at all the records in a table, culling them according to criteria you specify. It then takes those culled records and copies them to a brand new table. You're left with two tables, one being a subset duplicate of the other. (Now doesn't *that* sound intelligent and mathematical?)

Our scenario is this: You're still at Northwind Traders, and you've been given the job of listing all the discontinued products in the database. The list will need to be somewhat permanent because your boss wants a current snapshot of the discontinued data, and you know that's best done in a separate table.

SIDE TRIP

DO IT YOURSELF

Here's a bit of refinement for your query. The Products table includes a Yes/No field that tracks discontinued items. A Yes in that field means the item has been discontinued.

To an Access Yes/No field, anything other than a zero means Yes. That means you can modify this query so that you see only the active (non-discontinued) items by adding that field to your query and by including the number zero (0) as its criteria. Hint: You can leave the Total field as Group By. Give it a try!

To do the deed, you'll use a query similar to the one you just used to do the averaging and summing.

If you follow along, I'll show you how:

1. Create a new query in the QBE window using only the Products table. Save the new query as Discontinued Products Make query.

    It's not really a Make query — yet. It starts out as a normal, everyday Select query. You'll change it to a Make Table in just a moment.

2. Drag from the field list all the Product table's fields except for ProductID, UnitsInStock, and UnitsOnOrder. Because this table will consist entirely of discontinued items, these three fields would hold unnecessary data.

    There's one other detail I want to bring to your attention. Because the value of the Discontinued field in the new table will always be Yes, there's no need to include it in the new table. You do, however, have to include it in the query. Otherwise, the query wouldn't come up with the information you see, and there'd be no point to it! What you should do to solve the dilemma is to simply uncheck the Show checkbox for the Discontinued field. Doing so includes the Discontinued field in the query but leaves it out of the table that is the query's result.

3. The only criteria you need the query to look at as it decides which records to copy is whether the product has been discontinued. Accordingly, add Yes as a criteria in the Discontinued column of the QBE grid.

4. Here's where you do the magic. With the query still in design view, move to the ▭ Query ▭ menu on the menu bar and select ▭ **Make-Table Query** ▭. Access displays the Make Table dialog box, as shown in Figure 8-13.

Figure 8-13 Each new table gets its own name.

5. Type **Discontinued Items table** as the name for your new table. Because you'll want this new table to remain in the current database, be sure that the Current Database option button remains selected. When you're done, click ▭ **OK** ▭.

6. Next, you need to save your query again. Click ▦ on the toolbar and Access does just that for you.

7. Now — finally — you're ready to run the query. Click ▦ on the toolbar. Access displays a warning dialog box, as shown in Figure 8-14.

It's more scary than necessary, in my opinion. With a Make Table query, you're not destroying data, you're only duplicating it in a new table. Click $\boxed{\text{Yes}}$, and Access runs the query, creating a new object called Discontinued Items table.

Figure 8-14 In this case it doesn't matter that you can't undo your actions.

I don't know about you, but I'm curious at this point to see the new table. You'll find it in the database container under the Tables tab. Double click on its name and Access will show it to you. My version is depicted here in Figure 8-15.

ProductName	Cuisine	SupplierID	CategoryID	QuantityPerUnit	UnitPrice
Chef Anton's Gumbo Mix	Creole	2	2	36 boxes	$21.35
Mishi Kobe Niku	Japanese	4	6	18 - 500 g pkgs.	$97.00
Alice Mutton	Slavic	7	6	20 - 1 kg tins	$39.00
Guaraná Fantástica	Mexican	10	1	12 - 355 ml cans	$4.50
Rössle Sauerkraut	German	12	7	25 - 825 g cans	$45.60
Thüringer Rostbratwurst	German	12	6	50 bags x 30 sausgs.	$123.79
Singaporean Hokkien Fried Mee	Oriental	20	5	32 - 1 kg pkgs.	$14.00
Perth Pasties		24	6	48 pieces	$32.80

Figure 8-15 The newly created table — after I widened its columns a bit.

BONUS

Updating My Data

You've got enough experience with Access now to know that you can update any record by calling it up and directly changing it. That's not a bad process if you don't have a whole lot of records to deal with — or if you don't have to do the same thing over and over and... well, you get the idea.

That's because one thing you're good at is using the brain God gave you. You can think abstract thoughts, you can read with understanding, you can love. On the other hand, unless you're really — and I mean *really* — starved for something to do, you're probably not very good at mindless repetition. Computers, on the other hand, *love* mindless repetition, which is good given our continuing scenario.

SIDE TRIP

HERE'S A LITTLE OOPS PROTECTION

When you create and run an Update query, it actually goes into the table and modifies your data. That — for obvious reasons — can be very dangerous. One thing I've learned to do is to always and first save a copy of any table that I'm about to permanently modify.

It's a simple matter of copy and paste, just as if the table were a sentence in a word processor. Here's what you do:

1. In the database container with the Tables tab active, highlight the name of the table you're about to modify.

2. Press Ctrl+C to copy it.

3. Press Ctrl+V to paste it.

Access prompts you to give the copy a name. I usually use Copy of and the name of the table. For example, in this case I copied the Products table, structure *and* data, to what I decided to call the Copy of Products table.

Sure, that name's as obvious as dirt, but there's no chance I'll mistake it for something else. Once I've finished with this chapter and have successfully and accurately run the Update query, I'll just delete my copy.

And breath a small sigh of relief.

You're still at Northwind Traders and on a management career track. You're in the Accounting department, where inflation has taken its toll. Accordingly, you've been assigned to update the Products database by increasing the unit price of everything by the approximate current rate of inflation in the U.S.: 3 percent.

The process is straightforward. You create a query called an *Update query* that includes the table to be updated as well as any of its fields that will be used in the updating. The Update query starts out as a Select query, just as the Make Table query you created earlier in the chapter. Also, much as you did with the Make Table query, you turn this Select query into an Update query by choosing that option from the query menu while in design view.

The Update query has a special row in the QBE grid labeled Update to. This is the row where you put the mathematical expression that Access uses to do the necessary calculation.

Follow these steps and you'll see what I mean:

1. Create a new query just as you've done before, but this time using only the Products table.

2. Save the new query, again as you've done before, but this time using the name Products Update query.

3. Drag the UnitPrice field to the QBE grid. That's the field that contains the data you'll update.

4. Now you're ready to turn this Select query into an Update query. To do so, move your mouse cursor to the | **Query** | menu and select | **Update Query** |, as shown in Figure 8-16.

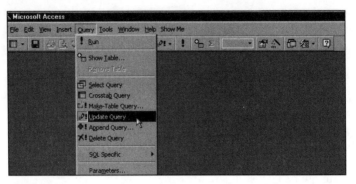

Figure 8-16 You make an Update query from a Select query.

5. Next, you have to tell the query exactly what to do. Move your mouse cursor to the Update to: row in the QBE grid. Type **[UnitPrice]*1.03**, as shown in Figure 8-17.

Figure 8-17 This update criteria will modify the data stored in the UnitPrice field.

In English, this means "take the value contained within the UnitPrice field and multiply it by one-point-zero-three times." Access uses the brackets ([&]) to understand that this is the name of one of its objects (a field, in this case) and not merely some other alphabetic text. If you wanted to be more specific, you could have typed, [Products].[UnitPrice], which to Access is analogous to a person's full name.

6. Save your query again. After you've done so, click  on the toolbar to execute the query. Access displays a warning dialog box, as shown in Figure 8-18.

Figure 8-18 Access does its best to protect you from mistakes.

7. If you're ready to go (you did make a copy of the Products table, just in case, didn't you?), click **Yes**. Access runs the query and updates all the UnitPrice values in the Products table.

So there you go. You can imagine that was a lot easier than doing the math and entering by hand the numbers for 77 records. And you didn't have to worry about introducing any typographical errors, either. This, friend, is the proper way to use a computer, in my most humble opinion.

Summary

Well we've done quite a bit here in this chapter. I hope you don't feel too overwhelmed — especially when I tell you that I've really only scratched the Access query surface, as it were. There is *a lot* more you can do with queries, but I've shown you the stuff you're most likely to use as an Access beginner.

By the way, I hope you've recognized that I was only joking when I said that I've been thrown out of more than 20 jobs. I mean, no one's *that* irresponsible. No way. I'm sure it couldn't have been more than 10 or 12 jobs — at the very most.

FORMALLY YOURS

KEY GOALS OF THIS CHAPTER

I've heard a familiar saying that goes something like this: "There are only two things you can count on this world: paying taxes and dying." It's true. I die a little every year when I have to fill out my income tax form. Not that I have to pay too much on a starving writer's income, of course; I would never complain about that, you know. What would be the point, after all?

No, what kills me are the forms, themselves. There's the basic 1040 with its schedules A, B, E, C, and F (did I miss any letters?). If you think you didn't make enough and so won't have to actually write them a check for the taxes they're already withholding, then you can try to fill out a form 1040EZ. "EZ"—yeah, right!

No matter what they call the form, I never know for sure from where to find the correct number to put in box 37 that I add to box 39 and then compare the result with box 24 and put any overage in box 40. Millions of taxpayer dollars have gone into designing those forms, and still they're often incomprehensible to someone as intelligent and good looking as myself.

Believe it or not, I've even seen Access forms like that. Huge, disjointed things, with sunken fields for data input scattered on them like holes in a dart board. Near some of the input fields they'll occasionally have a cryptic label; one that probably can be understood only by the form's designer.

While it's a handy tool, the datasheet view you've learned about can be limiting when you want to really zero in on your data. In this chapter, I'm going to show you how easy it is to create truly useful Access forms that let you do just that — forms that are so clear to use that they will allow anyone to use your database immediately and without questions.

Forming an Overview

First of all, what is a form, anyway? I'm glad you asked. A form is an Access object that can do one of two things.

* A form can display the fields of a single record in a table or dynaset and let you navigate among the records. This is called a "data entry form," although it's most often used as a data display form, if the truth be told.

* A form can serve as a holder for pushbutton controls — a switchboard, for example, such as the one automatically created in My First Address Book.

You've already seen a switchboard form when you created the My First Address Book database. Figure 9-1 is an example of a well-designed and implemented data entry form.

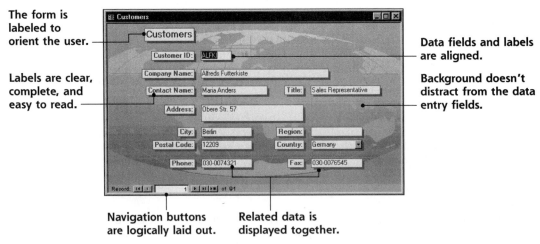

The form is labeled to orient the user.

Labels are clear, complete, and easy to read.

Data fields and labels are aligned.

Background doesn't distract from the data entry fields.

Navigation buttons are logically laid out.   **Related data is displayed together.**

Figure 9-1   This is a well-designed data entry form.

Let's stop for a moment and look at this illustration to see what makes this a "good" data entry form. First of all, notice that it's clean and neat. The data entry fields and labels aren't crowded together, nor is the form cluttered with extraneous information or visual effects.

There's also something else, something a bit more subtle. Here in the western world, we read from the top down and from the left to the right. As you can see, any user coming across this form is presented information in the same way. The first thing that you see is an orienting label at the top of the form. It leaves the user with no question that this form is about customer information. Next, you see the data entry labels that represent the form's real purpose. Each one is placed in what we've all come to accept as a "normal" name/address/phone number order. Finally, the navigation buttons at the bottom of the form are slightly out of sight, yet fall easily to hand when they're needed.

> **"A well-designed form doesn't get in your way as you work with the data."**

Notice how the data entry fields — and their labels — are aligned so that the data entry text boxes take precedence. With this kind of arrangement, you can easily notice, absorb, and then tune out the labels for the data entry fields. After all, you don't need a constant reminder that this field holds a name whereas that one holds a telephone number. The bottom line is: This well-designed form doesn't get in your way as you work with the data.

For what it's worth, here are some rules of thumb I've found useful in creating well-designed forms:

* Align all the data entry fields vertically with each other, and adjust their text to be left aligned within the fields. Then make each data entry field the same color — something different from the background color of the form.

* Put a descriptive label next to each text entry field and right align the label's text. Make sure that the label's text is easily readable against the form's background.

* Make sure that the form reads well from top to bottom and from left to right.

* Lay out the data entry fields so that they're together in logical order: names with names, addresses with addresses, telephone numbers with telephone numbers, and extraneous data with extraneous data.

An Automatic Form

Access seems to do so much automatically, I bet you're wondering if it does the same with forms. Well, wonder no longer friend: it does — and in spades!

Access has built-in wizards that help you create your basic, everyday form. Among these are three kinds of *AutoForms*: Columnar, Tabular, and Datasheet AutoForms.

A WORD ABOUT CONTROLS

As you work with Access forms, you'll typically enter data into little white rectangles and click buttons. Each of the things you work with in a form is called a *control object*, or a *control* for short. They're controls because you use them to control what Access does. For example, if you didn't click a button control, then Access would sit there and do nothing. If you never typed data into a text box, then Access would have no data to store.

I'd like to take a moment now and talk about these objects, or controls. As I do so, take a moment to look at the figure in this sidebar.

The most commonly used control is the text box. A pretty descriptive name, actually. Its sole purpose is to hold text — either text you type into it, or text that it retrieves from the contents of a field in your database. Text boxes work exactly the same as cells in a datasheet.

Near a text box, you'll usually see a label that identifies the text box for you. Another use for labels is to name an area in your form — a collection of checkboxes or option buttons, for example. You place labels on forms when you design them; labels can't be modified while you're actually using the form, as the contents of text boxes can.

Option buttons give you a way to select one of two or more options. They work much like the buttons on a car radio. You select one, and that's the option you get. If another button was already selected, then it becomes unselected when you select the next one.

Checkboxes are a clear and easy way for you to indicate Yes or No, or On or Off. You can tell which because if it's Yes or On, then the checkbox has a *checkmark* in it, provided its associated database field has a Yes or No in it. If the associated field is storing nothing, then the checkbox will usually appear as a simple gray square.

Creating an automatic form is a simple as this:

1. Open a database and have its database container visible.

2. With the Forms tab active, click New . Access displays the New Form dialog box, as shown in Figure 9-2.

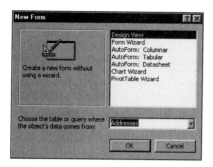

Figure 9-2 You can create all kinds of forms.

3. Highlight your choice of methods you want to use to create the form from among those in the list.

4. Indicate from which table or query the form's data is coming in the combo box below the list, and then click OK . What happens next depends on the kind of form creation method you chose.

We'll talk about the first two choices, Design View and Form Wizard, in just a moment. They're a bit more involved and so take a bit more explanation. Creating an AutoForm, on the other hand, is simplicity itself. Basically, all you have to do is click an AutoForm and then sit back for a moment until Access displays the completed form.

Here's what happens behind the scenes. When you choose one of the three AutoForms, Access starts cooking for a moment. It's looking at the table or query you indicated and noting what fields it contains so it can automatically lay out a form for you. Then, the next thing you see is the new table, displayed in Form view, ready for you to use. Like I said, simplicity itself.

A formal trio

As I've mentioned, Access can create three types of AutoForms. They are each a bit different, so I think it you should take a quick look at each of them. What I've done is create three different AutoForms from the Addresses table in the My First Address Book database. I'll show you each one in turn.

When it creates the Columnar AutoForm, Access takes your table's list of fields and stacks them in one or two columns, as shown in Figure 9-3. It's a pleasant enough form, if a bit mindless in its layout. The fields run in order from top to bottom along the left column and from top to bottom in the right column. I think the cloudy background is a nice touch.

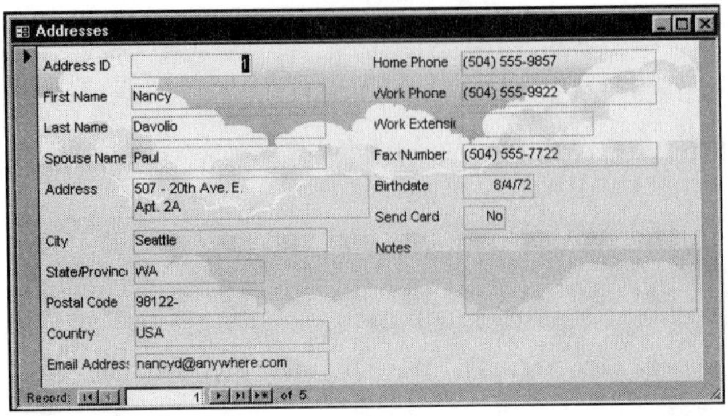

Figure 9-3 A Columnar AutoForm.

Unfortunately, I have a few basic problems with the columnar form layout. In the first place, there's no way for your user to know what the form is for, except to guess that it deals with names and addresses. The form really needs a header. Secondly, although the fields are aligned, the alignment is pretty hit and miss. Finally, the size of the data entry fields don't necessarily correspond to how big or small you need them to be.

We'll come back to this form in a moment and see if I can show you how to address these problems. First, however, I want to take a quick look at the other two types of AutoForms.

A Tabular AutoForm is shown in Figure 9-4. As you can see, it's pretty basic too, being more or less a glorified datasheet view. Admittedly, the Addresses table doesn't particularly lend itself to the Tabular format. Something like an inventory database would probably be more suited. Also, the tabular format works well as a subform, which you'll see later in the chapter.

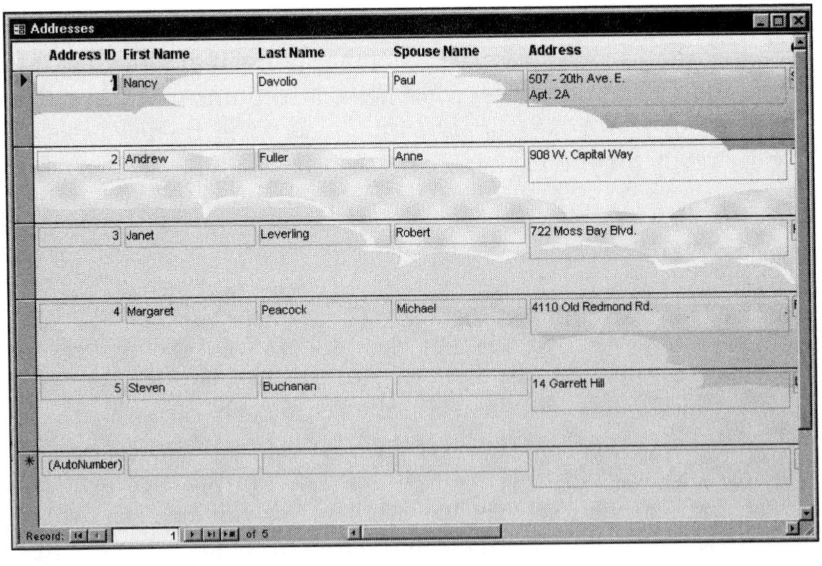

Figure 9-4 A Tabular AutoForm.

The last AutoForm is called the Datasheet, and that's exactly what it looks like. An example of a Datasheet AutoForm is shown in Figure 9-5. There's no immediately discernible difference between datasheets created by the AutoForm and regular, everyday datasheets. The only actual use for them is as subforms, about which you will learn shortly.

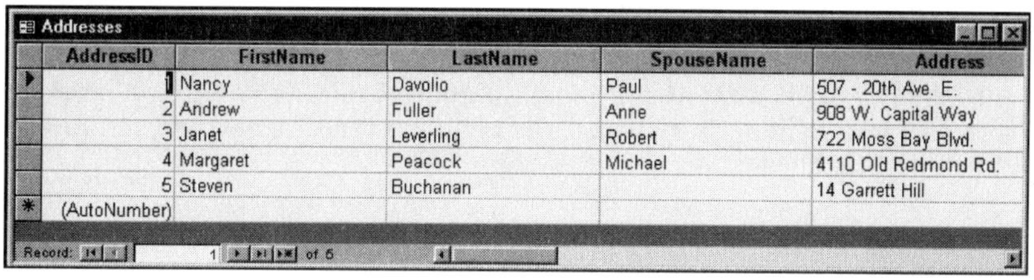

AddressID	FirstName	LastName	SpouseName	Address
1	Nancy	Davolio	Paul	507 - 20th Ave. E.
2	Andrew	Fuller	Anne	908 W. Capital Way
3	Janet	Leverling	Robert	722 Moss Bay Blvd.
4	Margaret	Peacock	Michael	4110 Old Redmond Rd.
5	Steven	Buchanan		14 Garrett Hill
* (AutoNumber)				

Figure 9-5 A Datasheet AutoForm.

Getting on the same page

Typically, the fastest and easiest way to create an Access form is to run a quick AutoFormat and then to modify it. That's exactly what you'll do with the columnar form I showed you in the previous section.

The first thing to do is to make sure that we're on the same page, so to speak.

Accordingly, follow these few steps, if necessary:

1. Open the My First Address Book database and close its switchboard form.

2. Display the database container, with the Forms tab active.

3. Click **New** to see the New Form dialog box.

4. With the Addresses table chosen as the table from which you want to take data, click AutoForm: Columnar in the list box, and then click **OK**. Access creates a columnar table such as the one I showed you earlier.

Doing it your way

Now that we're all on the same page, I can show you how to quickly and easily modify your new table. I'll show you how to move and resize the fields so that they're laid out better. At the same time, I'll show you how to create a header band that will orient your user. As a final flourish, you'll learn how to add your very own navigational buttons to your modified form.

VIEWS, VIEWS

Forms and queries have something in common. When you create and manipulate them — as opposed to manipulating their data — you work with them while they're in their respective design views. But while you usually browse queries in datasheet view, you browse forms in form view.

In this exercise, I have you switch back and forth between form design view and form view so that you can immediately see the effect of what you're doing. You should also feel free to jump back and forth between the views whenever you need to.

Follow these steps to modify the table:

1. Assuming that you've got the Addresses form open in form view, click ✏ ▾ on the toolbar. Access displays the form in design view, as shown in Figure 9-6.

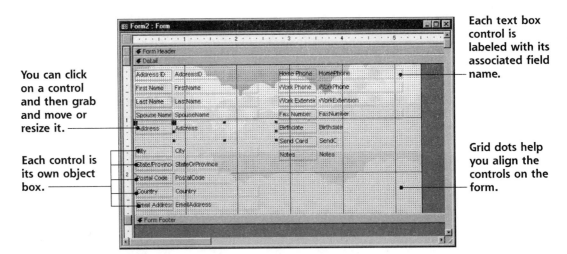

You can click on a control and then grab and move or resize it.

Each control is its own object box.

Each text box control is labeled with its associated field name.

Grid dots help you align the controls on the form.

Figure 9-6 The form in design view.

There are a few things I'd like you to notice about the form in design view.

＊ First of all, each control (text box, field label, or whatever) is surrounded by its own control box. You can move any control by clicking it to let Access know this is the control you want to move. You can read about how to move controls in more detail in the sidebar "Moving controls on a form."

* Access puts a grid on the form that makes it easier for you to align your controls. The grid is represented by rows of dots on your form in design view. By default, the controls on a form "snap" to one dot and then another as you move them along the form. You can vary the size of the grid, of course, and you can turn off the grid's "snap to" feature as well.

* There are three areas called "bands" in the form: a form header band (which is empty and very narrow right now — we'll be changing that in a moment), a detail band wherein the entry and display activity occurs, and a form footer band at the bottom of the form. The bands are analogous to the header, body text, and footer areas of a printed page.

* The colored area in the form detail band (the area that's of a different color from the background of the form design view window) represents the size limits of your form once it's in form view. You can vary the size by dragging on the right side or bottom edge. If the size you end up with is larger than your computer's screen, Access automatically puts in scroll bars that you can use to move around the form.

2. Now it's time for some adventure. What I want you to do is move and resize your form so that it's laid out in a more conventional manner — and for you to do it all by yourself. What I have in mind is for you to make the Address ID field shorter, put the person's full name all on one line, the phone numbers on another line, and so forth. Use your imagination and common sense for this exercise. There's no real right or wrong way to do the deed. When you're done, the form should look more like the one in Figure 9-7.

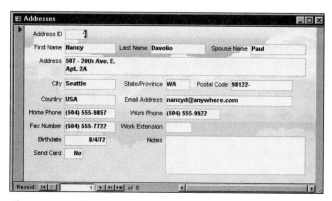

Figure 9-7 The columnar form as modified by me.

What I did

If you've already used your imagination to re-create the data entry form, that's fine. If you want to know what I did, however, here's a list:

* ✳ I first right aligned the text in all the field labels. This makes them visually "work better" with the data entry fields.

* ✳ I made the text in all the data entry fields bold. This makes their data stand out better against the background and when compared with their fields' labels.

* ✳ I changed the background of all the fields to opaque white. This makes the fields stand out better against the background.

* ✳ I moved the fields into a more standard order and positioned the other fields in a more logical grouping.

* ✳ I made the notes field larger to make it easier for people to include and read their notes.

* ✳ I saved my work!

SIDE TRIP

MOVING CONTROLS ON A FORM

Moving controls hither and thither on your form is easy. First of all, the form has to be in design view, of course. Then all you have to do is to click the control to let Access know it's the control you want to move. Access darkens the control box and activates the control's sizing and moving handles. Then you move and/or resize the control according to the information here:

The cursor as a
sliding finger. ————

Text entry fields and their associated labels kind of go together. Sometimes, however, you want to move them separately from one another. You grab one of the field moving handles — your cursor changes to a sliding finger — and slide it to where you want the object to be.

The cursor as a
pushing hand. ————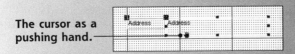

You move a field and label together simply by grabbing a control box — your cursor changes to a pushing hand — and pushing it to where you want the control to end up.

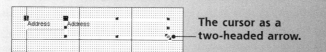

The cursor as a
two-headed arrow.

You resize a control by grabbing and dragging one of its resizing handles. When you do, your cursor changes to a double-headed arrow.

A BOX FULL OF TOOLS

When you modify or design a form, Access provides you with a virtual toolbox full of useful implements. Usually you'll find the toolbox to the left of your form (or whatever) while it's in design view. The following figure shows the Access toolbox.

There are two kinds of tools in the toolbox. The pair at its top are toggles — buttons you click on and off. The other buttons are tools that you select and use.

Using any of the tools is a two-step process: First you click the tool's icon. Then you move your mouse cursor to the form and click. Access places the tool on the form where you click. The tool's behavior is then determined by whether the wizard toggle is on and whether the tool has a wizard associated with it.

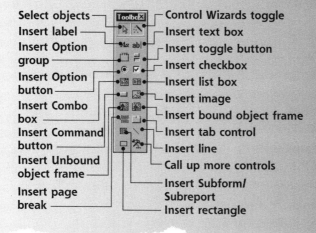

Select objects — Control Wizards toggle
Insert label — Insert text box
Insert Option group — Insert toggle button
Insert Option button — Insert checkbox
Insert Combo box — Insert list box
Insert Command button — Insert image
Insert Unbound object frame — Insert bound object frame
Insert page break — Insert tab control
Insert line
Call up more controls
Insert Subform/Subreport
Insert rectangle

FEATURE FOCUS The Tab control is new with Access 97. It lets you break up what you display on your forms into logical groupings, each one immediately available.

A Proper Look at Properties

 'd like to interrupt our regularly scheduled program here for a word about properties.

"Every control on your Access form — and the form itself, as a matter of fact — has properties."

When you're putting together a new form — or a report, for that matter — one of the most important buttons you can click on the toolbar is the properties button. The properties button opens the Properties dialog box. "What's that," you ask? Well, I'm glad you did. You can see an example in Figure 9-8. Here's what it does.

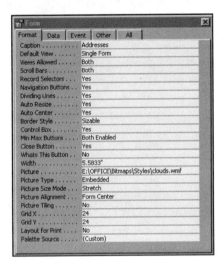

Figure 9-8 The Properties dialog gives you direct control over all your — um — controls.

You and I have certain attributes; two or so arms, legs, eyes, and ears. Further, each of these attributes can have properties. Eyes, for example, have the property of color — mine are green; yours may be brown or blue. Therefore, we can say that my eye color property is green and that your eye color property may be brown or blue.

Every control on your Access form — and the form itself, as a matter of fact — has properties. For example, each text box control has properties for background (color), border (color and style), and position (x and y coordinates). Forms, which are also controls, have properties such as position (x and y coordinates again), scroll bars (horizontal, vertical, or both), navigation buttons (yes or no), and caption (the text you see at the top of the form).

I think you get the idea.

Most controls possess four kinds of properties:

* Format properties have to do with how the control appears. I mentioned some of these in the previous paragraph.

* Data has to do with where the control's data comes from, its sort order (if any), and how it is to be edited or filtered.

* Event properties have to do with the kinds of actions that can occur when the control first opens or is closed, is pressed, or has its contents changed somehow. Normally, event properties are only important to you when you program an Access database application.

* Other properties are ones that don't fit into the preceding classifications. For example, a form control has such "other" properties as module (is there a programming module associated with this form?), popup (is this form a popup dialog box that stays on top of all other forms?), and cycle (what happens when you press the Tab key and you're on the last control of the form?).

As you design forms, you'll typically be interested in the properties in the Format tab. You can see any property by first selecting the control you're interested in, and then opening the Properties dialog box. Each property is listed there for you to see. If you want to change a property, you have two ways to do so.

The first way is to move your mouse cursor to the property you want to change and type in your change. Quite often, however, you don't even have to work that hard. If a property can have only one of a certain set of values, then the values are displayed for you in a drop down list box when you click on the property's line in the Property dialog box.

The second method has to do with text formatting. For the normal, run-of-the-mill kinds of bolding, italicizing, and aligning, you can click the appropriate button on the toolbar. Oh yes — don't forget to first highlight the control containing the text you want to format.

A Cloudy Picture

B efore I leave the subject of properties, I want to show you something neat. As I do so, I think you'll get a more intuitive idea of how properties actually work.

Have you noticed the cloudy picture that forms a backdrop for our example form? This picture is a bitmap called CLOUDS.WMF that comes with Access. You can use any bitmap picture (files with an extension of .BMP, .WMF, and .CGM) as a backdrop for your forms by including the filename as the Picture property of your form.

If you refer to the Picture property in Figure 9-8, you can see what I mean. And for extra credit, here are what the other picture properties mean:

* Picture Type can be either Embedded or Linked. Embedded means that a copy of the picture file itself is made part of the Access database. This is fast, but it can take up a lot of room. Linked, on the other hand, means that Access stores a pointer to where it can find the bitmap file. This method isn't as fast, but it takes up practically no room in your database. The latter method also isn't as trustworthy because if the bitmap file disappears for some reason, it would no longer be available for use in your form.

* Picture Size Mode lets you indicate how the picture should fit into the size allotted to it in your form; you have three choices.

* Clip means that the picture is displayed as close as possible to its original size. If the bitmap is larger than the available space, then it's simply cropped to fit. If the bitmap is too small, then Access shows it all, even though what's shown doesn't fill up the available space.

* Stretch causes Access to pull and tug the bitmap to fit the form. If that means the picture becomes distorted, then so be it.

* Zoom means Access tries to make the picture fit as best as possible without resizing it.

* Picture Alignment lets you indicate where Access should try to put the bitmap on the form. Your choices include any of the form's four corners or its center.

So, do you get the idea? When I told you that properties give you control over your forms, I really meant control! And for a hands-on guy like me, it's something I really like. Now, back to our regularly scheduled chapter.

Forms and Bands Without Music

We've accomplished quite a bit of new stuff here. We still have a couple of details to which we must attend, however. One of these has to do with what I told you earlier in the chapter about how a good form orients its user.

First, please allow me to belabor a point: It's not enough for your form's user to be able to read it from top to bottom and from left to right. The user must also be able to instantly identify what the form is all about without having to deduce this from the fields on the form.

Our tool for this instant identification is the form's header, or *header band* to be precise. We need to create a label and place it in the header band.

Follow along, and I'll show you how:

1. Open the Addresses form in design view.

2. With the form open, click the bar with the word Detail on it. Access highlights the bar to let you know it's activated.

3. Click the bar's upper edge and drag the bar down a little way — enough to leave room for a label in type bigger than that of the data-entry fields. When you click the bar, your mouse cursor changes to the resizing symbol, as shown in Figure 9-9.

This is what the mouse cursor looks like when you resize something on the screen.

The bar darkens when it's selected

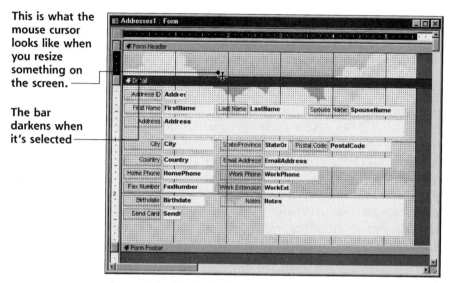

Figure 9-9   Resize the form header to make room for a label.

4. Click in the toolbox. Access changes the mouse cursor to a small cross as you drag it across the form.

5. Move the mouse cursor to the form's Header area that you've expanded, then click and drag to draw a box to hold your new label. Then wait just a moment — don't type anything; don't press any buttons!

The way Access works with labels is kind of strange, in my opinion. Access requires you to type your label immediately after drawing its container box. (That's why I told you to wait and not do anything at the end of the previous step.)

6. So, with the container box still visible, type **Names && Addresses** into it. You need to type the label exactly as I've indicated here, with two ampersands as shown in Figure 9-10.

Figure 9-10   You need to type two ampersands to get one in your label.

NOTE I know typing two ampersands together (like &&) looks strange — especially with my cursor in between them — but as with much of what I do, there's a method to my madness — snide comments by those who know me personally notwithstanding. The ampersand character has a special meaning in the world of Microsoft Windows programming.

When Windows sees an ampersand, it normally translates the ampersand into an underscore for whatever character comes next. This, for example, is how the underscored letters in your Windows menus and dialog box controls are produced. Then Windows uses the ampersand/underscored letter as a keyboard command shortcut.

So, if you type a single ampersand, Windows mindlessly does what it's been programmed to do: It formats the next character after the ampersand — a space, in this case — as an underscored space. On the other hand, if you type two ampersands back to back, Windows knows you really mean to have an ampersand character at that point and so reluctantly puts one there.

7. The next thing to do is format your label's text. So, after you've typed your label into its container box, press Enter. Then click the box to select it. Move to the font name box in the toolbar and select Arial. Give it a size of, say, 16 points. Access formats your label's text according to your selections. When you're done, your form in design view should look much like Figure 9-11.

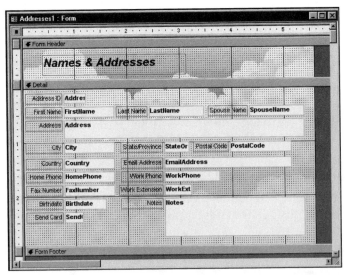

Figure 9-11 The form — almost finished — in design view.

That pretty much does it for this form. If you look at Figure 9-12, you'll see that it's a much more useful form than the one we started with. The form's label is easy to read and understand, and the fields are neatly and clearly laid out.

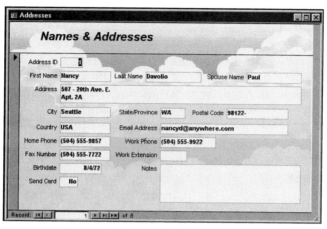

Figure 9-12 The completed form.

A Word About Form Bands

Forms have a schizophrenic quality to them in that they have at least two things going on at once. In the first place, there's the form itself. Its appearance and operation is controlled by Access and by Windows. In the second place, there's the data that's being displayed by the form and how it must appear. Although not immediately apparent, the two often have conflicting requirements. The way Access reconciles the demands of the two is by separating the form into up to three areas distinct in behavior and appearance called *bands*.

The form header band is at the top of the form. In form view, the header band remains at the same size and position no matter how big or small you make the rest of the form.

Below the header band is the detail band, where the data is displayed in data entry fields. While in form view, the detail band can be made smaller or larger, depending on your current computer display needs. As you resize your form, Access displays scroll bars in the detail area when appropriate. The scroll bars let you move up and down and from right to left in the form's detail area so you can view your data.

At the bottom, appropriately enough, is the footer band. Not always used, the footer band is handy for holding things like programmed navigation buttons (which I discuss later in the chapter).

A Form in Two Parts

So much for a simple form. With all this new knowledge, I bet you're raring to roll up your sleeves and tackle something dazzling: a form in two parts. I'm talking about what Access mavens call forms and subforms, and I'm about to show you how to use a two-part form as a way to display the data about parents and children in our running example.

Actually, to say that this type of form is a two-part form is something of a misnomer. It's more accurate to say that this type of form is two forms — one upon the other — with the two forms linked together.

NOTE A *subform* is an Access form that's embedded within another Access form. Most often, subforms come from queries in which you have two tables in a one-to-many relationship. The data from the one side of the relationship is depicted in the main form, whereas the data from the many side is depicted in the subform.

There are a number of ways to create a form with a subform. The easiest, in my humble opinion, is to create them both at the same time using the Access Form Wizard. You answer the wizard's questions to let it know that you're creating a form and a subform and which of the two is the "main" form.

Follow along, and you'll see what I mean:

1. You want to use the Form Wizard, so with the database container showing forms, click [**New**]. Access opens the New Form dialog box, as shown in Figure 9-13. Notice that I haven't put anything in the list box at the bottom of the dialog box. That information will come later.

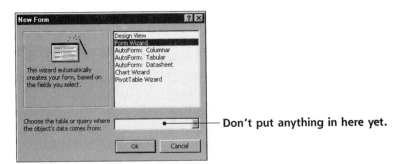

Figure 9-13 You start a form and subform with the Form Wizard.

2. In the New Form dialog box, select Form Wizard and click [**OK**]. Access opens the first Form Wizard dialog box.

3. This dialog box is where you tell Access which fields to use in both the main form and the subform. This is also where you tell Access from which tables or queries to get those fields. If you look at Figure 9-14, you'll see that I've started with the AddressID, FirstName, LastName, SpouseName, and HomePhone fields from the Addresses table. You do the same, please. After you've done so, *don't* click Next. We're not yet done with this dialog box.

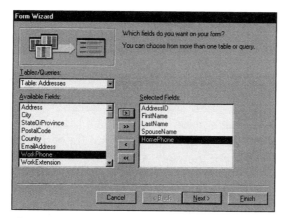

Figure 9-14 Start with fields from the Addresses table.

4. Next, select the Children table from the Tables/Queries list box at the top of the dialog box, as shown in Figure 9-15. Access displays the Children table's fields in the Available Fields text box.

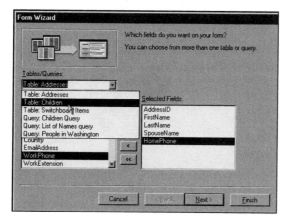

Figure 9-15 Now add fields from the Children table.

5. Move the FirstName, Birthdate, and SendCard fields from the Children table to the Selected Fields list. When you're done, your dialog box should look like the one in Figure 9-16.

6. Click Next and Access displays the next Form Wizard dialog box.

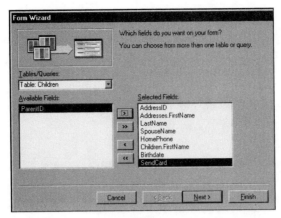

Figure 9-16 All of the fields you need have been selected.

7. Access knows now which fields we want to be included, and it knows from which tables to draw those fields. What it doesn't know is how to organize the data for our viewing. As you can see in Figure 9-17, I chose by Addresses. The effect of this answer is to cause the fields brought in from the Addresses table to be used in the main part of the main and subform. Because we want the forms to be together, make sure the Form with subform(s) option button at the bottom of the dialog box is selected. After you're ready, click ⌐Next⌐. Access displays the next Form Wizard dialog box.

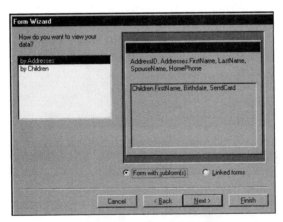

Figure 9-17 Next, you organize the data.

8. With the main part of the form pretty well defined, next you have to look at the subform part. As you can see in Figure 9-18, your choices are Tabular and Datasheet view. My preference in this case is Tabular, so select that option. Sure, it's really nothing more than a glorified datasheet, but that small bit of glory will make the final form more attractive. Click ⌐Next⌐ to move on.

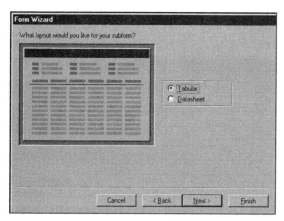

Figure 9-18 You have two similar choices for how you'll view the subform.

9. Now for the chintz. I simply couldn't make up my mind among all these background choices, so I simply chose Standard, as shown in Figure 9-19. You can use whatever background you like. If you choose Clouds, however, this form will have the same background as the form you created earlier in the chapter. There's nothing wrong with that, as far as I can tell. The trade-off is between a consistent look among your forms and having them appear so similar that your users might be confused. Anyway, pick a background and click ⬛**Next**⬛. Access displays the last Form Wizard dialog box.

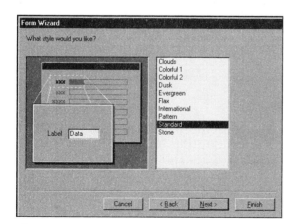

Figure 9-19 You can choose any background you wish for your form — choose Standard if you, like me, can't decide.

This is where you name your new forms. I haven't used Parents before, so that's what I used for the Form name, as shown in Figure 9-20. We already have a form named Children, so, breaking out the old mental thesaurus, I decided to use Kids as the name of the subform.

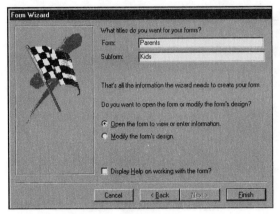

Figure 9-20 Because each form and subform is a separate entity, they must each have a unique name.

10. Click **Finish** and you're done. Access cooks for a moment and then displays your form and subform for you, as shown in Figure 9-21.

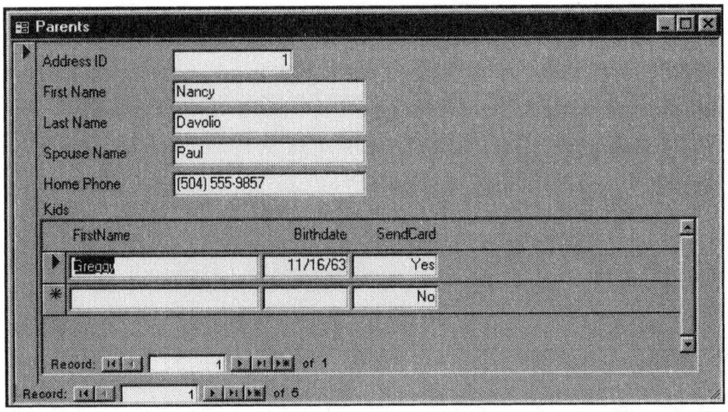

Figure 9-21 The finished form with its subform.

Now that you've finished with the form, play with it for a while. See if you can get a feeling for the relationship between the two forms and their data. Notice how the data in the subform changes as you move from record to record in the main form.

Pretty neat, huh?

Doing It My Way

It's not that I don't appreciate Access's efforts in creating the form for me, you understand, but no matter how long I look at the thing, it's still just plain ugly — not to mention the fact that it's not as useful as I'd like it to be. Correcting the situation is actually kind of interesting, so I thought I'd share it with you.

If you look at Figure 9-22, you'll see what the form looks like in design view once I reworked it. I moved and resized the fields just as I showed you earlier in this chapter. Oh yes, I also added a label for the form in its header.

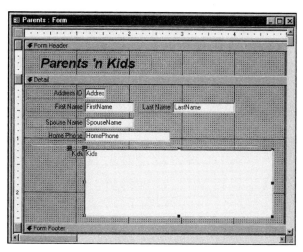

Figure 9-22 The main form with its place holder for the subform.

By the way, while you're still looking at Figure 9-22, I want you to notice something else. Can you tell that the subform doesn't actually exist in the main form? Instead, Access puts a place holder there, one the same size as the default size of the subform. If you want to modify it, you have to open the subform by itself.

As a matter of fact, if you take a look at Figure 9-23, you'll see the subform itself in design view. As you'll notice, it's a simple affair, including only the three fields we chose in the Form Wizard. If you look closely, you'll also notice that Access places the labels for the three fields in the subform's header — an intelligent and efficient use of space, I'd say.

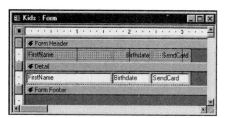

Figure 9-23 A subform is a form of its own.

And now for the payoff: the reworked form and subform in all its final glory, as shown in Figure 9-24. Not too shabby, if I do say so myself.

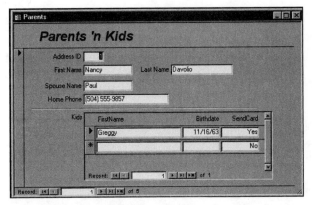

Figure 9-24 The final form, in all its glory.

BONUS

Buttons, Buttons

The last thing I want to do with you in this chapter is to have a little fun. I want to show you how easy it is to include command buttons on your forms. I hesitate to call it programming, although that's exactly what it is! In any case, this is something that's sure to wow your coworkers. Just don't tell them how easy it is.

The command buttons I'm talking about will take the place of the navigation buttons you find at the bottom of all Access data screens. Starting with the Address1 form from the beginning of this chapter, we'll put in four buttons: one for each navigation function.

Follow along, if you please, and allow me to reveal yet another mystery:

1. First, open in design view the Addresses1 form that we modified earlier. Then use your mouse cursor to grab its bottom edge, down below the form footer bar. When you do so, the cursor changes to the resizing icon. Pull the bottom edge of the footer bar down enough so that you'll be able to put some buttons on the footer bar. You can see the results when I did the same thing in Figure 9-25. You've just created a form footer!

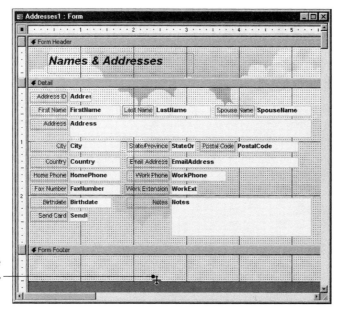

Your mouse cursor changes when you resize the form footer.

Figure 9-25 Pull down the bottom edge of the footer until it's big enough for some buttons.

2. Make sure that the Toolbox Wizard button is selected. Then click [icon]. Move your mouse cursor down to the form footer, hold the right button down, and move the cursor down and to the right to draw a button. Access draws a square that it fills with a button as soon as you release the mouse button. Access also gives the button a temporary caption of Command*nn*, where *nn* is a number, and calls up the Command Button Wizard. You can see what I mean in Figure 9-26.

NOTE The number in the name of the command button is just Access's way of making sure that each new control has a unique name. It's a temporary name that you can easily change.

3. The next thing to do is to let Access know what this button is for. In the Command Button Wizard dialog box, select the first option, Record Navigation, in the Categories list box. Then select Go to First Record in the Actions list box. When you've done so, click Next .

4. Now you need to give your command button an icon so people will know what it does. Using the information from the preceding dialog box, Access knows that this will be a navigation button that moves its record pointer to the first record in the database. For this reason, Access displays a list of "first record" icons. I picked the cartoon hand called (appropriately enough) Pointing Up, as shown in Figure 9-27.

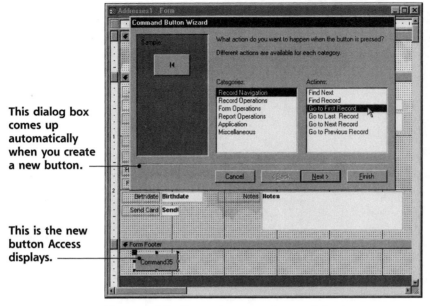

This dialog box comes up automatically when you create a new button. ⎯

This is the new button Access displays. ⎯

Figure 9-26 Draw a button and get a dialog box.

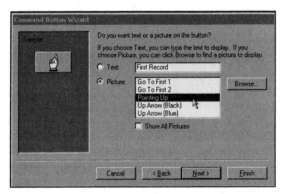

Figure 9-27 Each command button can have its own icon.

You can use practically any picture as an icon on a command button. If you have one you want to use instead of Pointing Up, click the **Browse** button and go get it. Otherwise, click **Next**. Access displays the next Command Button Wizard dialog box.

5. Now you should give your command button a name. Type it into the text box at the top of the dialog box. As you can see in Figure 9-28, I typed cmdFirstRecord.

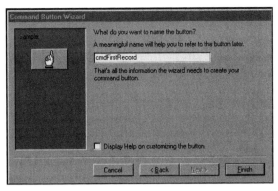

Figure 9-28 Each command button must have a name.

The prefix cmd is what we in the biz call "Hungarian" for command button. Hungarian is an obscure reference to Charles Simyoni, an early Windows programmer who came up with this kind of naming scheme. It's very efficient. If I want to write some programming later, I can simply call this button by its name, knowing what the button's function is just by looking at the name.

6. Anyway, when you've typed in the name by which you want the button to be known, click **Finish** . Access cooks for a moment, automatically writing the programming code that will make the button do its work whenever someone clicks it.

7. Now do the same process three more times, once each for the previous, next, and last records. Table 9-1 shows you what I did for these buttons.

TABLE 9-1 My Command Buttons

Button Purpose	Button Icon	Button Name
MOVE TO FIRST RECORD IN THE DATABASE	Pointing Up	cmdFirstRecord
MOVE TO PREVIOUS RECORD IN THE DATABASE	Pointing Left	cmdPreviousRecord
MOVE TO NEXT RECORD IN THE DATABASE	Pointing Right	cmdNextRecord
MOVE TO LAST RECORD IN THE DATABASE	Pointing Down	cmdLastRecord

8. With the buttons out of the way, the next thing to do is to get rid of the navigation buttons Access automatically puts at the bottom of its forms. With the form still in design view, select the entire form by clicking the little square that's at the form's extreme upper left. (You'll find it at the intersection of the two rulers.) Then display the property sheet and, in the Format tab, choose Navigation Buttons: No.

9. That's it! The last thing is to look at your super-duper form in form view. Click on the toolbar and admire your work. If you'd like to admire mine, you can see it in Figure 9-29.

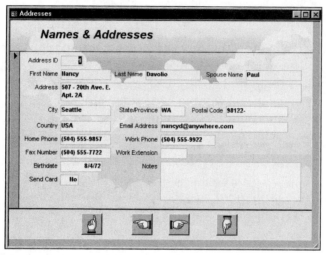

Figure 9-29 My handiwork!

Summary

Wow! What a lot of stuff to learn all at once. Forms are one of my favorite parts of Access. I love the control I have over their appearance. I appreciate all the tools available to me to format the form so it conveys the database's information to me and to others — and lets me quickly and easily manipulate my data.

As you can see, forms are very important in the database world. They're what your user — well — uses. They're where the rubber meets the road, to coin a phrase. Without forms, our databases would be nothing but datasheets. What an unattractive thought.

Next up is our means of sharing information from our database to the outside world: reports. You thought forms were interesting? Just turn the page...

ME, REPORTING FOR DUTY

10

KEY GOALS OF THIS CHAPTER:

Years ago, I started out life as a newspaper stringer. A stringer is a kind of freelance reporter who is paid by the length of his piece that's finally printed in the newspaper. They print your stuff in column inches, you cut out the columns and tape them end to end, and then you measure the result. (Then the editor checks your taping and your measurement.) The longer the taped-together column, the more farthings they throw your way. The idea is the better you are as a reporter, the more they use and so the more you get paid. Well, that's the theory, anyway.

I quickly learned that when you write news copy, your story doesn't necessarily flow in chronological order. First, you're supposed to put in the most important stuff, follow it with less important stuff, and so on. The trick was to know what your editor would find to be "the most important stuff." And all this to bring the best possible information to your readers.

Early in my tenure at the paper, I happened to cover a town council meeting. It was exciting and fun. The next year's budget was thoroughly debated. The council discussed cutting the speed limit on the road through town; the police chief and town constable were clearly in favor of that. Some guy got belligerent about garbage collection, using "bad" language and threatening any newspaper reporter who would dare to embarrass him by printing what he had just said. Towards the end of the meeting, some dear soul decried the street sign leading to the county cemetery.

I got it all down, as a good reporter should: budget first, garbage collection, speed limit, the interesting quote just slightly censored. Almost as an after-thought, I included the cemetery remarks. When I was through with my reporter's work, the information was all there.

The next morning I opened my copy of the paper, looking for my story. The editor had changed the lead a bit. Finding the cemetery angle somehow fasci-nating, he even sent out a photographer to get a picture of the "Dead End" sign on the street leading to it. I think that's where my disillusionment with reporting began.

As you've seen up to this point, the data in your database isn't useful until it's information. And information itself isn't useful until you can share it with someone. The end of this little conga line is reports: the means by which you share your information with your readers, who you'll find often behave much like editors.

In this chapter, I start by showing you the Old Faithful, quick and dirty, Access AutoReport. Then we'll look at modifying a report and making it look a bit fancy — and a lot more useful. We'll finish by creating what used to be the nemesis of many a working person: the mailing label.

Before we really get going, however, there's something I want you to know about reports. I'm assuming you recently waded through the preceding, really long chapter on forms. Well, in the world of Access, forms and reports have so much in common that they are more like fraternal twins than cousins. Just about everything you learned about forms, you can apply to reports as well.

Reporting, Automatically

Let's start with an AutoReport. Our scenario is that you're still working for Northwest Traders. Your boss has come into your office, and he's frantic. He has a shareholders meeting five minutes from now, and he's lost his list of the products sold by Northwind Traders. If he doesn't have that information for the meeting, he's toast.

"Please," he begs, "you gotta get me a list of all the stuff we sell." You, being the calm, collected person you are, sit back and smile. He doesn't realize how easily you'll get him off the hook, but you know the subject of your competence and helpfulness is sure to come up at salary review time. "Not a problem," you say, "I'll have it for you in a trice." (You always fall back on archaisms when you want to make an impression.)

Here's what you do:

1. You need data fast, so the first thing to do is to go to the right query. With the database container visible and the Current Product List query highlighted, click the Queries tab, as shown in Figure 10-1.

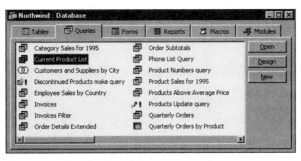

Figure 10-1 The first thing you need for a quick report is the data.

2. The next thing to do is create the report. Move your mouse cursor to the right side of the tool bar and click ▣, then select **AutoReport**, as shown in Figure 10-2. Access cooks for a moment and then displays the new report in print preview.

Figure 10-2 An AutoReport is a new object for Access.

3. Before you do anything more with the report, you really should save it. Choose **Save** from the **File** menu and give your new report the name Temporary Products List report.

FEATURE FOCUS Now in Access 97, you can automatically create a report by pressing its AutoFormat button.

NOTE Most printers nowadays will let you print in what they call *portrait* and *landscape* modes. These terms come from the photographic world, where pictures are most often rectangular. Portrait mode is where the paper is taller than it is wide. Paper in landscape mode, on the other hand, is wider than it is tall. For the purposes of this chapter, you'll want to be printing in portrait mode. You can adjust your printer's orientation by selecting Page Setup from the File menu, and then clicking on the Paper Size tab. You'll find the options for portrait and landscape orientation there.

VIEWS, VIEWS, AND PRINT

When you look at a report in design view, you can preview the report two different ways in Print Preview. You'll find the View button at the left end of the design toolbar. When you click it, a menu drops down. It contains three options, as shown in the following figure:

Design view is a kind of placeholder for the view you're looking at now. It's in the menu so that it'll be available when you're in one of the print previews.

Print preview shows your report just as it will look when it's printed, with the correct data in position and everything ready to go.

Layout preview shows your report correctly laid out — with its elements positioned correctly — but with "bogus" data. This is data taken from the first few records of your database, but used only to demonstrate position, not what the report will really look like.

4. Take a moment to look at the report in print preview, as shown in Figure 10-3. Access displays it this way so you can do a quick double check on your work. If this report contains the information you need, then you can go ahead and print it by clicking the Print button. If not, then you can close it without saving and try again.

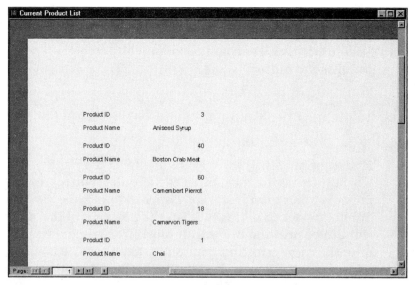

Figure 10-3 A new report in print preview.

Notice that you can move around the report using the scroll bars at the window's right and bottom edges. If there's more than one page to the report, you can get to the other pages by clicking the navigation buttons at the bottom of the window. Pretty familiar and consistent with the rest of Access, isn't it?

5. You can get an overview of the report by "zooming" out. If you look at Figure 10-4, you'll see what I mean. Click 🔍 on the toolbar to see this view.

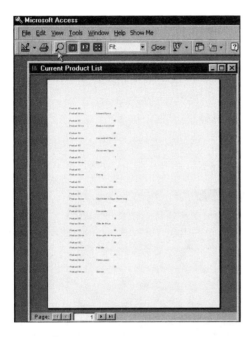

Figure 10-4 Here we have a zoomed out view of the report.

6. If everything looks okay, click 🖨 on the toolbar. Access prints the report. You hand it to your boss; he smiles gratefully; everything is sweetness and light.

A Slight Improvement to Automation

In my ever-so-humble opinion, the AutoReport is even more ugly than its formly sibling. I mean, just look at it! It has no title, so you can't immediately tell what it's for. The data just sits there, with constantly repeating labels. It's a report, certainly, but it shows its potential more than its maturity.

I think it would be worthwhile to spend a few minutes to fix that. Here's what needs to be done:

✳ The report, just like a form, needs a title to orient its reader.

✳ There's no good reason to repeat the words Product ID and Product Name throughout the entire report or to print each product name so far apart. I would format the product names and numbers as columns, with the labels at their heads.

✳ Reports, by their nature, are snapshots in time of your data. If you were to look at two reports printed at different times or on different days, you wouldn't know which was which unless they had a date and time stamp.

In the next few sections, I'll show you how to implement these fixes so you can get the most out of your reports.

A titled report

Titles on reports are much like titles on forms. If you know how to do one, you really also know how to do the other.

In any case, follow along, if you please:

1. First, let's see what we have to work with. Click ![icon] to open the Temporary Products List report in design view, as shown in Figure 10-5.

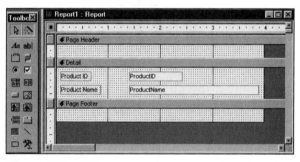

Figure 10-5 This report is not yet ready for prime time.

2. Now for the title itself. Click ![icon] on the toolbox. Then move to the Page Header band on the form, drag open a label rectangle there, and type **Northwind Traders Products** into it. If you like, you can also enlarge the Page Header band and some font sizes (as I did).When you've done that, your report should look much like the one in Figure 10-6.

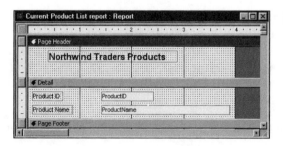

Figure 10-6 A label orients the report's readers.

3. Click on the toolbar to save your report.

Turning labels into column heads

Next, I want to show you how to turn data labels into column heads. Basically, all you have to do is move them up to the Page Header band. Of course, like a lot of things in life, it's not quite that simple.

The fastest and easiest way to move a report element from one place to another is to cut and paste:

1. Click a label.

2. Press Ctrl + X to cut it.

3. Move the mouse cursor to the Page Header band and press Ctrl + V to paste it.

That's pretty simple to do, really. The only difficulty, if you can call it that, is what Access does when you cut and paste from one band to the other.

"The fastest and easiest way to move a report element from one place to another is to cut and paste."

In this case, when you paste a label from the Detail band, you'll find that it automatically appears in the upper left corner of the Page Head. That's a default action by Access, because Access doesn't know where you want to put the label and it hasn't been programmed to guess. Yes, I know that's kind of mindless on Access's part, but what can you expect from a computer?

Perform these steps, and you'll see what I mean:

1. With your report in design view, move labels for the two data fields to the page header band using the cut and paste method you already know. There's something you'll want to watch out for, by the way. When Access pastes your labels automatically, for some reason it puts them one on top of the other. You can "unstack" them by highlighting the top one and moving it off the others.

2. Move the pasted labels into position in a row below the report title, and just above the Detail band. When you have them in the correct position, it'll be as though they were at the top of two columns — which is what they're going to be, as a matter of fact.

3. As long as you're working with the labels, select the Product ID label and format its text to be right-aligned by clicking ▤ on the toolbar. (That will make it match the default format of the ProductID data field below it.)

4. Next, move the data display fields into position under their respective labels. Because the data display fields are in the Detail band and the labels are in the Page Header band above them, this is where the report design grid comes in handy. By default, all the elements on a report snap to the design grid's dots. You can use that facility to get the labels lined up directly above their respective data display fields. After you've done this, your report should look like Figure 10-7.

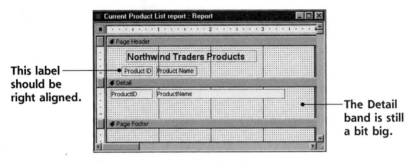

This label should be right aligned.

The Detail band is still a bit big.

Figure 10-7 We're almost there.

5. Click ▤ on the toolbar to save your report.

Squeezing the space

When Access puts rows of data together in an AutoReport, its choice of line spacing is often overgenerous. Our moving fields around simply made the situation worse. So, the next thing we need to do is tighten things up a bit.

If you were to click the Print Preview button right now, you'd see that each product would print with quite a significant space under it. That space comes from the height of the detail band, so we'll have to make the detail band shorter.

Here's how:

1. With your report in design view, make sure that the ProductID and ProductName data fields are flush with the bottom of the detail band bar. If necessary, you can select both data fields and move them up at the same time.

2. When the two data fields are where they need to be, click the Page Footer band and move it next to the bottom of the ProductID and ProductName data fields. When you're done, your report in design view should look like the one in Figure 10-8.

MOVING THINGS TOGETHER

Quite often when you're moving objects around on forms and reports you're design-ing, you'll want to move more than one at a time. Now, you already know that before you can move an object, you have to select it. I'll bet, however, that you didn't know that there are two ways to select more than one object at a time.

The first way is to press and hold the Shift key as you click a succession of objects. The other way involves the rulers you find at the top and left of a form or report in design view.

If you move your mouse cursor on a ruler and click, a small arrow appears on the ruler for as long as you hold the mouse button down. Coming out of the arrow's point is a straight line that goes entirely across (or down) the design view window, as shown in the following figure. When you release the mouse button, every object that was touched by that line is selected, as shown in the next figure.

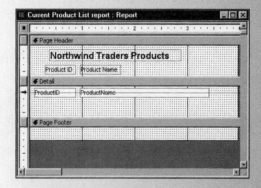

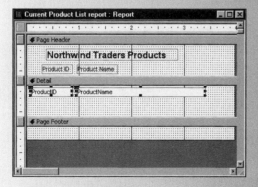

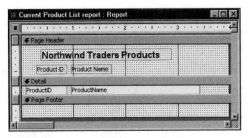

Figure 10-8 There's no more room to squeeze.

If you're curious, go ahead and take a look at your report in print preview. I did, and mine looked like Figure 10-9. As you can tell, it's a neat report, just about ready to go.

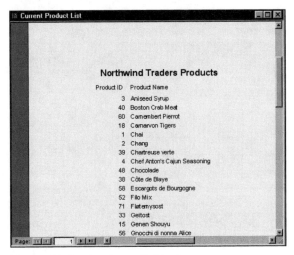

Figure 10-9 An almost finished report.

3. Click 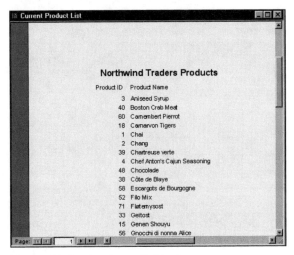 on the toolbar to save your report.

A finishing touch

Do you remember what I said about reports being a snapshot of your data? Well, it's true, of course — otherwise, why would I have said it? My point is: No report is really finished if it doesn't have at least a date on it. A time stamp and page number would be good too, you understand, but, in my opinion, a date is essential.

Follow along, and I'll show you how to add these to your report:

1. With your report in design view, click the **Insert** menu. Access displays the menu shown in Figure 10-10.

Figure 10-10 Choose Date and Time.

2. Choose [**Date and Time**] from the menu. Access displays the Date and Time dialog box, as shown in Figure 10-11. As you can see, you can check either date or time to include in your report, or you can include both. You can also choose the format in which you want these items to be printed.

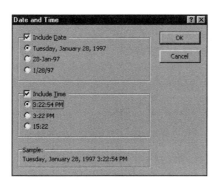

Figure 10-11 The Date and Time dialog box.

3. Click [**OK**], and Access puts into your report a label box containing the information it needs to be able to print the date and/or time.

4. Move this label to the Page Footer band and place it against the report's left edge.

5. Click [▣] on the toolbar to left align this label.

6. As an extra touch, add the page number to your report, too. You'll find [**Page Numbers**] on the same [**Insert**] menu as you found [**Date and Time**]. The Page Numbers dialog box looks much the same — and works exactly the same — as the Date and Time dialog box. An example is shown in Figure 10-12.

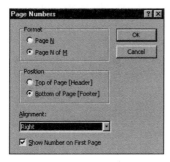

Figure 10-12 You can also add page numbers to your report.

For page numbers, I usually use the "Page N of M" format. (I especially like the way I can use that information to more easily organize a stack of pages if I drop it.) I typically right align the page number and put it at the bottom right of the report's footer band. If you've done everything as I suggested, your report will look much like the one shown in Figure 10-13.

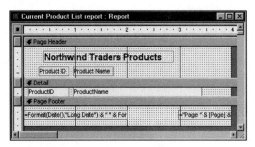

Figure 10-13   The report: designo el finito!

Well, there you go: one report designed and ready to print. Being eternally curious and not always confident in what I've just done, I also like to take one last look at any report I've designed.

7. To look at the report in print preview, click 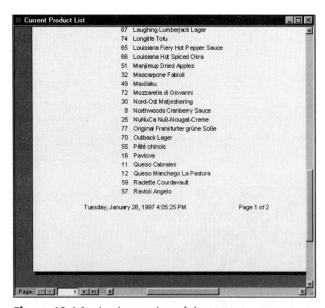. Access displays the report — well, a part of it at least. When I previewed my work, I saw the report as shown in Figure 10-14. By the way, you'll notice that when I previewed my report it was in portrait mode. You'll want to double-check that yours is as well.

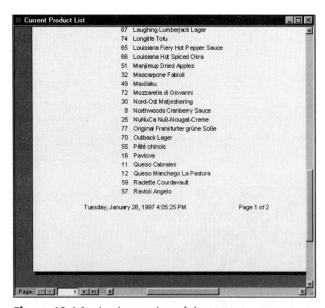

Figure 10-14   A print preview of the new report.

A LOOK AT WHAT LOOKS LIKE A FORMULA

The page numbers and the labels for date and time you put into your report contain what looks like a mathematical formula. Pretty close, anyway. What they really contain is called an Access *expression*.

Much like a mathematical formula, an expression is a way of combining some built-in Access functions (remember them?) so as to print a certain result. (You can find an explanation about any of these functions by looking them up in Access Help.) The functions used here include the following:

- `Format()` is a function that Access uses to know that whatever is contained within the parentheses should be displayed a certain way. The contents of the parentheses can include other functions such as `Date()` or `Time()`, or strings of literal text characters that are enclosed within quotation marks ("). Of course, there's always some type of complication. Refer to the figure below to see that the words `"Long Date"` and `"Long Time"` are also contained within quotation marks and yet are not literally printed. That's because these are the names of formatting variables that are hard wired within Access's `Format` function. When the `Format` function sees one of these, it "knows" how you want your date or time to appear.

- `Date()` is Access's way of using your computer's built-in clock to display today's date. If your computer is accurate, then the date, too, will be correct.

- `Time()` uses the computer's clock to display the current time in your part of the world.

- `Page` is the number of the page currently being worked with — or printed.

- `Pages` is a count of all the pages that can be printed in a document.

- `&` (the ampersand) is, in this case, what's known as a *concatenation operator*. *Concatenation* is the process by which different strings of text characters are strung together.

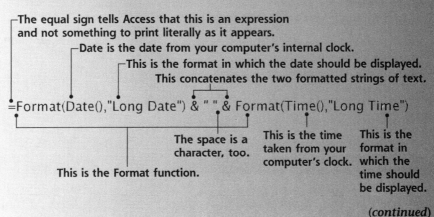

The equal sign tells Access that this is an expression and not something to print literally as it appears.

Date is the date from your computer's internal clock.

This is the format in which the date should be displayed.

This concatenates the two formatted strings of text.

`=Format(Date(),"Long Date") & " " & Format(Time(),"Long Time")`

The space is a character, too.

This is the time taken from your computer's clock.

This is the format in which the time should be displayed.

This is the Format function.

(*continued*)

┌─This tells Access that this is an expression.

This concatenates the Page variable with the literal text.

="Page " & [Page] & " of " & [Pages]

The literal word "Page."

This is the place holder for the page number taken from the report — after it's formatted, but before it's printed.

This is more literal text.

This is the place holder for the total number of pages in this report.

Wizardly Mailing Labels

Mailing labels are one of the big bugaboos in computerized databases. For some reason, we always need them, and yet labels always seem so difficult. Well, no longer. I'm about to show you how easy it is to create mailing labels using Access's built in mailing label wizard.

Here's our scenario: You're working in the Northwind Traders Marketing Relations department, and it's time to get out a warm and fuzzy greeting card to all your customers. Each card will be individually signed by the customer's account rep, but it's up to you to address and mail the little beasts.

The names and addresses you need are already collected for you; they're in the database, after all. The only thing you need to do is use the Label Wizard to format and to print the labels themselves.

I'm almost embarrassed at how easy this is going to be, but follow along anyway, and I'll show you how to do it:

1. With Access up and running and the Northwind database loaded, click the Reports tab on the database container to activate it.

2. Click New. Access displays the New Report dialog box you've seen before.

3. Not to belabor the obvious, but because you're making labels for customers, choose Customers as the source of your labels' data. Then, with the Label Wizard highlighted, click OK. Access displays the Label Wizard dialog box, as shown in Figure 10-15.

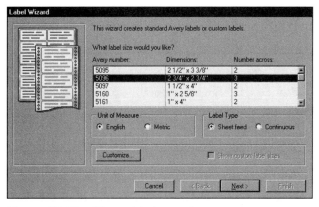

Figure 10-15 All new labels start here.

As you can see, the Access Label Wizard has the dimensions of all kinds of Avery labels already defined for you. All you have to do is choose one by its number. If you don't happen to use Avery labels, however, you have two choices: use a cross reference to find the Avery equivalent of the labels you're using or click **Customize** and define your own label.

4. I've decided to use Avery 5096s. They're nice and big, with plenty of room for an international address on them. If you want to do the same, click 5096 and click **Next**. Access displays the Label Wizard dialog box, as shown in Figure 10-16.

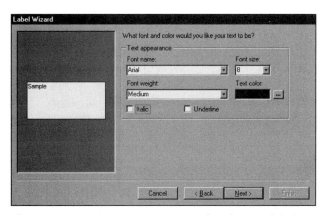

Figure 10-16 You can use any type font for your labels.

5. Select a font to use for your labels from the drop-down list. You can also change the font's size, color, and weight in this dialog box. If you like, you can also have the labels' type italicized or underlined by default by clicking on the appropriate checkbox. After you've made your choices, click **Next**. Access displays the next Label Wizard dialog box, as shown in Figure 10-17.

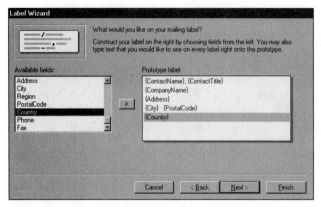

Figure 10-17 Here's where the meat and potatoes of creating labels begins.

This is where you lay out your label. On the right side of the dialog box is a list of available fields; on the left is a prototype of your label with a darkened line on it. The darkened line is a cursor to help you place fields where you want them.

6. Double click a field name on the list of available fields, and the field will appear on the darkened line in the prototype label. If you need spaces or punctuation, type them directly into the prototype label. You can see in Figure 10-17 the fields I chose to use. Copy my work, if you please, and then click ⎡ **Next** ⎤. Access displays the next Label Wizard dialog box, as shown in Figure 10-18.

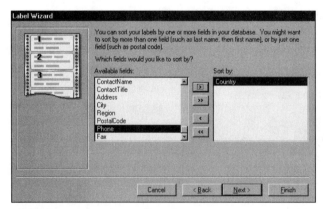

Figure 10-18 You can sort your label on any of the fields it contains.

7. You can sort your label on any of the fields it contains. That makes it very easy for you to comply with postal regulations if you're sending out a mass mailing here in the United States. However, because this is an international mailing, I've decided to sort the labels by country. To do

the same, double-click Country in the list of available fields and then click **Next**. Access displays the last Label Wizard dialog box, the one shown in Figure 10-19.

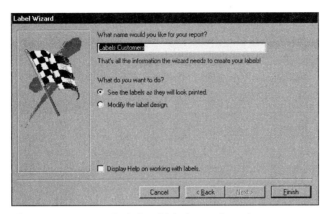

Figure 10-19 Each defined label must have its own name.

8. Access offers Labels Customer as a name for the labels. That's fine with me. If you want to use another name, you can type it into the text box at the top of the dialog box. On the other hand, if the default name is okay with you too, click **Finish**. Access cooks for a moment, and then displays the formatted labels in print preview, as shown in Figure 10-20.

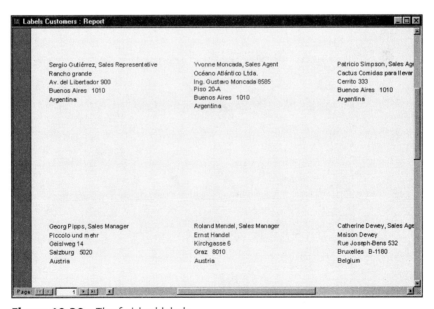

Figure 10-20 The finished labels.

That's about it for mailing labels, friend. The only thing left to do is insert the sheets of blank labels into your printer — with the correct side up, of course — and click the Print button on the toolbar. Oh, yes: You'll have to take the labels off the sheets and press them onto the envelopes. "Details, details," he muttered, shaking his head.

BONUS

Rolling Your Own

You can define your own labels, if you like. After they're defined, you can use them just as you'd employ any of Access's built-in labels.

Here's the process in a nutshell:

1. Start to create the new label just as you would any other one, beginning with the New Label dialog box from the database container.

2. When you get to the first Label Wizard dialog box, click **Customize**. Access displays the New Label Size dialog box, as shown in Figure 10-21.

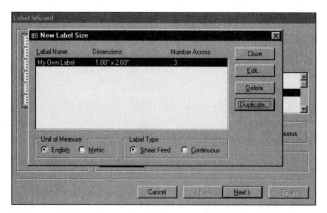

Figure 10-21   You can use your own labels just like any other.

3. If you've already defined a label, its name will appear here. If so, you can click the label's name and continue as you normally would. If you haven't yet defined a label, then click **New**. Access displays the New Label dialog box, as shown in Figure 10-22.

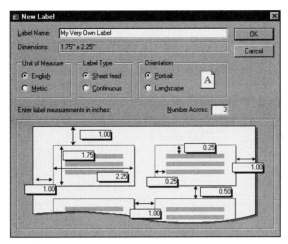

Figure 10-22 You can define a new label of just about any size.

4. The basic differences among labels have to do with their sizes and margins. Enter the size and margins for your label in the appropriate fields in this dialog box. All those places to put numbers might daunt you at first. Just take them one at a time, and you'll find that things will work out fine.

5. After you've defined your own label, give it a name at the top of the dialog box and then click **OK**. From that point on, you can use the newly defined label just as you would any other label.

Summary

You might not realize it, but this point is something of a watershed for you. You now have the skills to create a database from scratch, to create easy-to-use forms for data entry, to create queries that turn the data into information, and to create reports that let you share that information with others. It's similar to being a high school graduate, in that you know enough to be useful — and dangerous — at the same time. If you wanted to, you could put this book down right now and be able to do good work. Please don't, though. I've got more neat stuff to teach you.

In our next chapter, I get to open the world of Access charts for you. Bar charts, pie charts, you pick 'em, we've got 'em. All you have to supply is the data.

Oh, by the way... Do you remember the "dead end" that offended sensibilities back when I was a reporter, the one on the street leading to the cemetery? Turns out the town fathers in their wisdom decided to change it to a "No Exit" sign. Makes a fella kind of want to shake his head in wonderment.

PART THREE

FLEXING OUR MUSCLES

THIS PART CONTAINS THE FOLLOWING CHAPTERS:

CHAPTER **11** A THOUSAND-WORD PICTURE

CHAPTER **12** I WANT IT TO LOOK LIKE THIS

CHAPTER **13** A SEQUEL CAN COME FIRST

CHAPTER **14** I'LL TALK WITH MY FRIENDS

By now, you have enough understanding of Access that you could walk away from this book and accomplish quite a bit with databases of your own. In this part, however, you'll go a step beyond the essentials of the product and learn about the truly powerful aspects of Access that will enable you to flex your database muscles and impress the pros. Adding graphical elements, tweaking the design of your user interface, creating queries with the Structured Query Language, and sharing your database information across networks are all advanced Access features that will enhance your database knowledge and thus complete your well-rounded Access 97 education.

For decades, government agencies in oil- and gas-producing states had been collecting data — barrels and barrels full of data, in fact. In Texas, the job fell, oddly enough, to the Railroad Commission. In other states, the data gathering was done by a variety of industrial or natural resource commissions or departments. Eventually, the states found themselves with enormous amounts of data on oil and gas production, on condensate and casinghead gas, on disposal water, and on wells and pipelines.

Like the very oil and gas that it quantified, this data remained underground, stored in deep bureaucratic wells where almost no one could see it. Most of it resided on tape or in enormous flat database files on mainframe computers.

However, as three employees at a Texas oil marketer realized, data is not the same thing as information. What was needed were easy-to-use forms through which this mass of data in oil-producing states could be organized, accessed, and presented in meaningful ways.

In 1993, these three people — Bill Weddle, Claude Cobb, and Larry Robinette; one an accountant, another a middle manager, and the third a sales director — formed an Austin, Texas-based firm called HPDI, whose goal was to provide current and historical oil and gas data in a user-friendly, inexpensive, functional, and machine-readable format, either on CD-ROM or through an online service. They hired a Microsoft Access developer who had been working with Access version 1.1. He and two other developers wrote a generic set of code, created simple forms and reports, designed wildcard query screens, built various other specialized screens, and enabled the data to be organized and accessed in five different ways: by leases, by gatherers, by operators, by counties, and by districts.

HPDI now employs 12 people, including management personnel, professional and student developers, data collectors, and sales personnel. The company currently has 27 databases on the market.

The head developer at HPDI, Corey Rhoden, says that Access has proved to be an excellent tool for the company, in large part because so many clients and potential clients use Windows and Microsoft Office products. Access is very flexible and easy to use, he says, although one problem for HPDI is working around the one-gigabyte file-size limit.

Already making databases for almost 20 states, HPDI would like to expand to be able to publish data all across the country and even internationally, as well as to put out more historical products. Its biggest limitation is finding a way to keypunch mountains of data when, as is often the case, the data doesn't exist in easy-to-convert formats.

A THOUSAND-WORD PICTURE

IN THIS CHAPTER YOU LEARN THESE KEY SKILLS

I have nothing but admiration for those talented people who can create art using their hands, mostly because I can't. For the life of me, I couldn't draw even a decent doodle — let alone the occasional indecent doodle. Even my photographs come out with what polite professionals call "soft" focus.

So far, I've shown you how to create information from your data. I've even shown you how share that information with other people in a report. Now it's time to go a step further — into the world of information as depicted by graphical charts.

In this chapter, I show you how to create a report that has the "normal" list of data on it. Next to the data, however, I show you how to put a chart derived from that data, a chart that your reader should be able to instantly absorb. A chart that will convey the true meaning of the data without using words. A chart that is worth — dare I say it? — a thousand points of data!

The Creative Process

Access charts appear most often on reports, although they can be put on forms too. As you can imagine, however, creating a chart to graphically depict your data is rather more complicated than producing a simple report or form.

Between forms and reports, I've chosen to go the easier route and to show you how to put a chart on a report. Our scenario (you knew one was coming, didn't you?) is as follows: You're still in marketing, and your boss is again frantic. This time it's a meeting of the board of directors he wants to impress. A simple report simply won't do, no siree, Bob! The board will be deciding on the budget, and your boss needs to show some prior year's results. In this case, he wants them to see how much of each product category Northwind Traders sold in 1995.

As with most other things having to do with Access, the process is most easily done when broken down into its constituent parts.

In this case, you will:

1. Take the relevant query (Category Sales for 1995) and create one of Access's quick and dirty AutoReports with it.

2. Dress up the AutoReport just enough so that it's not embarrassing.

3. Create a blank report to hold the AutoReport and a chart.

4. Create a pie chart.

"Access charts appear most often on reports, although they can be put on forms too."

WHICH ONE WHEN?

Different data represents different information. That's fairly obvious. It follows that different information is best depicted by different kinds of graphics. Table 11-1 shows a list of what I think is the best kind of chart to use in various situations:

TABLE 11-1 Chart Types

Chart Icon	Chart Type	When to Use It
	COLUMN	To compare several series of data with each other or to show their differences — over time, for example. Each category of data is represented by a column, with increasing values resulting in taller columns.
	3-D COLUMN	Works like a column chart but can be used to compare two series of data with a third series, that's in turn related to them both.
	BAR	Works just like a column chart, but more laid back (or is that laid down?).
	3-D BAR	Works like a bar chart but can be used to compare two series of data with a third series, that's in turn related to them both.
	LINE	Depicts the trends of several variables over time.
	3-D LINE	Also known as a ribbon chart, it shows relationships over time in three dimensions.
	AREA	A variation of the line chart, the filled-in area below the lines highlights the differences between and among data series.
	3-D AREA	Much like the area chart, this one is also good for demonstrating the relationship of the individual series with the total.
	SCATTER	Depicts the relationships among two sets of numbers, disregarding time.
	BUBBLE	A variation of the Scatter chart, this one can also depict the value of a third series of data.
	3-D BUBBLE	A fancier Bubble chart.
	PIE	Lets you see the proportion of a single series of numbers compared with the proportions of all of them added together.
	3-D PIE	Just a fancier pie chart.
	DOUGHNUT	A pie chart within a pie chart, it can depict proportions to the whole of more than one series of data.

Access gets the information it needs to create charts from the data in your database. That data can be in a table or it can be in a query; it doesn't really matter. That means you don't really have to include a representation of the chart's underlying data in your report. I've found, however, that most people who read a report with a chart on it also want to see the data. Perhaps it's a natural kind of modern-day cynicism, but that's the way things are.

FEATURE FOCUS In days of old — during the early '90s — people put "charts" on their Access forms and reports. Nowadays, they use "graphics" instead. They're the same images, but are called something different. And that, my friends is how something on occasion becomes a software feature.

The final report I'm going to show you how to create in this chapter will incorporate both a chart and something you haven't seen before: a subreport. As you have probably guessed, a subreport is really nothing more than a normal, everyday Access report that's been stuck into ("embedded," as we in the biz say) another report. Although a subreport is an entity separate from a main report, in practical terms it becomes part of the main report. Also, because it's a separate entity, you create, modify, and manipulate the subreport separately from the main report.

"A *subreport* is a normal report that's been inserted into another report — normally called the *main report*."

A Quick and Dirty AutoReport

I showed you in Chapter 10, "Me, Reporting for Duty," how to create an AutoReport, so I won't bore you here with too much repetitive detail. I'll just quickly run through the process of creating one. Later, I'll show you how to embed it as a subreport into the main report.

Because the chart you're creating will depict Northwind's sales for 1995 by category, you start with the query that provides exactly that data.

Follow along, and I'll show you what I mean:

1. With Access running and the Northwind database loaded, activate the Queries tab on the database container. (When you click on the Queries tab, Access activates it.) As you can see in Figure 11-1, the query we'll use is already there. It's called Category Sales for 1995, and if it's not highlighted, please make it so.

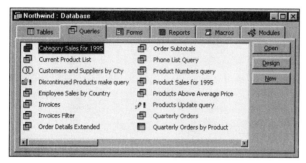

Figure 11-1 The query you need has already been created for you.

2. Because the Queries tab — and not the Reports tab — is active, you can't click New at this point to create a new report. Instead, move your mouse cursor to the ▣ on the toolbar and click the arrow that's part of its right side. Access pops down the menu shown in Figure 11-2.

Figure 11-2 Choose the AutoReport option to create a new report.

3. From the pop-down menu, select the ⬛ **AutoReport** option. Access notes that you've highlighted the Category Sales for 1995 query and uses it to create the new report. When it's done cooking, Access displays the report in print preview mode, as shown in Figure 11-3.

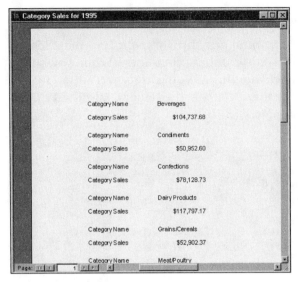

Figure 11-3 The subreport, just a-birthing.

A First Little Touch-Up

Well, you have the beginnings of what you need to use as a subreport. Before that happens, however, there are a couple of details you need to touch up.

For example, as it's formatted now, the report is simply too big (or is that "too long?"). In any case, as it is now, it would take up so much room on the main report that you would have no room left over for the chart!

Perform these steps, and the subreport will be in good shape in no time:

1. Click ![icon] on the toolbar. Access displays the report, as shown in Figure 11-4. As you can see, it needs to be "cleaned up" so that the data fields are by themselves in the Detail band and the data labels are in the Page Header band.

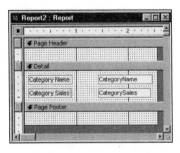

Figure 11-4 Click the design view button to see the new subreport in design view.

2. Move the field labels to the report's Page Header band. Then, move the data fields so that they're in a row by themselves in the Detail band.

3. After that's done, tighten up the height of all three of the report's bands — Page Header, Detail, and Footer — so that they're bunched right next to each other, as shown in Figure 11-5. If you like, you can also format as bold the text in the label fields, as I did. This isn't important; it's just an extra touch I like to make.

Figure 11-5 The subreport is now almost ready to use.

4. Save the report as Category Sales for 1995. Then click 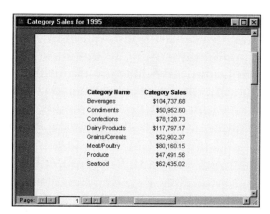 and take a look at your new report in its final form, as shown in Figure 11-6.

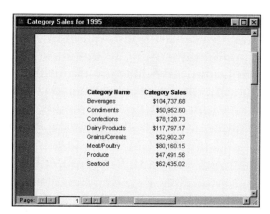

Figure 11-6 The report is saved and ready for use as a subreport.

There are a couple of things I'd like you to notice about the subreport. First, it sure looks like I've violated my own advice about giving every report a title and a date stamp. Well, as usual there's a method to my madness.

As you'll soon see, when Access puts a subreport into a main report, it uses only the subreport's detail band. Anything you've put into other bands is simply ignored. The reason I made the field labels bold is to make it easier for me to know what's what if ever I need to look at the subreport on its own.

Adding a Blank Main Report

With the subreport out of the way, the next piece of this pie is a blank main report that you can use to hold it — and the chart too, of course. When I say "blank main report," I mean exactly that. It's like a blank piece of paper on which you copy the chart and subreport.

Follow along, and you'll see more of what I mean:

1. With the Category Sales for 1995 query under the Queries tab highlighted, move your mouse cursor to the 🖼 on the toolbar. Select ⌈ **Report** ⌋, as shown in Figure 11-7. Access calls up its New Report dialog box.

Figure 11-7 This time, select Report to open the New Report dialog box.

2. Take a moment now to look at the dialog box in Figure 11-8. Notice how it already has the name of the query entered for you as the chosen one. (Sounds almost religious, doesn't it?) Access does this as a kind of courtesy, even though you don't need it for your present purposes. You can simply ignore it. I'm bringing up the subject just so you aren't confused, perhaps thinking that you'll need it because Access put it there.

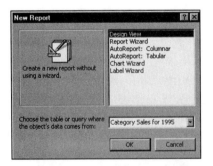

Figure 11-8 Your query is already there.

3. By default, the New Report dialog box should also have Design View highlighted. That's good, because that's something you *do* need. Click ⌈ **OK** ⌋, and Access opens a new, blank report in design view, as shown in Figure 11-9.

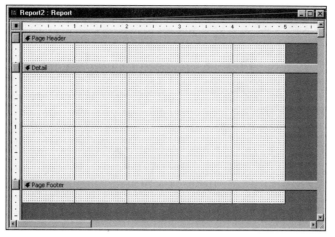

Figure 11-9 Access opens a new, blank report.

4. Assuming that up to this point you haven't been on the edge of your chair, just waiting to get to the end of one page so you could get to the next, this is where things begin to get interesting, in my view. Click in the toolbox. Then move your mouse cursor to the blank report and drag open a box in which you'll place the subreport, as shown in Figure 11-10.

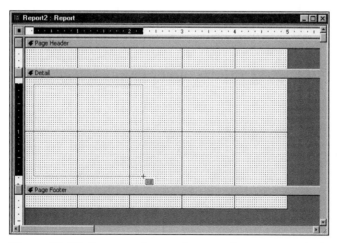

Figure 11-10 To put a subreport into a main report, you have to first make a place for it.

As you start dragging, you might notice that Access has changed your mouse cursor to an icon that resembles the Subform/Subreport toolbox button. That's just Access's way of keeping you oriented. When you let up on your mouse button, Access knows where to put the subreport, and so it goes on to the next step, that of opening the Subform/Subreport Wizard. Please see Figure 11-11.

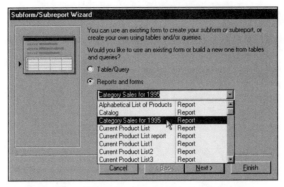

Figure 11-11 This is the first dialog box of the Subform/Subreport Wizard.

Working with the Subform/Subreport Wizard

The Subform/Subreport Wizard guides you as you enter a subreport into your main report.

Please follow these steps:

1. Look at the first Subform/Subreport dialog box, as shown in Figure 11-11. Notice that you can create the subreport from a table or query, or you can do it the way we did: by first creating another report. I prefer doing it this way because it gives me more hands-on control than I'd get by relying on the wizard. In any case, click the Reports and forms option button and then select the Category Sales for 1995 report from the drop-down list. Click **Next** and Access displays the second Subform/Subreport Wizard dialog box, as shown in Figure 11-12.

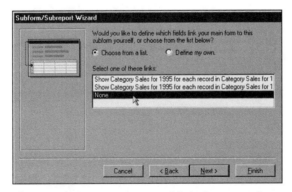

Figure 11-12 You won't need links for your subreport.

Quite often, a subreport's data needs to be linked somehow to the data displayed on the main form. A good example of this is a report in which you list each customer along with all the stuff they've ordered over a period of time. In this case, however, you don't need links between the two reports because the main report isn't depicting data, as such. It's merely a holding place for the subreport and the chart.

2. Select None from the list displayed in the dialog box and then click Next . Access calls up the third Subform/Subreport Wizard dialog box, as shown in Figure 11-13.

Figure 11-13 Each report and subreport needs a name.

3. As you know by now, each object you create has to have a name. Access offers you here a perfectly good name for the subreport. So, unless you want to go back and redo your answers on one of the preceding Subform/Subreport Wizard dialog boxes, go ahead and click Finish . Access cooks for a moment and then displays the no longer blank report. As shown in Figure 11-14, Access has put a place holder for the subreport in the main report's Detail band.

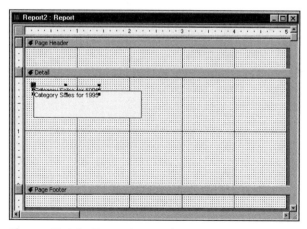

Figure 11-14 Every element that goes on your report has its own place to be.

A second bit of touch-up

When Access puts a placeholder for the subreport in your blank report, it automatically also includes a label for it. I don't normally have a problem with this. After all, Access has no way of really knowing what kind of information appears in the subreport. In this case, unfortunately, the label gets in the way, so you need to get rid of it.

Do you remember that I told you earlier that Access only uses the information in the detail band of a subreport? Well, this is one time when that's inconvenient. Because Access does so, you need to also add the labels to the blank report.

Follow along as I go through the process:

1. Select and then delete the label from the subreport placeholder in the main report.

2. One at a time, add two labels just above the subreport placeholder. In one, I'd like you to type **Category**, and in the other please type **Sales**. If you like, you can also format the labels' text to be bold and align them so that their text is against the labels' left and right edges, respectively. When you're done, your main report should look like the one shown in Figure 11-15.

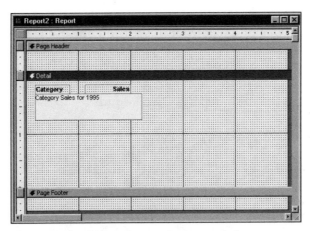

Figure 11-15 The subreport is almost ready.

3. When it prints the main report, Access by default includes a thin border around any subreports. My preference is to delete the border in this case. Accordingly, right click the subreport placeholder and select ‖ Properties ‖ from the menu Access pops up.

 TIP If you had left the data labels in the detail band of the subreport, then they would have been repeated in the subreport for each category. Clearly, you don't need that kind of repetition, so that's one reason why I had you move them to the Report Header band.

4. On the Properties sheet, first click the Format tab to activate it. Then move down to the `Border Style` property and click it. When the down arrow appears, click it and choose `Transparent` from the list, as shown in Figure 11-16.

Figure 11-16 You don't need a border around your subreport.

5. There's one more detail you need to attend to if you want this report to be excellent instead of merely very good. Click 🔍 on the toolbar.

Take a look at the subreport and note how well the labels on the main report line up with the data items in the subreport. When I first put this report together, they weren't even close. To correct this, I toggled back and forth between print preview and design view, moving the labels a bit each time until they looked "right." If you like, you can do the same.

6. I almost forgot another detail: SAVE YOUR REPORT. Then, once you're ready, you can move on to putting in the chart itself.

At Last: the Piece de Resistance

Talk about dessert after a full meal — we're there! We're finally at the point where I can show you how to put in the chart for which you've been waiting.

This is how to do so:

1. With the report in design view, move your mouse cursor to the **Insert** menu and choose **Chart**, as shown in Figure 11-17. Then move your mouse cursor to the main report and drag open a box in which to place the chart, as shown in Figure 11-18.

Figure 11-17 Charts are opened from the Insert menu.

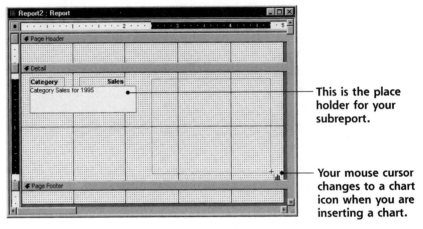

This is the place holder for your subreport.

Your mouse cursor changes to a chart icon when you are inserting a chart.

Figure 11-18 You need to prepare a place for your chart on the main report.

2. When you release the mouse button, Access cooks for a moment and then opens the first Chart Wizard dialog box, as shown in Figure 11-19.

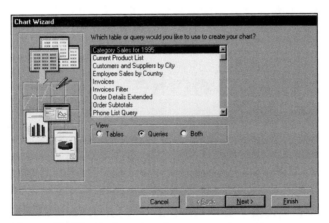

Figure 11-19 You're using the same query again.

3. Because both the subreport and the chart are based on data from the same query, you need to choose its name here in the dialog box. To see a list of queries only, click the Queries option button in the View box. Then make sure the Category Sales for 1995 query is highlighted.

4. When you've done so, click [**Next**]. Access displays the next Chart Wizard dialog box.

5. Select both fields from the list of those available and move them over to the Fields for Chart list, as shown in Figure 11-20.

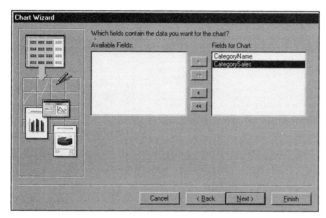

Figure 11-20 Access needs to know which fields to use.

6. Click [**Next**], and Access opens the next Chart Wizard dialog box, as shown in Figure 11-21.

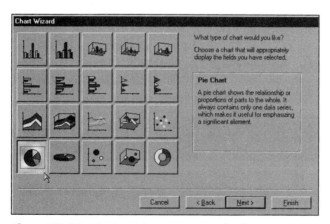

Figure 11-21 You're going to create a pie chart.

7. I think a pie chart would best depict the results of the Category Sales for 1995 query. That's because a pie chart contains a single list of numbers and comparing each of the category amounts to the whole is easiest and most informative. Accordingly, click the pie chart icon at the lower left corner of the dialog box and then click [**Next**]. Access opens a specialized Chart Wizard dialog box, as shown in Figure 11-22.

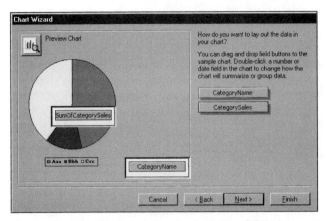

Figure 11-22   Pie charts use a single series of data.

I call this a specialized dialog box because it appears only when you choose to create a pie chart for your report. It "knows," for example, that pie charts employ a single series of data for their calculations. By the same token, other specialized dialog boxes are displayed when you choose to create other kinds of charts.

Notice that the potential field names for the chart are collected in buttons under the instruction text at the dialog box's right. Notice also that Access has placed a calculation — SumOfCategorySales — into position on the chart icon itself. That makes perfect sense because Access will use two values to create the pie chart: each category's sales figure, which is then compared as a fraction of all the categories' sales figures added together.

8. Once you're satisfied with your choice of chart type, click ▐ **Next** ▌. Access displays the next Chart Wizard dialog box, as shown in Figure 11-23.

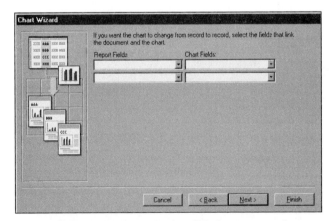

Figure 11-23   You don't need to link the report and chart fields.

A HANDY HELPER

I often can't keep track of what's what when I'm creating charts. To help people like me, Access includes a Preview Chart button at the top left of the Chart Wizard dialog box. When you click this button, Access displays a preview of the chart, as shown in the following figure.

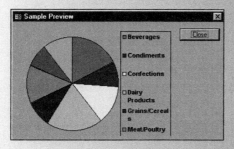

If you're in the same boat, try changing the fields around and then clicking the Preview Chart button. Each time you do, Access takes the fields you've indicated, in the order you've indicated, and creates a preview chart. If it looks okay, then go with it. If not, on the other hand, then keep adjusting the fields until the preview chart looks right to you.

9. With some combinations of charts and their underlying data, you might want the chart to immediately reflect changes in the data. If so, you'd link the two using the drop-down list boxes in this dialog. Because you're using a query that is a summation of other data, that wouldn't work well in this case. So, to leave the fields blank, select No Field from the combo box and click ▐ **Next** ▐. Access displays the last Chart Wizard dialog box, as shown in Figure 11-24.

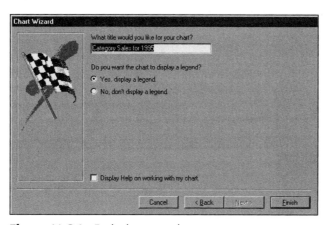

Figure 11-24 Each chart must have a name.

10. Enter the title **Category Sales for 1995** for your chart in the text box at the top of the dialog box. When you've entered the title, click [**Finish**]. Access cooks for a moment and then puts your chart in the place you prepared earlier. When I did the same, my report and its chart looked like the one in Figure 11-25.

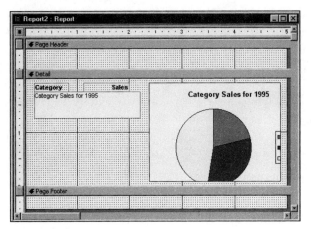

Figure 11-25 The report is nearly finished.

11. Click 🖫 on the toolbar to once again store your report on your computer's hard disk.

Finishing a Chart

Quite often, when left to its default devices, Access gets you "almost there" and not "all the way there." I've found it to be the same when Access creates charts.

Here's what I mean: Take a look at your report in print preview. Does it look okay, or is it or its legend poorly formatted?

When I previewed my work, the pie part of the pie chart looked okay, but its legend was off. Its size was wrong, it was partially hidden by the edge of the chart's area, and so on.

What you see is likely to be off by a different amount than mine was. That's because you and I are likely to have placed our charts and reports differently on our own computer screens — not to mention the fact that we may be using different screen resolutions.

An Access chart is a discrete object, one that is embedded in your report. As such, you can modify and manipulate it on its own. As a matter of fact, if you're going to adjust it at all, you have to work with it individually.

To modify your chart, double click it. Access opens the Microsoft Graph applet that's built into Windows 95. You can see an illustration of it in Figure 11-26.

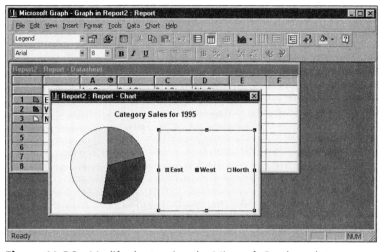

Figure 11-26 Modify charts using the Microsoft Graph applet.

A complete discussion of how to modify charts is way beyond the scope of this book, and that's frustrating to me. On the other hand, I know that it could take an entire book to do justice to the subject.

I feel almost as though I'd be confounding you if I told you too little, and confusing you if I told you too much. My only choice is to take the middle road, give you some directed hints, and rely on your intelligence and common sense, so here goes.

"An Access chart is a discrete object, one that is embedded in your report. As such, you can modify and manipulate it on its own."

What's most unfortunate is that the Graph applet shows you only a generic representation of your actual chart. I wish they had thought instead to build into the product a more definitive representation of the chart with which you're working. This leaves you with a situation in which you manipulate the generic chart, then close the applet and finally look at *your* chart in print preview. You repeat the process until the chart looks good enough — or you run out of time because your boss *must have it now!*

TIP A *legend* on a chart is a list of labels that tell you what each of the parts of the chart represent. In Access, a chart legend will usually include a small colored box next to each of the legend's labels that corresponds with the color of that label's data item.

Just like any other Access (or Windows) object: To work on it, you first select it, and to select it, you click it. So, to modify a part of your chart, click the part of its generic representation that you want to modify. For example:

✳ If you want to move the pie chart itself, then click right next to it. The applet draws a box around the pie chart that you can move, reduce in size, or enlarge. The size of the chart changes in direct proportion to the size of the box.

✳ If you want to move a slice of the pie chart, then click it. The applet draws handles on it that you can use to change the size of only that piece or to move it around. You can use this facility to create an "exploding pie chart," one whose "slices" are drawn separated from the others.

✳ If you want to change the size of the legend — a distinct possibility in this case — then click the legend. The applet draws a box around the legend that you can use to change its size or move it.

In any case, I went back and forth moving my legend, adjusting the proportions of the chart, and changing the size of the pie, until the report in print preview looked like what's shown in Figure 11-27.

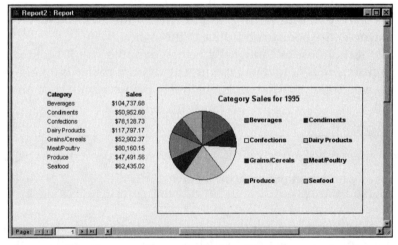

Figure 11-27 The report is now finished to all but the professional's eye.

BONUS

Finishing Your Report

I f you really needed to, you could go ahead and print out your new report and chart. Before you do, however, I'd like to recommend that you add two standard finishing touches: a title and a date stamp.

Follow these steps to do that:

1. With your main report in design view, add a label to its Page Header band. I used Northwind Traders 1995 Sales by Category, centered above the subreport and chart. I formatted the text in 12-point Arial Bold.

2. Enter a date stamp by clicking **Insert** and then **Date and Time** . You can choose the format you want to use for the date and time from the dialog box. Access places the expression field into your Detail band, so move it to the Footer band. When you're done, your report in design view should look much like the one shown in Figure 11-28.

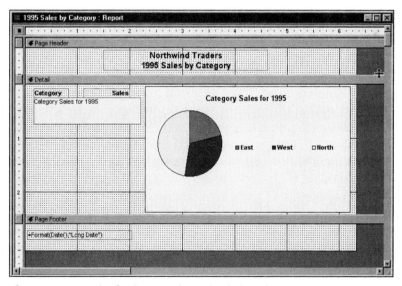

Figure 11-28 The final report shown in design view.

 TIP Can you see how the title I put in my report is written in two neat lines? Believe it or not, even with the lines broken like that, it's a single paragraph. You can do the same thing by pressing Shift+Enter wherever you want to insert a line break without a paragraph break.

3. Save your report again and then get the payoff: Take a look at it in print preview. When I did, it looked like what you see in Figure 11-29.

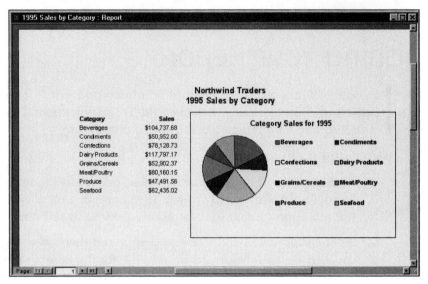

Figure 11-29 Here's the final report in all its glory.

Well, that's that. We're done with the report, and if I may say so: like Ricardo Montalban, it looks marvelous.

Summary

The difference between a user and a power user is the quality of his product. After going through the exercises in this chapter, you are very well on the way to becoming a power user.

If there's anything you've gained from this chapter, I hope it's this: Don't be afraid to press buttons and to experiment. You won't break anything, and you'll learn much.

Coming next, I'd like to expand on your new skills by giving you some more advanced tools to use as you work with databases.

I WANT IT TO LOOK LIKE THIS

12

I've got a toolbox in the garage. Actually, I've got three. One's from my growing-up days, full of odds and ends I thought I'd be able to use some day. Every now and then I find myself rummaging through it for some old part or half-squeezed tube of distributor lube (27 years old, not yet used up, and still completely useable).

Another toolbox comes from my college course in aircraft technology. As part of the degree, I had to learn how to fix and fly airplanes. There are specialized tools for that, you know, almost none of which I've thrown away. Most of the tools are funny kinds of pliers used for inserting tools to hold metal together or to twist safety wire or to simply put the squeeze on recalcitrant parts.

The third toolbox is the family toolbox. It has in it tools that belong to the whole of us. The screwdrivers the kids used to pry up driveway concrete when they were younger, the hammers they used to kill bugs and to set off rolls of caps, the wrenches with which they chased away neighbor girls. (In time, they put an end to *that* by themselves.) This is the box in which tools gone from the other two mysteriously appear.

What I want to do in this chapter is give you a kind of toolbox. It'll be more intellectual than physical, of course, but you'll find what you learn here to be at least as useful as a screwdriver.

We'll start with a look at the table design view window, where I'll show you some tools you can use to control what your user is allowed to enter into the database. We'll go on from there to create a new kind of switchboard, something even more intuitive to use than the one Access automatically creates. We'll finish with me showing you how you can provide data to your user, so that they don't even have to type to enter data into the database.

A User Interface Is Really for You

I f you're a living, breathing, carbon-based life form today, you've heard the buzzwords "user interface." By this point, you've got more than a merely intuitive idea of what a user interface really involves. Now it's time to get to the nitty gritty.

If you remember nothing else from this chapter, remember this: The basic reason for a good user interface is to keep your user from making mistakes.

In actual fact, the user interface you create for your database bears more on you than it does your user. That's because you're the person who has to deal with problems allowed by any deficiencies in your design. If your users can't orient themselves on a form or your boss can't understand a report, you will be the one with whom they want to — um — "speak." Believe me: It's worth it to take a bit of time in the beginning to get things right.

The right beginnings of a user interface

All good database user interfaces start at the point where you design a table. With a few keystrokes then, you can actually *require* that what your user tries to enter as data is correct. ("Correct" in terms of fitting correctly into your database, of course. The data itself might be as bogus as a three dollar bill, but you have almost no control over that.)

"If you remember nothing else from this chapter, remember this: The basic reason for a good user interface is to keep your user from making mistakes."

If all good user interfaces begin with a table's design, then it makes sense for us to begin by taking a close look at the user interfaces of a table in design view. Look for a moment at Figure 12-1. It's the top half of the Addresses table from the My First Address Book database. I've highlighted the HomePhone field, and we'll get to it in a moment. For now, I want you to look at all three columns you see in the figure.

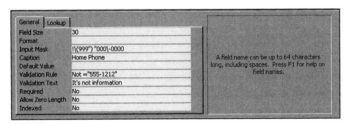

Field Name	Data Type	Description
AddressID	AutoNumber	ID number automatically generated by Access
FirstName	Text	First name
LastName	Text	Surname
SpouseName	Text	Spouse name
Address	Text	Street address
City	Text	City of residence
StateOrProvince	Text	State or Province
PostalCode	Text	Postal or Zip code
Country	Text	Country of residence
EmailAddress	Text	Email address
HomePhone	Text	Home telephone number
WorkPhone	Text	Work telephon number
WorkExtension	Text	Work telephone extension
FaxNumber	Text	Fax telephone number
Birthdate	Date/Time	Date of Birth
SendCard	Yes/No	Should we send this person a card?

Figure 12-1   This is a good beginning.

I want you to notice first that each and every field includes a description. Many of them are only two or three words long, but each one is easily understandable. If you were to come back to this database in five years, you'd instantly know what kind of data is stored in each of its fields.

Next, look at the field names themselves. Each of them is also a complete English word; well, words in some cases. Access, because of how it works with the Visual Basic for Applications programming language, requires that field names comprise a single word. If more than a single word was needed for clarity, however, then each is capitalized before they are run together. For example, First Name becomes FirstName. That way, you can look at the field name, even if it looks kind of funny, and still know what goes in it.

Masks and validation

Now I want you to turn your attention to Figure 12-2, the bottom of the Addresses table in design view. This is a kind of repository for all the details having to do with each field in your database. The words at left are properties, just like the ones you'd find on a property sheet. I'll discuss them one at a time.

General	Lookup
Field Size	30
Format	
Input Mask	!\(999") "000\-0000
Caption	Home Phone
Default Value	
Validation Rule	Not ="555-1212"
Validation Text	It's not information
Required	No
Allow Zero Length	No
Indexed	No

A field name can be up to 64 characters long, including spaces. Press F1 for help on field names.

Figure 12-2   Here's where you really keep your user from making mistakes.

TIP   A *byte* is the most common unit of measurement in the computer world. It stands for eight *bits* (the smallest unit of measurement) and is the size of one alphabetic character stored in your computer's memory.

The Field Size is a number that tells you how big (in bytes) your field is. In this case, we've allowed 30 bytes of space to hold the home telephone number. Because we're storing the data as text, this is really generous. Most telephone numbers (in the United States) can be stored in ten bytes. When you hand write a telephone number on a paper form, you may very well see a pair of parentheses "(" & ")" that you know is for the area code, with room for two numbers separated by a hyphen "-" which you also know to use for the seven-digit telephone number. This familiar format is a mask. It almost forces you to put the numbers into the familiar telephone number format. Computer masks look much the same and work much the same. The only difference is that when you use a computer mask, although the punctuation is displayed in your data entry field, it's not also stored in the database.

The Format is where you customize exactly how you want the contents of the field to be printed. The Format is necessarily different depending on what kind of data you're storing in each field.

* For text data, you can require that a certain number of characters are always entered in the field, and you can force whatever characters your user types to be upper or lower case.

* For numbers, you can specify how many decimal digits should be displayed. (Although it doesn't change the numerical value of the data itself, Access automatically rounds the number it displays up or down if the number of display decimal digits is less than the actual number of decimal digits.) You can also show numbers as percentages, in scientific notation, and as currency.

* Although dates and times are part of the same format function, you can display either dates or times alone. You can also choose how you want your dates and times displayed — spelled out, in military time, and so forth.

The next field is the Input Mask, which is a way of allowing only the data appropriate for a particular field to be entered. For example, the mask for the HomePhone field is (999) 000-0000. When a person enters a telephone number into this field, the 9's indicate that area code is optional, and that although the user doesn't have to enter an area code, if he does it will have to comprise numbers; Access won't allow alphabetical characters in place of the 9's. The 0's, on the other hand, indicate that the user is required to enter data here in the form of numbers; Access again disallows alphabetical characters.

If you take a moment to look at Figure 12-3, you'll see me entering a postal code into the database. Notice that Access has taken the mask information and is using it to show me with underscore lines the correct size for the data for the PostalCode field.

The Caption is what Access uses as a label for the field. If you don't put anything in as a caption, Access simply uses the Field Name as the label.

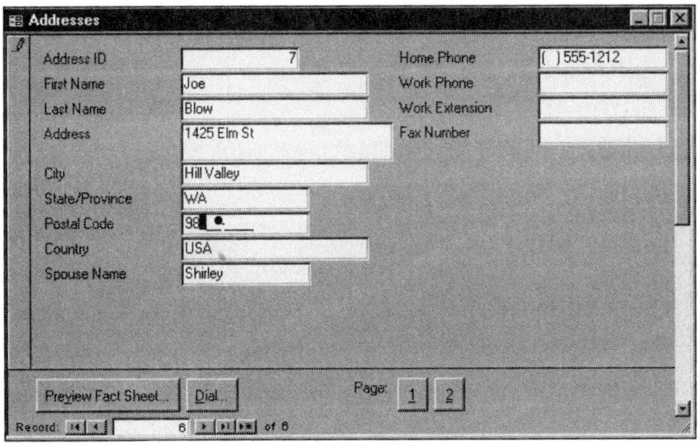

Figure 12-3 shows a form titled "Addresses" with fields including Address ID (7), First Name (Joe), Last Name (Blow), Address (1425 Elm St), City (Hill Valley), State/Province (WA), Postal Code (98), Country (USA), Spouse Name (Shirley), Home Phone (( ) 555-1212), Work Phone, Work Extension, Fax Number. Labeled "This is the mask."

Figure 12-3 A mask guides your data input.

The `Default Value` is useful in those situations where you have some data that's almost always entered into a field, and you don't want to have to type it all the time. For example, if most of the people in your address book live in your state, then you can put in the state's abbreviation as a default value. Access will display it each time you enter data into a new record. If the person lives in your state, then you merely press Enter when you get to that field; if not, you type the different state's abbreviation in the field instead.

"A field name can be up to 64 characters long, including spaces."

The `Validation Rule` is your instruction to Access that describes any particular requirements you might have to ensure that correct data is entered into this field. For example, you can enter "between 1 and 100" here to allow only numbers that fall within that range to be stored in this field. In this case, I've told Access to disregard the data if some smarty pants tries to enter the number for information as his home number.

The `Validation Text` is what Access displays in a warning dialog box if the `Validation Rule` is violated. Look at Figure 12-4 to see the warning box Access displayed when I tried to be a smarty pants.

The `Required` field is where you tell Access if the user *must* enter data for this field. If yes, Access won't save the record until this field is correctly filled.

`Allow Zero Length` is kind of technical. It has to do with how Access handles blank fields for text, memo, and hyperlink fields. If this is yes, then you can put in what's known as a *zero-length string* (a text string that's of no length!). Access then differentiates a zero-length string from a simple empty record. It's not something you'll need to work with for a while, but I thought I'd at least tell you about it for completeness' sake, if for nothing else.

`Indexed` is another yes/no field. If yes, then Access maintains an index for this field, which allows you to sort the field a bit more quickly.

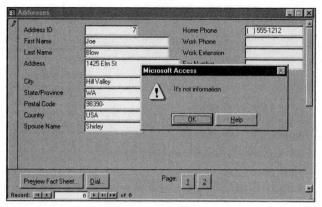

Figure 12-4 The validation text can tell your user what she did wrong.

Making the Computer Do Its Job

There's one thing I really like about computers and databases. If I type something into a database once, I never want to have to type it in again. Or, if there's some AutoNumber field that's associated with other data — names, for instance — I don't want to have to remember the number *and* the name. If I play my cards right, I don't have to; I can make the computer do its complete job.

What's coming next are two examples of how to do this. Incidentally, they also improve your user interface tremendously. The first thing I want to show you is how to put a combo box into a form. It will be one that automatically looks up the data you need and then stores that data into your database. The second thing I show you is how to make yes/no data easier for your user.

Looking it up, automagically

Back at the beginning of this book, in Chapter 3, "I'd Like to Jump in and Give it a Try," I showed you how to create a form called Children to add children's names to your database. You can see it in Figure 12-5. Now I want you to open that form again so we can work with it.

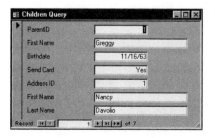

Figure 12-5 The Children form from the beginning of this book.

Now follow along as I show you how to put in the combo box:

1. With the Children form visible, click  on the toolbar. Access changes its view from form view to design view, as shown in Figure 12-6.

Remove this field and label.

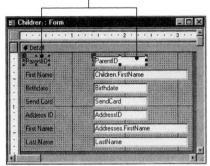

Figure 12-6 The Children form in design view.

2. Remove the ParentID field and label from the top of the form. When you've done so, your form should look like the one in Figure 12-7. Then save your form, if you please.

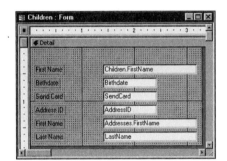

Figure 12-7 The Children form sans ParentID.

3. Click  on the toolbar. Access changes your mouse cursor to reflect the current task (creating a combo box). Move to the form and draw a place for the combo box, as shown in Figure 12-8.

Figure 12-8 A place for what's to come.

4. When you release the mouse button, Access opens the first Combo Box Wizard dialog box, as shown in Figure 12-9.

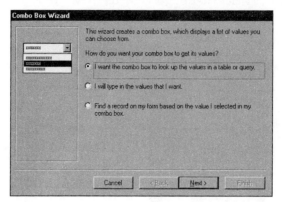

Figure 12-9 You'll automatically get the values you need.

5. Make sure the first option button, I want the combo box to look up the values in a table or query, is selected, then click Next . Access displays the second Combo Box Wizard dialog box, as shown in Figure 12-10.

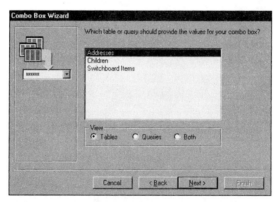

Figure 12-10 The Addresses table holds the data we need.

6. Access offers the Addresses table as the one from which it will get the combo box's data. That's fine, so with Addresses highlighted, click Next . Access displays the next Combo Box Wizard dialog, as shown in Figure 12-11.

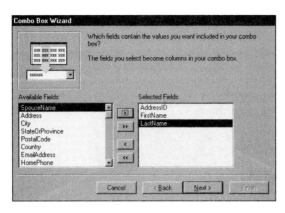

Figure 12-11 You only need three fields.

7. You only need three of the available fields from the Addresses table: AddressID, FirstName, and LastName. Move these fields from the available fields list to the list of Selected Fields. When you've done so, click **Next**. Access displays the Combo Box Wizard dialog shown in Figure 12-12.

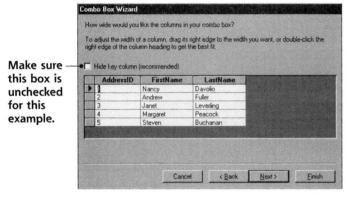

Make sure this box is unchecked for this example.

Figure 12-12 This is the meat and potatoes of combo boxes.

8. Here's where things can get a bit tricky. First, uncheck the Hide key column checkbox. Access knows that the AddressID is a key field and so automatically hides it. You need it, however, as a datum for the Children table, so you'll need to see it here.

9. The data in combo boxes appear in columns, three in this case. Often, the size that Access offers as a default is more — or less — than you need. In this case, it's too big. Move your mouse cursor to the line between the AddressID and FirstName column headings, and scoot it to the left. That'll make the column holding the AddressID narrower. If you like, you can also adjust the size of the columns holding the names, as shown in Figure 12-13. When you're done, click **Next** so that Access displays the next Combo Box Wizard dialog box, as shown in Figure 12-14.

**Make this
column narrower.**

**You can resize these two
columns too, if you like.**

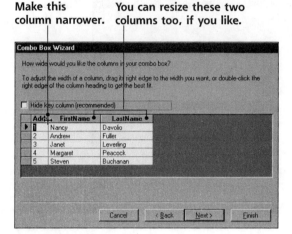

Figure 12-13 You can adjust the size of your
combo boxes' columns.

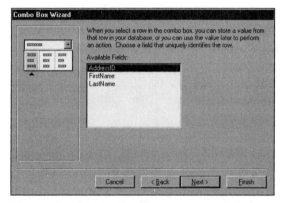

Figure 12-14 Here's where you get your data.

10. This is where you tell Access where it should get its data from. You'll recall that when you created the Children table, you took the **AddressID** from the Addresses table (in effect, the Parents table) and used it as the **ParentID** number in the Children table. Accordingly, with the **AddressID** field highlighted here, click **Next**. Access displays the next Combo Box Wizard dialog box, as shown in Figure 12-15.

11. Now that Access knows where to get the data from, you need to tell it where to put the data. Click the Store that value in this field: option box. Then select ParentID from the dialog's combo box. With that accomplished, click **Next** so that Access displays the next Combo Box Wizard dialog, as shown in Figure 12-16.

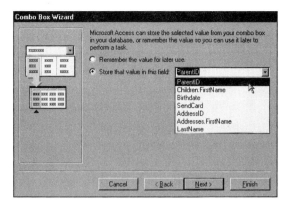

Figure 12-15   Here's where you put your data.

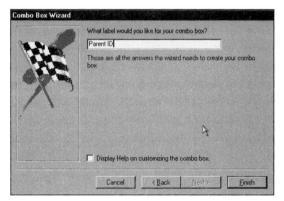

Figure 12-16   Access knows that everything should be labeled.

12. You remember that for a good user interface, everything should be labeled, don't you? Yes? Good! Type a label for your combo box in the text box at the top of this dialog. That's it for designing this combo box, so click ▐ **Finish** ▌. Access cooks for a moment and then puts the finished combo box into your form, as shown in Figure 12-17.

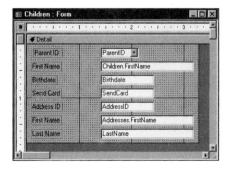

Figure 12-17   The combo box has been inserted into the form.

13. Before you do anything else, be sure to save your form again.

Trying it out

After you've put the combo box into your form, aren't you just dying to try it out? Well go ahead! I think, by the way, that you'll find the best way to do so is to add a new record to your Children table. Choose a parent to give to the child and continue filling out the form as you would have otherwise. This process is shown in Figure 12-18.

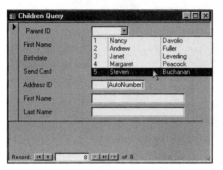

Figure 12-18 Here's an example of using the new combo box.

"Always save your work whenever you make changes to your form."

Checking for Yes and No

I hope that you're beginning to get the intuitive idea that the essence of a good user interface is convenience. Actually, there's a one-to-one correlation between the two. If it's convenient, then it's probably good.

By that measure, as you can probably see in Figure 12-19, the Children form still isn't "good." I mean, it's okay, and perhaps also somewhat usable, but it still isn't good. One problem lies in the Send Card field. It holds *Boolean* (yes/no or true/false) data, but it's inappropriately a text box. Sure, you can type "Yes" or "No" into the field, but that's not — um — "good." Let's change it.

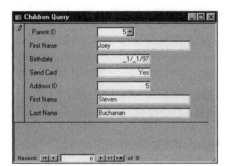

Figure 12-19 My Children form has a combo box, but it's still inconvenient to use.

TIP Just as a reminder: Click the design view button on the toolbar to put your form into design view. Then you can do the steps in this example.

Follow these steps:

1. With the Children form in design view, select and then delete the Send Card textbox field and its label, as shown in Figure 12-20.

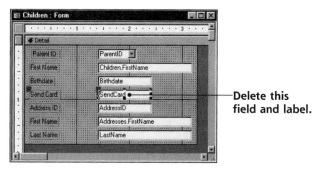

—Delete this field and label.

Figure 12-20 Cut this out!

2. Next, click ☑ on the toolbox. Move your mouse cursor over to your form — into the space opened by deleting the Send Card field — and draw a place for the new checkbox control. Access places the new control into your form, along with a label for it, as shown in Figure 12-21.

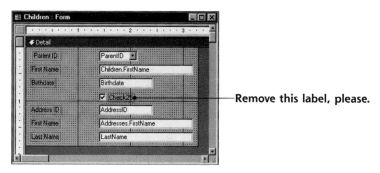

—Remove this label, please.

Figure 12-21 Here's a checkbox.

TIP *Bound* refers to the fact that a control is connected — "bound" — to an underlying field. When a control such as a text box is bound, then Access automatically displays in it the underlying data. If, on the other hand, the control is *unbound* (not connected to the underlying data), then Access can't automatically display anything in the field. You have to do that yourself, programmatically.

3. Access put this checkbox into the form as an unbound control. You have to bind it to the SendCard field in your database. Accordingly, highlight the checkbox in the form and then open the form's property sheet.

4. In the Properties sheet, click the Data tab. The first property, `Control Source`, is the one you need. Click its combo box arrow and select SendCard from the list it displays, as shown in Figure 12-22. This makes the connection — "binds," as we say in the biz — the form's checkbox and the Children table's SendCard field. Then, in the label Access automatically put on the form when you placed the checkbox, change its text to **Send card** and move it from the right of the checkbox to the left, aligned with the other labels.

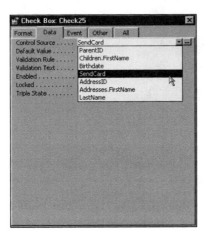

Figure 12-22 The control is now bound.

5. When you've done all that, save your form again. Then take a look at it in Form view, as shown in Figure 12-23.

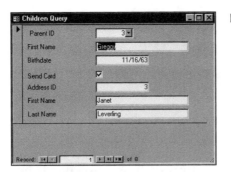

Figure 12-23 The Children form is now in much better form.

Well, that's pretty much it, don't you think? Well, no, as a matter of fact. The point of this chapter is your user interface, after all. I was hoping that when you first saw this form at the beginning of this discussion that something would jump out at you.

BONUS

If It Isn't Labeled, It Isn't Finished

So, it jumped out at you, did it? Good! You created this form at the beginning of this book, at a time when you had much less skill using Access than now. A simple and bare-bones form was good enough then, but no longer.

To finish this form, you need to add a label to it — not to mention move and resize its fields. You can see the form when I did just that in Figure 12-24.

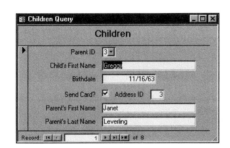

Figure 12-24 Now the form is really finished.

Here's a list of what I did:

1. First, I added a Form Header band into which I put a label. The label's text is centered, with 12-point bold type.

2. I right-aligned all the field labels and moved them over near their associated data entry fields.

3. I added text to the name fields' labels in order to make it clear which data these fields are displaying.

The last thing I did was sit back and congratulate myself on having done such a great job. I suggest that you do the same thing.

Summary

Well, that's yet another chapter of information into the old brain bucket. I won't talk much about user interfaces in the rest of this book, but I think you now have all the important stuff you need to know about it.

By the way, all living, breathing, carbon-based life forms have heard the buzzwords "user interface" by now. Lower-order carbon-based life forms may not understand the term, but they've certainly heard it. Higher life forms can recognize good interfaces. If you remember nothing else on the subject, please keep in mind the correlation between convenience and a good interface. That one fact is often what separates a professional's and an amateur's results. Just like it's a fact that the biggest difference between humans and lower life forms is that we're not afraid of vacuum cleaners.

Coming next is another look at queries — well, actually at what underlies queries: the structured query language called *SQL*.

A SEQUEL CAN COME FIRST

13

When I'm not writing books, I like to think of myself as a pilot — oh, excuse me: aviator. Not only do *I* think of myself as that, but so does our wise and gracious Uncle Sam. He even gave me a pair of bright and shiny wings to wear on special occasions: weekends, for example. One of the things I like best about flying — other than the bird-like freedom and touching the hand of God — is flying blind.

"Flying blind" is something of a misnomer. That's what they call it when you're flying in the middle of a cloud. You're not really blind. (They don't really let blind people actually fly airplanes, let alone drive out to the airport.) What's really going on is that you simply can't see anything useful outside the airplane then. All you have to direct you — and keep you "upright" — are the dials and instruments on the panel in front of you. And there are many dials and instruments, some telling you how high you are or how fast you're going, others showing you the right way to go.

The dials and instruments are all indirect. What's direct are my hands on the controls.

I even love the dials and instruments in my car. No mere idiot lights for me: No siree, Bob! I want to know exactly how fast my engine is turning over, and what kind of pressure the oil pump is putting out. My wife, on the other hand, likes things simple. If the car and its lights work: fine; if not: she knows I'll fix 'em. She hardly even uses the instruments. Indirect is fine with her.

How my wife and I are with cars is a kind of metaphor for the two different types of people who use Access queries. There are those who like the simple and quick query by example (QBE) approach, and there are others who like to delve behind the scenes. They are the ones who want to know exactly how queries work — people who like direct control. This chapter is for just that kind of individual.

You already know how to create queries using the QBE grid. While it works and is very convenient, in the final analysis it's a pretty indirect way of creating queries. Now I'm going to show you how to create queries with absolute control. This chapter is an abbreviated introduction to SQL (pronounced "sequel"). The acronym is short for "Structured Query Language," which is what underlies Access queries.

I want to start by giving you a bit of historical background to SQL. Then I show you how it and the QBE window work together as you create queries. This chapter ends by giving you a kind of SQL bestiary containing some of my favorite SQL keywords.

How SQL Came About

SQL came about because of E. F. Codd, Ph.D. He was one of the original thinkers behind relational databases. His 1970 paper, "A Relational Model of Data for Large Shared Data Banks," enumerated 12 rules that laid out a model of relational computing.

NOTE Actually Dr. Codd came up with 13 rules. He numbered them using the normal computer numbering system, which also counts zero (0) as a number, but the publicity people who wrote about it ignored rule number zero and called them "Codd's 12 Rules." Go figure.

Codd's rules take into consideration everything you can think up about relational databases. This includes ideas such as the following: That all the data in a database is explicitly represented as values in tables, that data integrity can't be affected by changing data or using low-level computing languages, and that there must be a Comprehensive Data Sublanguage to manipulate the data.

I bet you can see what I'm getting at: SQL is one such Comprehensive Data Sublanguage. It was actually invented at IBM during the mid '70s as part of a research project. At that time, the IBM researchers called their new language SEQUEL. Knowing how efficient engineers like to be with their English, it's no surprise that the name rather quickly lost half of its letters.

The technology and thinking behind SQL was early recognized for its importance. Within just a few years, in the mid '80s, the American National Standards Institute (ANSI) codified it as a standard called SQL-86. That standard has been refined until its latest incarnation as SQL-92. Nowadays, computer systems as large as US government mainframes and as small as personal laptops use databases that speak SQL.

First, Some Background

When you see a query in Access, most often it will be called a *select query*. That's because underlying your Query by Example is a specialized computer language called *Structured Query Language*, or *SQL* for short. It chooses the data you ask for in your queries by selecting only those data that meet your criteria. Here is an example of SQL:

```
SELECT * from Employees
```

This query would select all the data from a table called Employees. We'll take a closer look at this later, but for now, do you see why it is called a "select" query?

The QBE window is not alone

By now, you know all about the QBE window. You remember that it's composed of a top half holding a field list or two and a bottom half called the QBE grid. Further, you remember that you drag a field name down to the QBE grid, and can add to it criteria and expressions.

When you pose your question through the QBE window, Access automatically writes the SQL instructions it needs behind the scenes. As a matter of fact, what you see in the QBE window is really for your benefit alone.

SQL looks much like English in that it uses statements such as `Select FirstName, LastName from Employees` to get a list of all the people who work at, say, Northwind Traders, for example. Access has the ability to "read" SQL statements and to follow them as instructions.

This may sound to you like it's the long way around to your destination, but it's really not. You see, Access is actually two things. First there's the user interface that you see as you do your work, something commonly referred to as the *front end*. Underlying the user interface is the database engine itself; something the people at Microsoft decided to call the Jet database engine. This is the system's *back end*. When you run Access, you're really using it to control that back-end Jet database engine.

> **TIP** A front end is the part of the computer or software that does the initial manipulation and processing on data or instructions. It usually contains any necessary humanly understandable user interface. The front end sends the results of its work to the back-end processor, which takes care of detailed processing and housekeeping (making sure the data is stored correctly, remembering where exactly the data was put, and so on).

Access is set up this way to make it very flexible to use. You can have it (and the Jet engine) loaded on your computer and simply work away. But what if your computer were connected to a network? Well, if there's a Jet database engine to be found somewhere else on the network, you could use it almost as easily as if it were in fact on your computer. The same thing goes for just about any SQL-based database engine. The SQL engines — and Access — speak the same language.

How SQL Works

SQL is a language that can easily be read by humans as well as by computers. That's quite a feat when you understand that humans are very facile with the nuances of language and that computers are basically very stupid machines — two widely varying capabilities.

The only way it's possible for this to work is if the humans who write instructions for the computers to read do so using a very structured set of rules. That way, when the computers read their instructions, they'll be able to find what they're looking for. If the humans get the commands in the programming language even a bit wrong, then the computers will be confused. (I told you computers are stupid.)

SQL syntax is structured using logic that looks like this: SELECT *these fields of data* FROM *this table* WHERE *these conditions are met.* All you have to do to keep the computer from being confused is keep that logical order in mind, and that's simple, actually, especially if you take in little pieces at a time.

As you can see, there are only three words — called SQL *keywords* — for the computer to work with in this statement. (There are other keywords, but we're starting out simply.)

* SELECT is kind of an alert, telling the database engine that there's about to be a request for some data and what fields contain that data.
* FROM tells the database engine in which table in the database to find those fields.
* WHERE is an optional keyword that carries with it some criteria the database engine should use when choosing the data to display. (You remember criteria, don't you?)

Let's jump in and take a closer look.

SQL and QBE Working Together

Now I want to run a few SQL queries with you looking over my shoulder. After just a couple of examples, you'll be diving in all by yourself, I'm sure. First, I'll open a blank query. Next, I'll get into its SQL window, and then I'll write an SQL query.

With that done, I'll run it and show you the result. Here goes:

1. Access has no good way for beginners to get at its SQL windows, so the easiest thing to do is simply open a blank query. With your Northwind Traders database container visible, click the Queries tab to make it active, then click ⬚ **New** . Access displays the New Query dialog box, as shown in Figure 13-1.

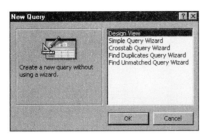

Figure 13-1   The New Query dialog box, ready to create a new query.

2. You'll notice that, as usual, Design View is highlighted in the dialog box. Go ahead and click ⬚ **OK** so that Access will show you a blank query behind the Show Table dialog box, as shown in Figure 13-2.

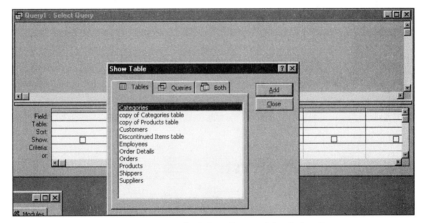

Figure 13-2   You need to get rid of this Show Table dialog box.

3. Because you're going to write your own SQL query, you don't need Access to put any tables into the QBE window. Accordingly, click **Close** in the Show Table dialog box. Access obeys, displaying an empty query, as shown in Figure 13-3.

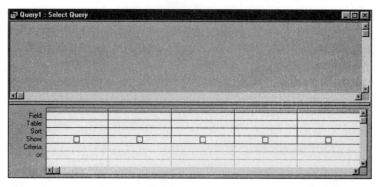

Figure 13-3 Access displays a blank query.

SIDE TRIP

THREE VIEWS OF THE BEAST

As you know by now, Access offers three ways for you to view a query: datasheet, design, and SQL view. You can select among the three choices by moving your mouse cursor to the upper left corner of the Access application window and clicking. The following figure shows you the pop-down menu you see when you click whichever icon is visible there.

A sequel that's first

Now you're all set for me to show you how to write a SQL query. Just for starters, why don't we simply snatch the whole enchilada?

Follow along with these steps, amigo:

1. Move your mouse cursor to the upper left corner of the Access application window and click ![SQL]. Access closes the QBE window and opens the SQL window, as shown in Figure 13-4.

   Notice that Access has already written SELECT here for you. Notice also that the word SELECT is immediately followed by a semicolon (;). That semicolon is what's known in the biz as a *statement terminator*. It signals the end of an SQL query.

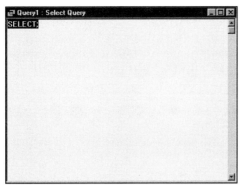

Figure 13-4 The SQL window is ready for input.

2. Move your mouse cursor between the word SELECT and the semicolon. I want you to select everything stored in all of the fields in the Employees table. To do so, type the following between SELECT and the semicolon:

```
*{Return}
from [Employees]
```

(Be sure to leave the semicolon there). This SQL statement is the same thing as saying, "Select everything (the asterisk) from the Employees table." You can clearly see what I mean by looking at Figure 13-5.

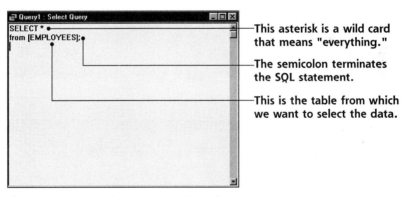

This asterisk is a wild card that means "everything."

The semicolon terminates the SQL statement.

This is the table from which we want to select the data.

Figure 13-5 Your first SQL query is ready to run.

TIP The square brackets around the word Employees is shorthand for "this is an Access object, which has this name." Truth be told, you don't really need to use the brackets in a query as simple as this one. I used them in this case because doing so makes the statement completely unambiguous to Access. For that reason, you'll often want to enclose your tables' and fields' names in square brackets when you create more complex queries.

3. Save your query as Everybody Query, and then click ❗ on the toolbar. Access runs your SQL query and displays the resulting dynaset, as shown in Figure 13-6. Just like the query told it to, Access selected every darn thing to be found in the Employees table.

Employee ID	Last Name	First Name	Title	Title Of Courtesy	Birth Date	Hire Date	A
1	Davolio	Nancy	Sales Representative	Dr.	08-Dec-48	01-May-92	507 - 20tl
2	Fuller	Andrew	Vice President, Sales	Dr.	19-Feb-52	14-Aug-92	908 W. C
3	Leverling	Janet	Sales Representative	Ms.	30-Aug-63	01-Apr-92	722 Moss
4	Peacock	Margaret	Sales Representative	Mrs.	19-Sep-37	03-May-93	4110 Old
5	Buchanan	Steven	Sales Manager	Mr.	04-Mar-55	17-Oct-93	14 Garret
6	Suyama	Michael	Sales Representative	Mr.	02-Jul-63	17-Oct-93	Coventry
7	King	Robert	Sales Representative	Mr.	29-May-60	02-Jan-94	Edgeham
8	Callahan	Laura	Inside Sales Coordinator	Ms.	09-Jan-58	05-Mar-94	4726 - 11
9	Dodsworth	Anne	Sales Representative	Ms.	27-Jan-66	15-Nov-94	7 Hounds
11	Lee	Christian	Photographer	Mr.	30-Jun-80	12-Jan-97	13306 22

Figure 13-6   Here's the dynaset from the SQL query.

4. I'd be amazed if you're not curious to see what the QBE window looks like at this point. After all, it — like the SQL window — is another way of looking at the query before it's run. Click ⬚ ▾ on the toolbar, and you'll see much the same thing as shown in Figure 13-7.

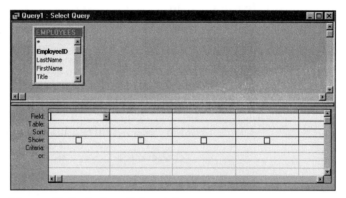

Figure 13-7   Is that all there is?

I don't know about you, but I find that QBE window to be something less than impressive. Somehow I thought there'd be more.

Taking names

I know what we can do. Let me show you what happens when you snatch just a couple of fields.

Follow along as I refine the SQL query to get the employees' names:

1. If you're not looking at your SQL window, click ⬚ ▾ to open it.

2. Type the following SQL query in the SQL window:

```
SELECT [FirstName],[LastName]
from [Employees];
```

3. Save your query. When you're done, your SQL window should look like the one shown in Figure 13-8.

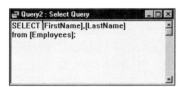

Figure 13-8 Your query is now a bit more explicit.

4. Now click ![run] on the toolbar to run the newly revised query. The *dynaset* you get should look like the one shown in Figure 13-9.

Figure 13-9 The resulting dynaset shows a list of employees.

5. If you click ![QBE] on the toolbar, you'll find that the QBE window is now much more interesting. I did, and you can see my result in Figure 13-10.

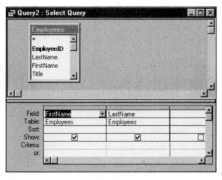

Figure 13-10 This is a much more interesting QBE window.

Well, I guess you can see how easy this SQL business is. There are a couple more things I want you to notice, however. First, can you see how I had you enclose the field names and the table name in square brackets. I don't mean to belabor the point, but the brackets go a long way toward making the query unambiguous to Access.

That's for Access; there's also something to notice for you. When you typed in your query, did you break your lines at the same place I did? I write my SQL code like that because it's easier to read. SQL syntax has much in common with its English cousin. There are verbs, objects, predicates, and such, and there are clauses. Without being too compulsive about it, I like to place each SQL clause on a line by itself. It doesn't make a bit of difference to Access, but it makes it much easier for me to read.

Adding a criterion

It's time to flex our SQL muscles now. Let's see about adding a criterion to the SQL. For this example, let's request a list of all of Northwind Traders's North American employees. We can do so by having Access look at the Country field in the Employees table — Employees.Country in Access computer shorthand — and display only those that contain the value USA.

Follow these steps to see how it's done:

1. Open the query you just ran in SQL view.

2. Enter the following code into the SQL window — and don't forget to include the commas (they're mandatory in SQL). Please forgive me if I belabor the obvious, but you'll probably find that it's easiest to simply change and add to what's already there.

```
SELECT
[Employees].[FirstName],
[Employees].[LastName],
[Employees].[Country]

FROM [Employees]

WHERE [Employees].[Country]="USA";
```

If you look at Figure 13-11, you'll see my computer's version of this same code. Notice that I've formatted it a bit differently from what I showed you earlier. I've broken up each SQL clause so that each one is more legible. You don't have to do this too, of course, but I think you might find it easier to read in the future.

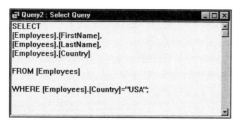

Figure 13-11 Here's an SQL query with a criterion.

3. Save your query and then run it. Figure 13-12 shows you what my dynaset looked like when I did the same thing.

Figure 13-12 The resulting dynaset shows all of Northwind Traders's North American employees.

4. If you're interested, you can compare the QBE window shown in Figure 13-13 with the simpler Figure 13-8 and Figure 13-10. As you can see, the criterion is right there for you.

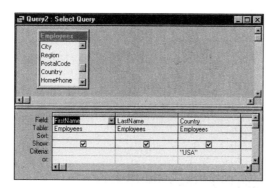

Figure 13-13 Here's the same query as seen in the QBE grid.

Are you starting to get an idea of how SQL works? Good. There's one more thing I want to show you before I finish this chapter.

SQL, grouping, and crunching numbers

X-REF In Chapter 8, "Let's Make Some Changes," I told you about how you can use queries to do calculations. You even created such a query if you followed along. Well, now I want to show you a query that comes with Access that also does calculations — and something more besides.

Follow along, if you please:

1. With the Northwind database open and its Queries tab active, highlight the Category Sales for 1995 query. Click 🖾 on the toolbar, and Access displays the query for you in QBE view, as shown in Figure 13-14.

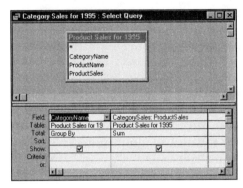

Figure 13-14 Access shows the query in QBE view.

This query looks at each of the products sold by Northwind Traders, sums all the values in each category as a group, and then displays the result for each.

2. Click 🗐 to see the code behind this query. You can see an example of it in Figure 13-15.

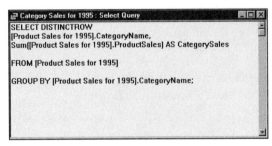

Figure 13-15 This code shows a group by query in SQL view.

As you look at Figure 13-15, you might notice a few new SQL keywords, described in this list:

a. DISTINCTROW tells Access to ignore duplicate rows. This way the same number isn't included twice in the categories' sum.

X-REF

b. SUM() is a function I mentioned in Chapter 8, "Let's Make Some Changes." In this case, Access is being told — by the information it finds within the parentheses — to take the ProductSales field from the Product Sales for 1995 query and to sum its values.

c. AS is the SQL way of temporarily renaming a field or group of fields when it's displayed. You usually use this to make clear what comprises a group.

d. GROUP BY tells Access where to collect the values contained in certain fields into groups and what fields to use for that process.

3. Click ![!] on the toolbar. Access runs the query and displays the result, as shown in Figure 13-16.

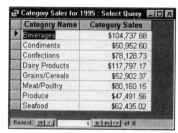

Category Name	Category Sales
Beverages	$104,737.68
Condiments	$50,952.60
Confections	$78,128.73
Dairy Products	$117,797.17
Grains/Cereals	$52,902.37
Meat/Poultry	$80,160.15
Produce	$47,491.56
Seafood	$62,435.02

Figure 13-16 The fields have been grouped and summed.

BONUS

My Favorite SQL

I thought I was finished, but I still have one more thing I want to do in this chapter. I want to give you a kind of bestiary on the SQL language itself. This isn't meant to be exhaustive, and there are a number of really good books written on the SQL language that can tell you more, but I think it's important that you at least have a basic reference of SQL keywords.

The very core of the SQL language is its SELECT statement. You'll usually find clauses that refine its scope incorporated into SELECT. Along with SELECT, there are a number of keywords that more fully describe your query's purpose to Access. Table 13-1 contains a list of the keywords I use most often, along with a bit of description for each.

TABLE 13-1 A Few SQL Keywords

Keyword	Description
SELECT <field names>	This command tells SQL which fields to use in this query. If you use more than one field name, then be sure to separate them with commas.
FROM <table name>	This command let's SQL know in which tables the fields are to be found.
IN <location>	Sometimes you'll want to use fields that are in another database. This keyword lets you tell Access what that other table is and where it's found.
WHERE <criteria>	This command refines the query according to the specified criteria. It applies to individual records before the data in their fields are grouped.
GROUP BY <field names>	This command tells Access which fields to use as groups.
HAVING <search criteria>	This command is a further refinement of the data, much like the WHERE clause. The biggest difference between the two is the fact that HAVING applies to groups of records.
ORDER BY <field names>	Specifies the order in which fields are displayed in the query dynaset.

Summary

While this chapter hasn't been an exhaustive exposition, as they say, it's a really good beginning for you and your understanding of SQL. I recommend that you get a good SQL reference book and that you create some queries using SQL on your own. As you get deeper into the subject, you'll find the direct, hands-on control to be very convenient in those situations where you can't use the QBE grid to get at the data you want.

So, with that said, I bet you're curious what more goodies are in store. Actually, what's coming next is a bit of sociability. I'm going to show you how to leverage your use of Access and databases on a single computer with other people working with other computers — but with the same database! If you'll quickly turn the page, we can get started....

I'LL TALK WITH MY FRIENDS

KEY GOALS OF THIS CHAPTER:

I've got teenager offspring in my house. Boy teenagers. With telephone handsets making very interesting — and semi-permanent — patterns on their ears. Teenagers who are not content to merely speak with their teenager girlfriends, but who have to e-mail them too: kilobytes worth.

Talk about being connected and transferring data. I know of networked government computers that spend less time communicating.

On the other hand, even we grownups often need to communicate — or at least have our computers communicate for us and share our data. Every time we go to the local record store for tickets to the theater or to our travel agent for tickets to faraway places, we're indirectly using computers that share data.

In this chapter, we're going to look at how you can share Access data among computers. Not only that, we're also going to import and export data from completely different kinds of software applications, let alone database applications. Along the way, I'll tell you a little about what it takes to network computers together and some of the security concerns you might want to take into consideration.

Working with External Data

Up to now, whenever you've opened a table or query, it was part of a database that exists on your own computer. In the "real world," that is often not the case. You can be using a table and data that actually exist on a computer halfway around the world. Because of the way Access works, you might not even be aware of that fact.

As you already know, a table is just another object to Access. Access can create a link between the database you're using and the one that actually holds the table. After that's done, Access and you can easily use the table no matter where it resides. Now I want to show you how easily you can link a table in another database to your current database.

Among the sample database applications that are automatically installed with Access is one called Solutions. It is very much an extension of the Northwind database that we've been using all along. The Solutions database contains a number of advanced programming examples for people who are involved in Access database development. (This is more than what you'll probably be doing, for a while, anyway.) In the Solutions database, there is a table that holds the sales goals for Northwind Traders' salespeople.

Follow along, and I'll show you how to link the sales goals table to the Northwind database.

1. Start Access and load the Northwind Traders database.

2. You're going to get data that's external to your Northwind database. Accordingly, move your mouse cursor to the Access ` File ` menu and select — you guessed it — ` Get External Data `. Access pops up a submenu, as shown in Figure 14-1.

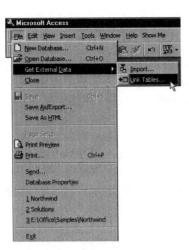

Figure 14-1 You're getting external data.

3. Select Link Tables from the pop-up menu. Access displays the Link dialog box, as shown in Figure 14-2. The Link dialog box works just like the File Open dialog box in that it shows you a list of file names from which you can choose one. If you weren't sure of the name of the database that held the table you wanted, you could use the options in this dialog box to search for it.

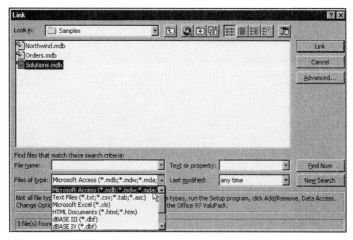

Figure 14-2 Here is a list of databases from which to link.

There's another thing I want you to notice about Figure 14-2. At the bottom left of the Link dialog box you'll see a combo box labeled, Files of type. Access lets you link files from all kinds of different database programs. It even lets you link spreadsheets from spreadsheet programs such as Excel. When Access links such files, these other kinds of files appear to be Access tables. You indicate in this combo box what kind of file you are linking to your Access database.

4. Make sure that the Files of type combo box indicates Microsoft Access, then highlight Solutions.mdb, which is the name of the database that holds the table you're going to link. After you've done that, click Link. Access displays a list of tables in the Link Tables dialog box, as shown in Figure 14-3.

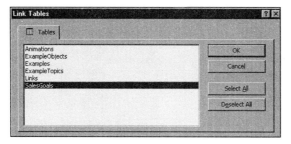

Figure 14-3 These are all the tables in the Solutions database.

So what's a link, anyway?

Before we get any further along, I want to share a word or two with you about the nature of links. A link to a table in another database is really a connection between your database and the other one, with a special coupling with the table you're linking. Part of that special coupling you've created causes Access to make a note of where it can find the other data. As long as that data stays where it's at — the table isn't deleted from the other database, or the other database isn't erased or moved to another location — Access will be able to find the linked table.

This points up an obvious question: What happens if Access isn't able to locate the linked table? If this happens, you have something of a problem, I'm afraid. Therein lies one of the weaknesses involved in linking objects.

A corollary situation is where the person who "owns" the database from which you've linked a table changes the table in ways you haven't anticipated. For example, what if the other user deletes data from the table that you need to find there? That's the second (potential) weakness of linking: You don't have control of the data to which you're linking. Paradoxically, another user adding and deleting data is also a strength — *if* you want the table to reflect all the latest changes.

One other thing you'll want to factor into your decision has to do with the table's size. If it's a big one, then having it stored somewhere else and not on *your* hard disk might be more efficient for you. The bottom line is this: If you decide to link a table from another database, you're going to have to coordinate with whomever "owns" that database. If you can't do that or if you can't be assured that the database and the table to which you're linking will always be available, then you'll be better off importing the table and maintaining it yourself.

5. Listed here are all the tables contained by the Solutions database. You can link all of them by clicking Select All , if you like. In this case, however, all we're interested in is the SalesGoals table. Accordingly, highlight its name and click OK . Access cooks for a moment and then places the table's name into the Northwind database's database container, as shown in Figure 14-4.

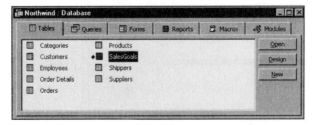

Figure 14-4 Now you can use the SalesGoals table.

At this point, the SalesGoals table is ready for you to use just as you can any other table in the Northwind database. Notice though that Access has placed a small arrow next to the table's icon. This arrow tells you that the table is linked: available to the database, but not really a part of it.

Importing Data into My Database

One obvious way of gaining control of your data — and thereby increasing the chance that it will be useful to you and others using your database — is to import a file instead of merely linking it.

When you import a file, Access takes a copy of the file from its source and makes the file an Access table. Once Access does so, the copy becomes part of your own database.

Do you remember how you can link many different kinds of files to your Access database? Well, the same thing goes for importing. As a matter of fact, I now want to show you how you can import an Excel spreadsheet into your Access database.

The file I want you to import is called common.xls; it is one of the sample files automatically put on your hard disk when you installed Microsoft Office '97. You should be able to find it in the \Office\Library subdirectory.

Go ahead and open common.xls. The sidebar "Opening an Excel Spreadsheet" contains pointers for doing so.

When we get to it, you'll find that the actual process of importing a file is almost identical to linking. The only real difference as far as your keystrokes or mouse clicks are concerned is that you select Import instead of Link from the appropriate menu, but because you're about to import an Excel spreadsheet (something that isn't an Access table), I think we need to first take a bit closer look at that file itself.

14

SIDE TRIP

OPENING AN EXCEL SPREADSHEET

You can open an Excel spreadsheet in one of two ways, both virtually the same as opening an Access database:

- Using Windows Explorer, click your way to the folder holding the common.xls file. When you see it, double click the file name. Windows loads Excel and opens common.xls.
- From the Programs menu, select the Excel icon. After Excel is loaded and running, select File and then Open. Use the File dialog box to navigate to the \Office\Library subdirectory where you can find common.xls.

A preliminary adjustment

When you see an Excel spreadsheet, there's one thing you'll notice right away. It looks an awful lot like a database table in datasheet view. That's because they have much in common with each other. Take a quick look at Figure 14-5 and you'll see what I mean.

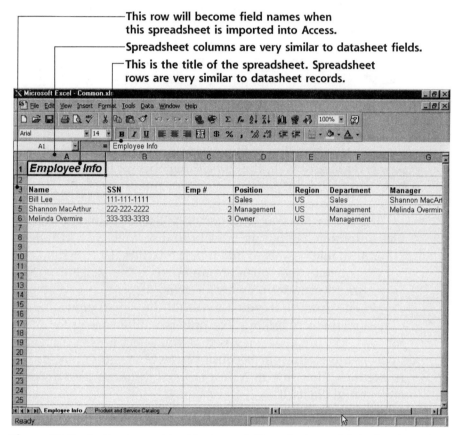

Figure 14-5 An Excel spreadsheet looks much like a database table in datasheet view.

Spreadsheets are an electronic metaphor for accountants' ledgers, which are arranged in columns and rows. Notice that the spreadsheet's data is also arranged in columns and rows — just like a datasheet. There are some essential differences between spreadsheets and datasheets, however.

One of these differences is the fact that you can place a title and other extraneous text on a spreadsheet. You can't do that on a datasheet. Also, if you want your columns labeled on a spreadsheet, you have to do it yourself. With datasheets, on the other hand, Access takes care of that chore, getting the labels from the field names of the underlying table.

For you to be able to easily import this spreadsheet, you need to do some clean-up to make it look more like a datasheet.

Perform these steps and you'll quickly have everything shipshape:

1. The spreadsheet's title, Employee Info, will only be in the way when you import the spreadsheet. So, with the common.xls spreadsheet open, move your mouse cursor to the number 1 that labels the first row.

2. With your mouse cursor (which looks like a cross at this point) over the 1, press your left mouse button and drag down to the 2 of the next row. Excel highlights both rows, as shown in Figure 14-6.

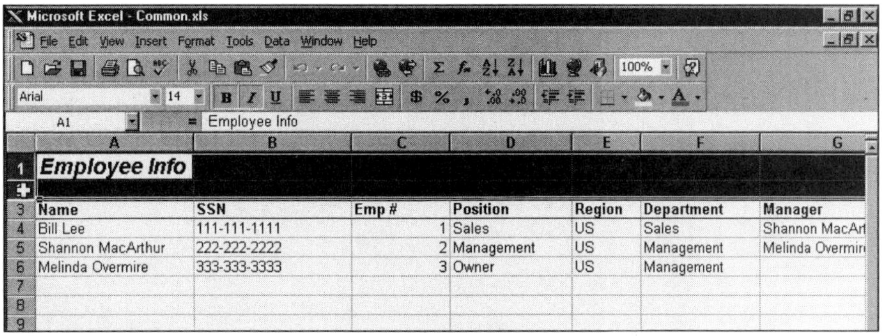

Figure 14-6 The first two rows of the spreadsheet are about to be deleted.

3. With both rows highlighted, right-click your mouse button. Excel displays a formatting menu. Select ⎡ **Delete** ⎤ from this menu. Excel removes those two rows from the spreadsheet and moves up the rows below them. If you've done this correctly, your spreadsheet should look like Figure 14-7.

4. Save the common.xls spreadsheet by clicking 🖫 on the toolbar.

That's about all you need to do to prepare common.xls for its transformation into an Access table. And that comes next. Oh, yes: If you like, you can close Excel at this point. If you'd like to keep the spreadsheet as it was before you deleted the two rows, then just click No when Excel asks you in a dialog box whether to keep your changes.

TIP You might be wondering why I had you go through the process of selecting Delete from a menu instead of what would seem to be the easier and more direct way of accomplishing the same task: simply pressing the Delete key. Well, allow me to explain.

"Delete" has two meanings within Excel. One meaning — obtained when you merely press your keyboard's Delete key — is: "Clear the contents of the highlighted rows." That meaning instructs Excel to make the rows empty and not to remove them completely. Selecting Delete from the menu, on the other hand, instructs Excel to remove the rows completely, and that's what you need to do for this exercise to be successful.

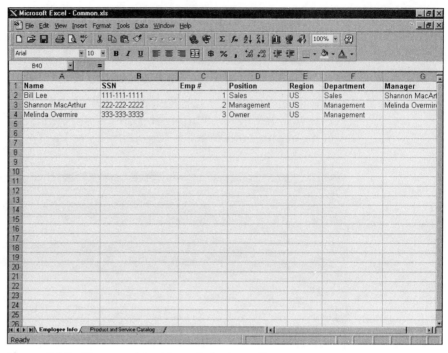

Figure 14-7   The spreadsheet is ready for importing.

Doing the import

After you've prepared the file, importing common.xls is a fairly straightforward process.

Follow along and you'll see what I mean:

1. With Access up and running just as it was before, select the
   Get External Data option from the File menu. Access displays
   the same pop-up menu as it did before.

2. Select Import from the pop-up menu. Access displays the Import dialog
   box, as shown in Figure 14-8.

3. Make sure that Microsoft Excel (*.xls) is displayed in the Files of Type
   combo box, then navigate to the subdirectory on your computer that
   holds common.xls.

4. Highlight common.xls and click Import . Access displays the first of its
   Import Spreadsheet Wizard dialog boxes, as shown in Figure 14-9.

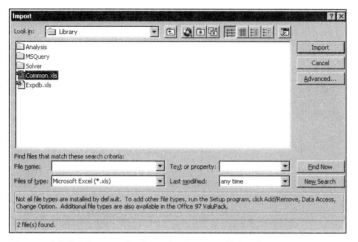

Figure 14-8 Access displays the Import dialog box.

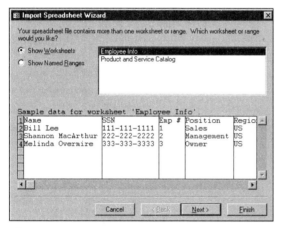

Figure 14-9 You have to choose which spreadsheet to import.

5. Excel workbooks can comprise a number of spreadsheets; up to 256, as a matter of fact. Accordingly, the Import Spreadsheet Wizard shows you a list of spreadsheets from which to choose. In this case, you want to select the one called Employee Info, so make sure it's highlighted. Access displays a portion of the spreadsheet. This preview lets you double-check that this spreadsheet is in fact the one you want to import. It is, so click Next . Access displays the next Import Spreadsheet Wizard dialog, as shown in Figure 14-10.

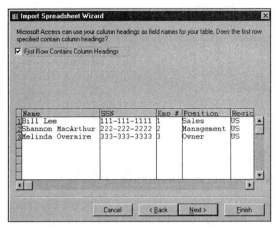

Figure 14-10 The spreadsheet column headings become field names.

6. Do you remember the clean-up you did on this spreadsheet? Well, this is the dialog box you were preparing for. At its top, check the box labeled, First Row Contains Column Headings. Access changes the first row of the example spreadsheet to reflect that it now contains field names and not mere data. With that done, click [**Next**]. Access displays yet another Import Spreadsheet Wizard dialog, as shown in Figure 14-11.

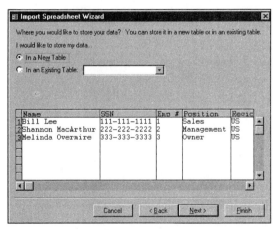

Figure 14-11 Where do you want to put the new table?

7. Next, you must decide where you want to put the new table. You can make it a new table, standing alone as the others do, or you can make it part of an existing table. For this example, select the first option button, In a New Table, and click [**Next**]. Access displays the next Import Spreadsheet Wizard dialog, as shown in Figure 14-12.

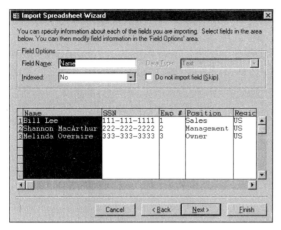

Figure 14-12 Access needs to know the new table's data types.

8. As you know, each field in an Access table holds data of a particular type. In this dialog box, you tell Access what type to use for each of the new table's fields. Access uses some intelligence here, looking at the data contained within each field and making an assumption regarding the kind of data it holds. For the most part, Access chooses Text as the data type, unless what the new field contains is clearly a number of some type (simple numeric data, a currency figure, and so on). In this case, you can accept Access's decisions, so click Next. Access displays the next Import Spreadsheet Wizard dialog, as shown in Figure 14-13.

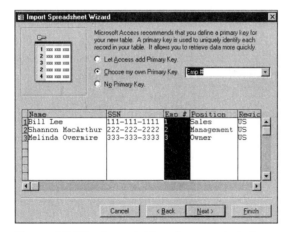

Figure 14-13 Access tables often contain indexes.

9. We're getting close to the end now. About all that's left is to decide on an index for the new table. You don't have to define one, of course, but in this case, I recommend using the Emp # field as an index, so choose the Choose my own Primary Key option button and select Emp # from the combo box. With that out of the way, click ⟦ Next ⟧ so Access can show you the last Import Spreadsheet Wizard dialog box, as shown in Figure 14-14.

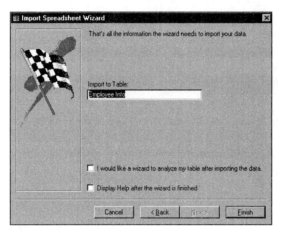

Figure 14-14   At last, you can name your new table!

10. Knowing the name of the spreadsheet it's working with, Access offers the spreadsheet name as the potential name for your new table. I couldn't think of anything better, so I accepted the recommendation. If you want to use something different, type it into the Import to Table text box. When you're done with naming the table, click ⟦ Finish ⟧. Access cooks for a moment and then displays the dialog box shown in Figure 14-15 to let you know that it is finished importing the new table. Click ⟦ OK ⟧ and you're on your way.

Figure 14-15   Another job has been finished.

If you're curious, you can look for the new table in your database container. Figure 14-16 shows you what mine looks like. As you can tell, there isn't really all that much to see — and that's the point. The imported table is *exactly* like any other table in your database.

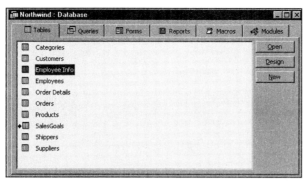

Figure 14-16 There's the new table, sitting quietly among its siblings.

Every now and then, I run across a reader who is terminally cynical. For that person, I offer Figure 14-17 to show the spreadsheet *cum* table in datasheet view, ready for input or any other manipulation.

Name	SSN	Emp #	Position	Region	Department	Manager
Bill Lee	111-111-1111	1	Sales	US	Sales	Shannon MacArthur
Shannon MacArthur	222-222-2222	2	Management	US	Management	Melinda Overmire
Melinda Overmire	333-333-3333	3	Owner	US	Management	

Figure 14-17 The new table is ready for use.

TIP You can go through this entire procedure to import a file into your Access database, but it might not be necessary. If the file you're importing is an Access table and if that table is on your own computer, you don't have to. You can simply copy and paste it instead, just as if it were a paragraph in a word processor.

Access can import and link data from any other Microsoft product, of course. These include FoxPro and Excel. It can also work with data from dBASE and Paradox databases and Lotus 1-2-3 spreadsheets. Access imports text data from delimited and fixed-width ASCII text files. Finally, Access works very well with SQL tables and other Open Database Connectivity (ODBC) applications.

Exporting Data

Sending your Access data out to another program — what we in the biz call *exporting* the data — is even easier than importing it. Access is able to export data in all kinds of other software formats, from databases (of course) to spreadsheets to word processors.

Here's a scenario to illustrate this: You've been assigned to provide the name and address data for boilerplate marketing letters that will be sent to each of

Northwind Traders's customers. Five minutes later, you tell your coworker that the data is ready for him to use.

That quickly? You can bet your bippy on it. Exporting data is even easier than importing data.

Look fast, and I'll show you how:

1. With the Northwind database open and its database container visible, select the Customers table as shown in Figure 14-18.

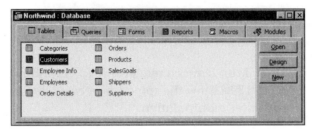

Figure 14-18 You can export a copy of the data in any table.

2. Select [**Save As/Export**] from the [**File**] menu, as shown in Figure 14-19.

Figure 14-19 Exporting and saving: They both start the same.

3. When you export data from a table, all you're doing is exporting a copy of the data — you're not exporting the table itself. So, when Access displays its Save As dialog box, shown in Figure 14-20, indicate where you want the copy of the data to go: either within the current database (as another table) or to an external file or database. In this case, you want to send to an external file, so select the first option. Click [**OK**], and Access displays the Save Table dialog box, shown in Figure 14-21.

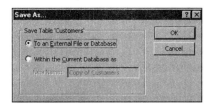

Figure 14-20 In or out: That's the question.

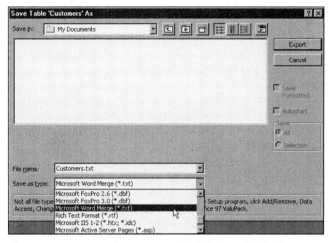

Figure 14-21 You have a myriad of choices for the format of the data you export.

4. This dialog box looks much the same as the other file management dialog boxes used by Access. One difference that's important here is the Save as type combo box. In this scenario, the data is to be used by someone writing letters in Word, so select Microsoft Word Merge (*.txt). Access automatically offers a file name of Customers.txt. That works just fine in this case, so click ⟨ **Export** ⟩. Access again cooks for a moment, creating the file and placing it into the My Documents folder by default. Just to make sure, I double checked by looking in the My Documents folder, as shown in Figure 14-22.

Figure 14-22 The new text file is full of data and ready to be used.

When Access exports text files, it does so in what's called *Tab-delimited ASCII* format. That means the data from each field is enclosed within quotation marks and separated by a tab character. This format is as common as dirt in the computer world. For that reason, almost every word processing application is able to directly take the data in that format and use it.

Access can export data in Microsoft FoxPro and Excel formats. It can also export data to dBASE, Paradox, and ODBC databases. Additionally, Access can export to Lotus 1-2-3 spreadsheets as well as to fixed-width and to delimited ASCII text files.

Networking Access

Up to this point in the chapter, I've discussed using your database for the most part by yourself. Now I want to introduce you to working with Access on a network. Sure, I've mentioned linking, but that's not really the same thing.

When you work on a network, your database efforts are leveraged with those of the other people on the network too. Imagine, for example, what would happen if all the travel agents in the world suddenly couldn't work on the same network, and you had to fly somewhere. Nobody could tell you for sure which seats were still available on your flight. They couldn't even tell you the latest and greatest price! And forget even thinking about renting a car once you got to your destination.

When you think about working with databases and networks, there are some fairly technical things you need to consider. I realize that you're a beginner — although not as much of a beginner as you were when you started this book. I'm going to touch on the technical aspects, however, so that you have an idea what's going on with your own computer and its network.

The most important factor to consider is just how the data is to be shared. It's normal on a computer network for more than one person to look at the same data. It's also normal for them to be able to modify that data and for each of them to see the modifications as soon as they occur.

To share, or not to share: That's the question

When you open an Access database, you have a choice of doing so for your exclusive use or not. You indicate your choice in a checkbox at the right side of the Open dialog box. You can see what I mean by looking at Figure 14-23.

When you open a file with the Exclusive checkbox checked, no one else can use that database as long as you have it open. If they try to do so, they see a warning dialog box such as the one shown in Figure 14-24.

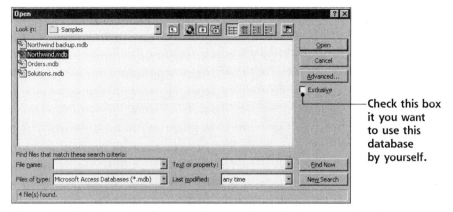

Check this box it you want to use this database by yourself.

Figure 14-23 Access databases can be open for exclusive use or shared use.

Figure 14-24 Only one at a time, please.

Okay, I'll share

So, let's say you want to share your database. If you do, you have to make some choices as to what kind of access users have to the data, how often users' views of the same data is updated, and so on. Let me go over some of the decisions you have to make and let you know about some of their ramifications.

First of all, take a look at Figure 14-25. This is the Advanced tab of the Options dialog box. You get to this dialog by selecting Options from the Tools menu. This dialog box is a kind of central repository of information that tells Access how to handle sharing data in terms of what happens when you have a table open. The following list describes your various options.

* **Default Record Locking:** While everyone should be able to see the same data at the same time, it can be awfully confusing if everyone can simultaneously change that data. This is the case if you select No Locks, as shown in Figure 14-25. Use this option with great caution. On the other hand, if you choose All Records, no one can change any data in the table as long as you have that table open. The middle course is to select Edited Record, where only the record that you're editing is locked — that is, until the record is automatically saved by Access.

* **Default Open Mode:** You can decide on a database-by-database basis whether you open it by default for your exclusive use or if it's to be shared by others on the network.

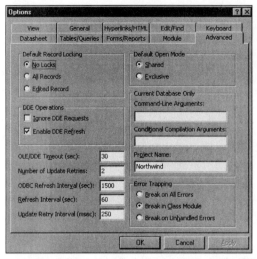

Figure 14-25 This is where you indicate how you want to share your data.

* **DDE Operations:** DDE is an acronym for *Dynamic Data Exchange*, a method that some Windows programs use to "talk" with each other. When I say talk, I do so advisedly. That's because the way the two Windows programs exchange data is called a *conversation*. Anyway, your choices here are to allow Access to listen for a potential conversation of such type and whether it should take part if it "hears" the beginnings of one.

* **OLE/DDE Timeout (sec):** This is where you indicate how much time Access should take to wait for an answer from other programs when it attempts to communicate with them.

* **Number of Update Retries:** This is where you indicate how persistent Access should be when trying to save a record that you've changed and which is locked by another user on the network.

* **ODBC Refresh Interval (sec):** This is where you indicate the interval between times when Access checks with other users on the network to see if they've changed any data.

* **Refresh Interval (sec):** This is where you indicate the interval between times when Access exchanges data with other users on the network when it knows that data has been, or is being, changed.

* **Update Retry Interval (msec):** This is where you indicate the interval (in thousandths of a second) that Access should wait to change a record that's been locked by another person on the network.

An Extra, Advanced Word

Not all of the options on the Advanced tab have to do with sharing data. I thought you might be curious about the other options, so I thought I'd tell you just a little about them too.

- **Current Database Only** is a group of three text boxes that have to do with how Access reacts to external commands and to programming.
- **Command Line Arguments** are parameters Access looks for when the program opens.
- **Conditional Compilation Arguments** have to do with how Visual Basic for Applications (VBA) is to handle code modules that a developer has programmed. Programming Access through VBA is a rather advanced topic that's beyond the scope of this book.
- **Project Name** is the name by which the database is to be known programmatically. It can be the same thing as the database name, which is the case with the Northwind database, or it can be something completely different. Again, this has to do with programming and is really beyond the scope of this book.
- **Error Trapping** has to do with how Access handles mistakes it finds in how its modules perform their programs. This is yet another option that doesn't involve sharing data.

A Question of Security

When you prepare to share data with other people, one of your prime considerations is the integrity of that data — and the potential of data being embarrassing to someone. You know that, being inanimate, data doesn't corrupt itself, and you know that data that knows about itself isn't embarrassing to itself. When other people become involved with the data, all this changes. Accordingly, you need to take steps to control, but not necessarily restrict, access to your data.

This is what people are really talking about when they mention database security. Let's take a more nitty-gritty look at it. Select Security from the Tools menu, and Access displays a pop-up submenu, as shown in Figure 14-26.

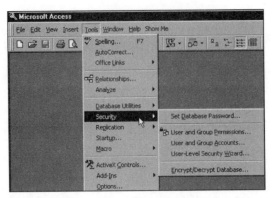

Figure 14-26 Security has to do with protecting data and its information.

The first menu item, Set Database Password, lets you create a password you can use to protect your entire database. When you select this option, Access displays the Set Database Password dialog box, as shown in Figure 14-27. If you want to use a password with a database, type it into the top text box. Just in case someone's looking over your shoulder, Access doesn't show you what you're typing. You have to retype it — exactly — in the Verify text box. From now on, anyone who wants to work with this database will be prompted for the password upon opening.

Figure 14-27 Every database can have its own password.

Users, groups, and permissions

When a bunch of people work with Access on a network, Access has to have a way of categorizing them. Sounds pretty judgmental, doesn't it? Well, the computer is necessarily arbitrary in how it goes about its work. Accordingly, everyone gets to be part of some group or other.

Access doesn't know you as an individual, of course. It does know what it's been told can be done or what data is allowed to be accessed by various groups of people. So, to share some or all Access tables over a network, a person must be part of a defined workgroup. With that said, here's the basics of how to secure an Access database:

✴ Collect the names of people who need to access the database into defined workgroups. A workgroup can be thought of as a specific group of people who need to work with the same data and so are given the same access to it.

* Make sure that anyone who logs on to your database does so by password. In that way, they "tell" Access right up front who they are. In that way also, Access knows what data they are allowed to work with.

* If you want to go the extra step, then also encrypt your database file. That way, if an unauthorized user tries to look at the file, they'll see only random characters instead of your data.

Grouping people together

As you've probably guessed by now, the basic unit of security is called a *group*. Every Access database starts out with two groups: *Admins,* who can do anything, and *Users,* who can do, well, anything too by default. You might be wondering how you create a group or include a person in a group.

The basic tool you use to do all this is the User and Group Accounts dialog box. Open this dialog by selecting Tools→Security→User and Group Accounts.

The first thing is to add users. You do so by selecting the Users tab of the User and Group Accounts dialog box, which is shown in Figure 14-28. When you click the New button, Access displays the dialog box shown in Figure 14-29. Type a person's name into the text box. At the same time, you'll be prompted for a Personal ID for that individual. Access combines the two into a unique internal identifier it uses to keep track of who has permission to do what.

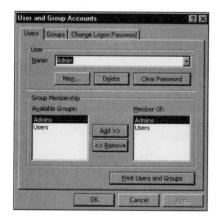

Figure 14-28 A new user is born.

Figure 14-29 Enter a new user and his personal ID.

Once you've added users, you also need to create groups. The tool for this chore is the Groups tab in the same User and Group Accounts dialog box, as shown in Figure 14-30. As you can see, this group will comprise people who work in the Northwind Traders accounting department.

Figure 14-30   A group is born.

Permitting what's allowed

When you do something in Access such as read or update data or look at a table in design view, you do so because you have permission to do so. Who gets permission to do what is determined by checkboxes in the User and Group Permissions dialog box, as shown in Figure 14-31.

Figure 14-31   If you want permission, here's where you get it.

Open this dialog box by selecting User and Group Permissions from the Tools→Security menu. As you can see, to allow a group of people to do something, you check one of the permission checkboxes. Every Access object — table, query, report, and so on — has its own set of permissions that you can allow or disallow.

As you can also see in Figure 14-31, all members of the group called Sales have permissions necessary to read and update data in the Customers table. They don't, however, have permission to delete any customer accounts. The same kind of thing can be done with users in the Personnel group and the Employees table, for example.

BONUS

Keeping a Secret

The last aspect of security I want to discus has to do with keeping an entire database secret from prying eyes. You do so by encrypting it according to a scheme that's built in to Access.

If you want to encrypt your copy of the Northwind database, follow these steps:

1. Close the Northwind database, but *don't* close Access.

2. From the Tools menu, select Security and then Encrypt/Decrypt Database. Access displays its Encrypt/Decrypt Database dialog box, as shown in Figure 14-32.

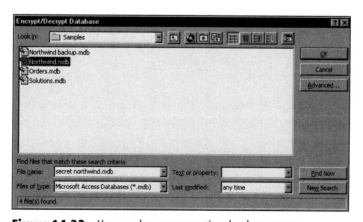

Figure 14-32 You can keep your entire database secret.

3. Type a name for the database in the File name text box near the bottom of the dialog box. Because Northwind is closed, you can put its name here. As you can see, I took a different tack and entered the name Secret Northwind instead.

4. You want to make sure that Access knows which database you want encrypted. Accordingly, highlight Northwind.mdb, and then click OK. Access cooks for a moment, encrypting the database.

After it's done, you can use the encrypted database just as you would if it were still "wide open." If you take a look at Figure 14-33, you'll notice that other than the database having a different name, there's no obvious difference from before it was encrypted.

Figure 14-33 An encrypted database looks the same as any other to an authorized user.

Summary

Well, it looks like we've come to the end of our adventure with Access. You've come a long way — from knowing perhaps nothing about databases to being able to make one a complete secret. Congratulations! Now go out and do some good with your new knowledge.

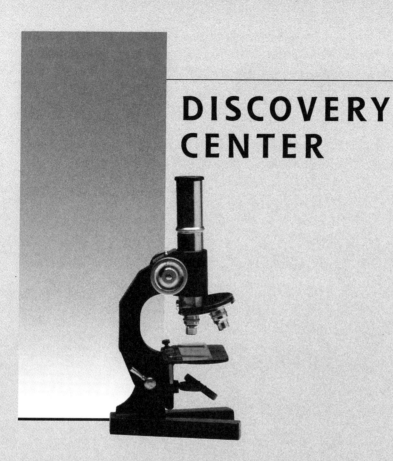

DISCOVERY CENTER

This section of the book is designed to aid your discovery of Access 97 by speeding you to the most important procedures you need to know. To get a compact overview of the most prominent capabilities found in Access — and a handy reference as you progress in your control of this powerful software — turn to the Discovery Center and explore at will.

CHAPTER 1

How to Start Access (page 10)

1. Click the `Start` menu.

2. Select the `Programs` menu.

3. Select the `Microsoft Access` item.

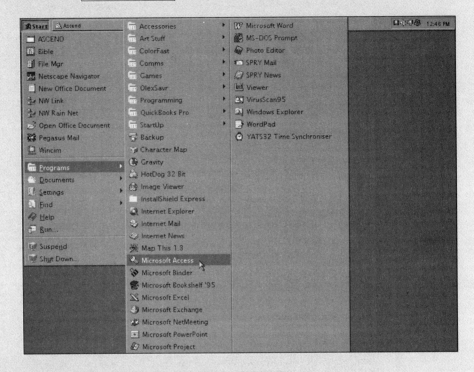

How to Create a New Database (page 18)

1. Start Access, and it displays the New Database dialog box.

2. Choose <u>B</u>lank Database from the choices in the New Database dialog box.

3. Type a name for your new database in the text box labeled File <u>n</u>ame.

4. Make sure the Save as type: field is set to Microsoft Access Databases.

5. Choose where on your computer's hard disk you want the new database to be saved.

6. Click <u>Create</u>.

CHAPTER 2

How to Get Help (page 37)

1. Press the F1 key. Your Office Assistant pops up, ready to help you.

2. Choose one of its suggestions or type in a question.

How to Search for Almost Any Word in the Access Help System (page 46)

1. Select <u>Help</u> → <u>Contents and Index</u> from the menu bar. Windows displays the Help Topics: Microsoft Access 97 dialog box.

2. Click the Find tab and enter the word for which you're looking in the #1 combo box. Windows displays forms of the word in the #2 list box.

3. Highlight one of the forms, and Windows displays the titles of appropriate help topics in the #3 list box.

4. Double-click one of the help topics to see it.

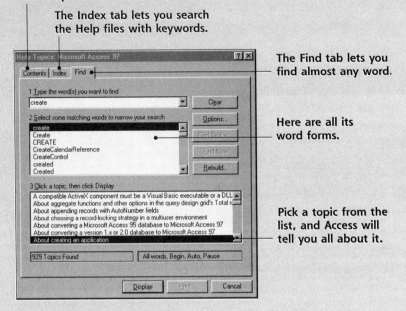

The Contents tab lets you browse the Help files table of contents.

The Index tab lets you search the Help files with keywords.

The Find tab lets you find almost any word.

Here are all its word forms.

Pick a topic from the list, and Access will tell you all about it.

How to Find a Chapter in the Help Table of Contents (page 44)

1. Select `Help` → `Contents and Index` from the menu bar. Windows displays the Help Topics: Microsoft Access 97 dialog box with the Table of Contents visible.

2. Highlight one of the titles you see there and click `Open`. Windows displays the help topic for you.

CHAPTER 3

How To Create a New Database Using the Wizard (page 58)

1. Click ▢ on the Access toolbar.

2. Click the Databases tab in the New Database dialog box and choose a template from the list of those displayed.

3. Click `OK` and answer the wizard's questions.

4. Click `Finish` when you're done.

How To Create a New Table Using the Wizard (page 70)

1. With your database open, click the Tables tab.
2. Click New and then choose Table Wizard from the New dialog box.
3. Click OK and answer the wizard's questions.
4. Click Finish when you're done.

How To Create a New Query Using the Wizard (page 76)

1. With your database open, click the Queries tab.
2. Click New and then choose Simple Query Wizard from the New dialog box.
3. Click OK and answer the wizard's questions.
4. Click Finish when you're done.

How To Create a New Form Using the Wizard (page 82)

1. With your database open, click the Forms tab.
2. Click New and then choose Form Wizard from the New dialog box.
3. Click OK and answer the wizard's questions.
4. Click Finish when you're done.

How To Create a New Report Using the Wizard (page 69)

1. With your database open, click the Reports tab.
2. Click New and then choose Report Wizard from the New dialog box.
3. Click OK and answer the wizard's questions.
4. Click Finish when you're done.

CHAPTER 4

Before You Create a Database (page 87)

Sit down with a piece of paper and plan it first.

* Know the difference between data and information (page 88)
* Find out what data is available (page 90)

* Decide what tables are necessary (page 90)
* Plan what queries will best provide the needed information (page 93)
* Lay out reports that will best convey the information (page 94)

How to Analyze a Table (page 96)

1. Select `Tools` → `Analyze` → `Table` from the menu bar.

2. Select the table you want to analyze and then click `OK`.

How to Analyze Database Performance (page 103)

1. Select `Tools` → `Analyze` → `Performance` from the menu bar.

2. Select the objects you want to analyze and then click `OK`.

3. Once Access finishes analyzing the objects' performance, it displays a list of recommendations, suggestions, and ideas.

CHAPTER 5

This is your table's name.

The record selector shows you which record you are working with.

Each row is a complete record.

Each column is a field in the record and is topped by a field selector.

Slide this up and down to move up and down your records.

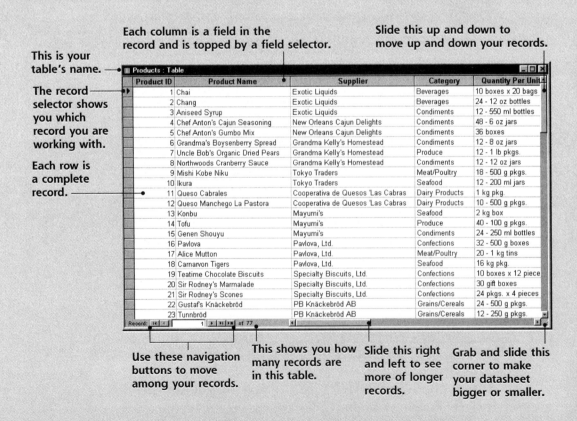

Use these navigation buttons to move among your records.

This shows you how many records are in this table.

Slide this right and left to see more of longer records.

Grab and slide this corner to make your datasheet bigger or smaller.

The record selector is the little button at the extreme left of each record on your datasheet. When you put your mouse cursor into a field, the record selector changes according to what's going on with that record.

This is the current record. ────● ▶
This is a new record. ────● *
This record is being edited. ────● ✎
This record is locked by another user on this network. It can be
∅ ●──── read, but not edited and saved.

How to Edit a Record (page 110)

Put your mouse cursor into the field you want to change and simply start typing.

How to Add a New Field to a Table (page 118)

1. Move your mouse cursor onto the field selector and right-click.
2. Select `Insert Column`. Access creates the new field in your record, giving it the name Field1.

How to Remove a Field from Your Table (page 120)

1. Move your mouse cursor to its field selector and right-click.
2. Select `Delete Column`.
3. Click `Yes` in the warning dialog box.

How to Move a Field from One Column to Another in Your Datasheet (page 118)

1. Move your mouse cursor to its field selector.
2. Click once on the field selector.
3. Click and drag the field selector to the position where you want the field to appear.

How to Sort Your Data (page 120)

1. Move your mouse cursor to the field selector of the column you want to sort.
2. Right-click your mouse button and choose `Sort Ascending` or `Sort Descending` from the utility menu.

CHAPTER 6

How to Create a New Query (page 127)

This is the query window.

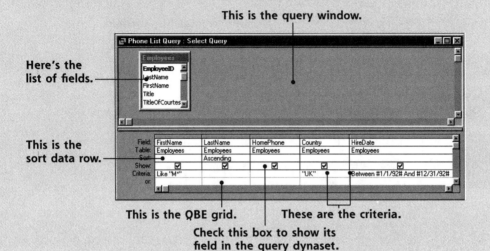

Here's the list of fields.

This is the sort data row.

This is the QBE grid.

Check this box to show its field in the query dynaset.

These are the criteria.

1. Click the Queries tab in the database container,
2. Click New .
3. Select Design View.

How to Add a Table or Other Query to a Query (page 128)

In the Show Table dialog box, double click the name of the table or query you want to add.

Click here to see a list of queries. You can add any of them to this query.

These are your tables. You can include any or all of them in your queries.

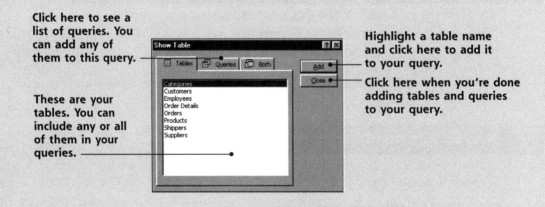

Highlight a table name and click here to add it to your query.

Click here when you're done adding tables and queries to your query.

How to Add a Field to a Query (page 129)

Drag the field's name from the field list to a column in the QBE grid.

How to Hide a Field from Appearing in a Dynaset (page 130)

Uncheck the Show field checkbox in that field's column in the QBE grid.

How to Add Criteria to a Query (page 133)

Type the criteria into the criteria rows in the QBE grid.

How to Delete a Field from a Query (page 129)

Highlight the field's column in the QBE grid and press Delete.

CHAPTER 7

How to Join Two Tables (page 144)

1. Select `Tools` → `Relationships` on the menu bar.
2. Add the tables or queries you want to relate to the Relationships dialog box by dragging one of the fields you want to relate over to the other one. Access creates the join.

How to Enforce Referential Integrity (page 151)

Click Enforce Referential Integrity in the detail Relationships dialog box.

How to Open the Relationships Dialog Box (page 144)

Select `Tools` → `Relationships` from the menu bar. Access displays the Relationships dialog box.

CHAPTER 8

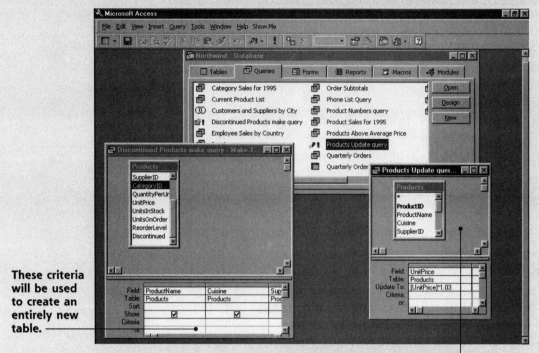

These criteria will be used to create an entirely new table.

Action queries are almost as easy as select queries.

Update your data all at once.

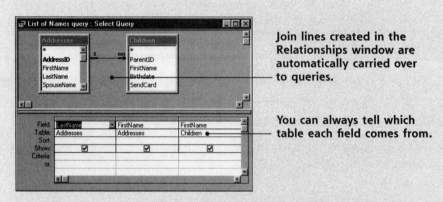

Join lines created in the Relationships window are automatically carried over to queries.

You can always tell which table each field comes from.

You can make a query with two tables as easily as making a query with one table.

How to Create a Query Using More Than One Table (page 154)

Drag each table's field list from the Show Table dialog box into the QBE window. Drag the fields you want to use down to the QBE grid.

How to Create an Update Query (page 159)

1. Create a normal select query.

2. With the query in design view, select | Query | → | Update Query | from the menu bar.

3. Add your update criteria to the Update to: row and run the query.

How to Create a Make Table Query (page 164)

1. Create a normal select query.

2. With the select query in design view, select | Query | → | Make Table Query | from the menu bar.

3. Add your field lists to the QBE window. Drag your fields to the QBE grid from the field lists in the QBE window.

4. Add any criteria you want and then run the query. Access prompts you for the name of a new table.

CHAPTER 9

When it's on, the wizard toggle automatically calls up tool wizards when you select certain tools.

The toolbox contains controls you can put on your forms.

The design grid helps you align controls on your form.

The header band holds the form's label.

Data is displayed in the detail band.

The footer band can hold control buttons.

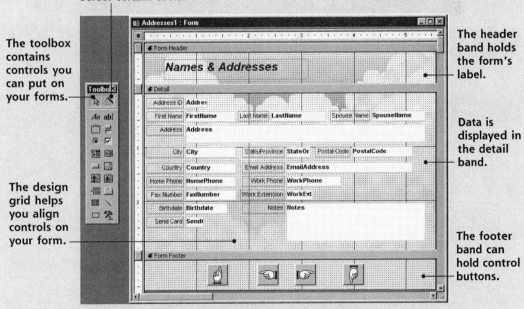

A form in design view, ready for you to modify.

How to Create an AutoForm (page 173)

1. With the Forms tab in the database container active, select the table or query that will underlie the form.
2. Click [New].
3. Select one of the three AutoForm Wizards from the New Form dialog box.

How to Add Navigation and Control Buttons to a Form (page 194)

1. With the form in design view and the Toolbox Wizard button active, click ▣.
2. Move your mouse cursor to the position on the form where you want the button to appear.
3. Drag your mouse cursor down and to the right to draw the button's shape.
4. Make your selections on the Control Wizard dialog boxes.

How to Resize a Control (page 181)

1. Select the control.
2. Click one of its sizing handles and move it.

How to Select Several Controls at Once (page 173)

Hold the Shift key down as you select each control.

How to Delete a Control (page 173)

1. Select the control.
2. Press Delete.

CHAPTER 10

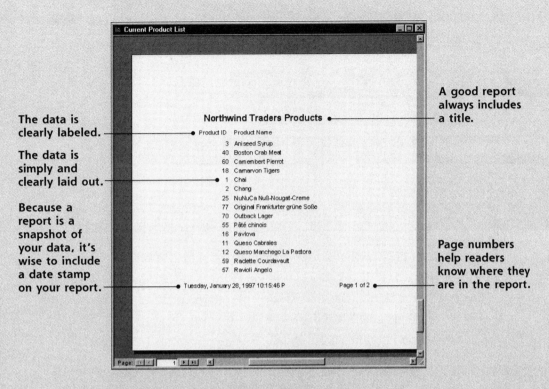

The data is clearly labeled.

The data is simply and clearly laid out.

Because a report is a snapshot of your data, it's wise to include a date stamp on your report.

A good report always includes a title.

Page numbers help readers know where they are in the report.

This is the report title.

The Header band appears on all pages.

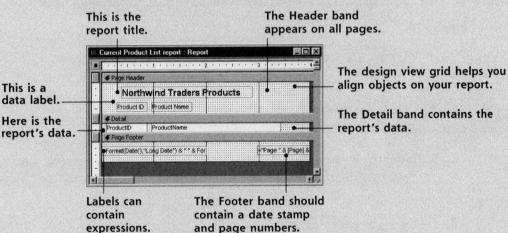

This is a data label.

Here is the report's data.

The design view grid helps you align objects on your report.

The Detail band contains the report's data.

Labels can contain expressions.

The Footer band should contain a date stamp and page numbers.

How to Create an AutoReport (page 200)

1. From the database container with the Reports tab active, click New .
2. Select one of the AutoReports from the New Report dialog box.

How to Preview a Report (page 202)

Click the 🔍 button on the toolbar.

How to Change the Size of a Report Band (page 206)

Click and drag its bar.

How to Add a Date and Time Stamp to a Report (page 208)

1. While in design view, select Insert → Date and Time from the menu bar.
2. Select the date and time format you want in the Date and Time dialog box. If you don't want one or the other to be included, make sure the corresponding check box is unchecked.
3. When you're done, click OK .

How to Add Automatic Page Numbers to a Report (page 208)

1. Select Insert → Page Numbers from the menu bar.
2. Select the format you want in the Page Numbers dialog box.
3. Click OK .

How to Create a Mailing Label (page 212)

1. With the table or query from which you'll get the mailing labels' names, and with the database container with the Reports tab active, click New .
2. Select Label Wizard from the New Report dialog box.
3. Follow the prompts on successive wizard dialog boxes.

CHAPTER 11

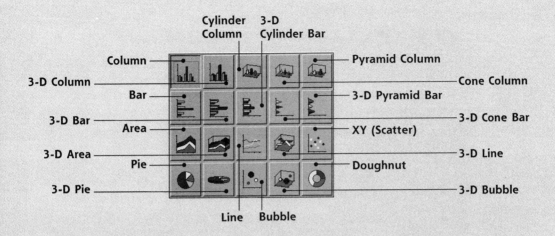

Cylinder Column
3-D Cylinder Bar
Column
Pyramid Column
3-D Column
Cone Column
Bar
3-D Pyramid Bar
3-D Bar
3-D Cone Bar
Area
XY (Scatter)
3-D Area
3-D Line
Pie
Doughnut
3-D Pie
3-D Bubble
Line
Bubble

How to Insert a Chart into a Form or a Report (page 233)

1. Select `Insert` → `Chart` from the menu bar.

2. Follow the prompts of the Chart Wizard dialog boxes.

How to Modify a Chart (page 238)

1. Double click the generic representation of the chart in your form or report.

2. In the Graph applet, click a chart object to select it.

3. Modify it as necessary.

How to Preview a Chart (page 237)

With your form or report in design view and the chart in position, click the 🔍.

CHAPTER 12

Field names are complete and understandable.

Each field is described.

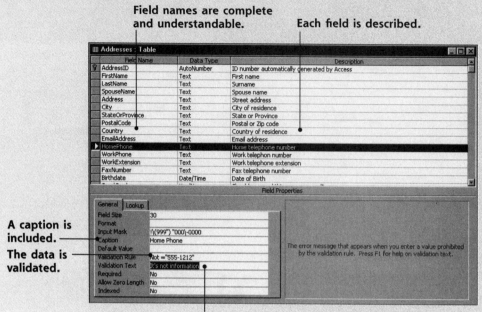

A caption is included.

The data is validated.

Users find out what's wrong when they put in the "wrong" kind of data.

How to Bind a Control (page 254)

1. With the control highlighted, open the Properties sheet.
2. Use the `ControlSource` property to make the connection between the control and its underlying data.

How to Create a Good User Interface   (page 244)

Make the form or report as easy as possible for the user to employ.

How to Create a Mask for Input (page 245)

Enter the mask — according to the type of data to be stored — into the table as you design it.

How to Remove a Control (page 255)

1. Highlight the control with the form in design view.
2. Press the Delete key.

CHAPTER 13

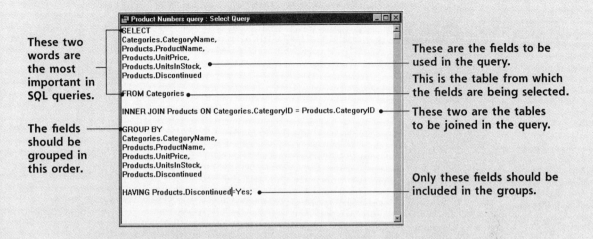

These two words are the most important in SQL queries.

The fields should be grouped in this order.

These are the fields to be used in the query.

This is the table from which the fields are being selected.

These two are the tables to be joined in the query.

Only these fields should be included in the groups.

The fields are grouped as per the query's instruction.

Only the fields complying with the HAVING clause are included.

How to Create an SQL Query (page 262)

Create a normal query with Access. (They are all SQL queries.)

How to Enter SQL Code into a Query (page 264)

1. With the query in design view, click 🔲 on the toolbar. Access displays the SQL window.

2. Type in your SQL code there.

Click ▣ on the toolbar, just as you would with any other Access query.

With a blank SQL window visible, type in the keyword SELECT, an asterisk (*), the keyword FROM, the name of the table from which to select all the fields, and end with a semicolon (;).

CHAPTER 14

Take out this label from the spreadsheet to use the data in an Access table.

Fields are in columns.

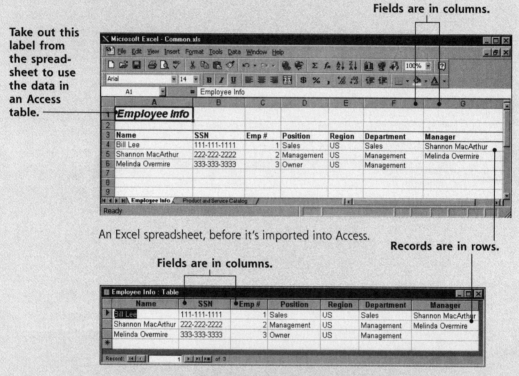

An Excel spreadsheet, before it's imported into Access.

Records are in rows.

Fields are in columns.

A new Access table created from the imported Excel spreadsheet.

How to Export a Data File from Access (page 287)

1. Select `File` → `Save As/Export` from the menu bar.
2. Indicate a name for the file to be exported as well as a format in which it is to be exported.
3. Click `OK`. Access converts the file and saves it in its new format.

How to Link an External File to an Access Database (page 276)

1. Select `File` → `Get External Data` → `Link Tables` from the menu bar.
2. Indicate a name for the file to be linked.
3. Click `OK`.

How to Encrypt a Database (page 297)

1. Close the database to encrypt.
2. Select `Tools` → `Security` → `Encrypt/Decrypt Database` from the menu bar.
3. Enter a name for the database in the Encrypt/Decrypt Database dialog box.
4. Click `OK`. Access encrypts and saves the database.

How to Open an Encrypted Database (page 297)

Select the database from the Explorer or the Documents menu just as you would an unencrypted database.

VISUAL INDEX

Getting Help with Access

How to see a Help Table of Contents — page 44

How to open an Index of Help topics — page 45

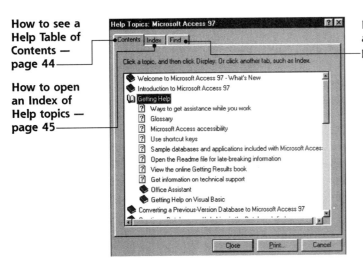

How to find almost any helpful word — page 46

Get help from the Office Assistant — page 37

Choose your own Office Assistant — page 39

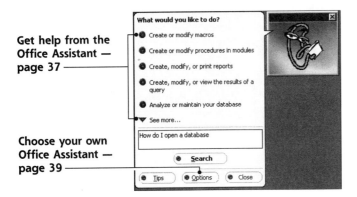

319

Forms, Reports, Queries, and Tables

How to create a
table — page 23

How to create a
query — page 76

How to create a
form — page 82

How to create a
report — page 200

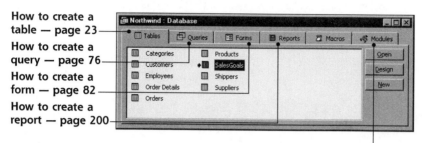

How to import or link a table — page 282

Working with Forms

How to include
a label for your
form — page 184

How to format a
form — page 192

How to add a
subform to a
form — page 188

How to navigate
your form — page 23

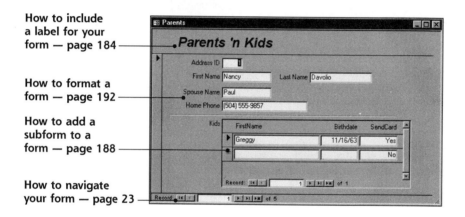

Working with Reports

How to change the size of a page header or footer — page 206

How to add a label to each page on a report — page 204

How to add a datasheet to a report — page 228

How to add a chart to a report — page 233

How to include the date in the report footer — page 208

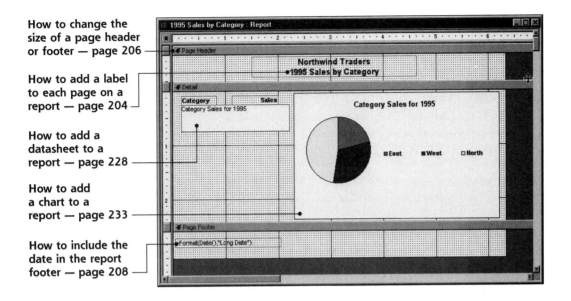

How to move controls on a report — page 232

How to include the date and time that your report was printed — page 208

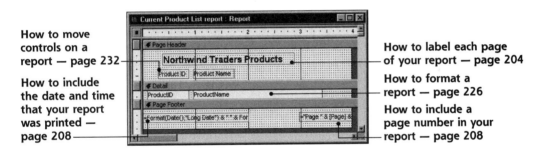

How to label each page of your report — page 204

How to format a report — page 226

How to include a page number in your report — page 208

Working with Queries

How to write an SQL query — page 264

How to choose only certain fields from more than one table — page 266

How to create and use joins — page 268

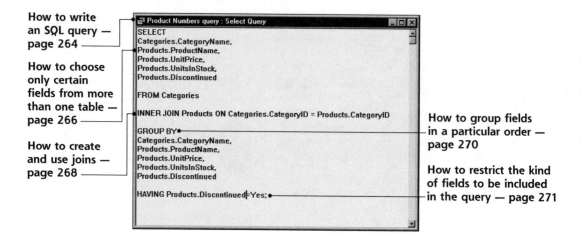

How to group fields in a particular order — page 270

How to restrict the kind of fields to be included in the query — page 271

Working with Tables

How to create a table — page 70

How to choose what data type to use — page 91

How to include an input mask — page 245

How to validate data that's input — page 245

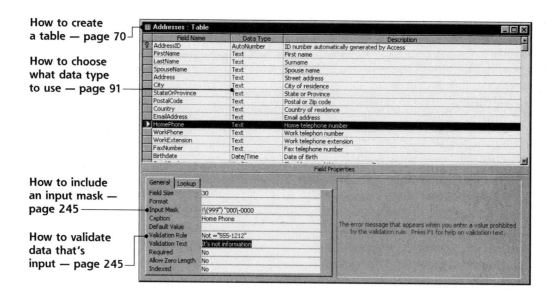

Working with Databases

How to create
a new database
using a wizard —
page 58

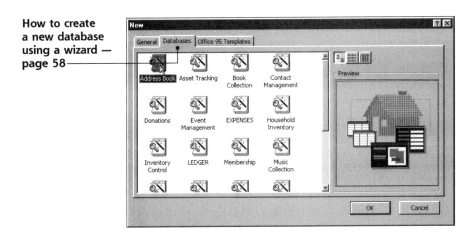

How to save —
page 26

How to print out
a hard copy of
your database —
page 200

How to use a
datasheet — page 27

How to add a new
record to your
database — page 112

How to navigate
your database —
page 28

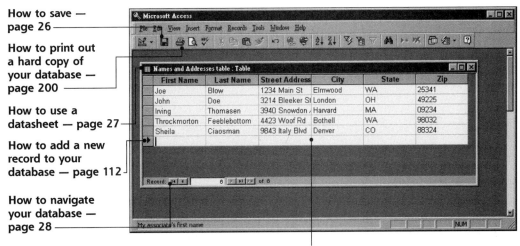

How to change the size of columns in a datasheet — page 108

How to secure
your database —
page 293

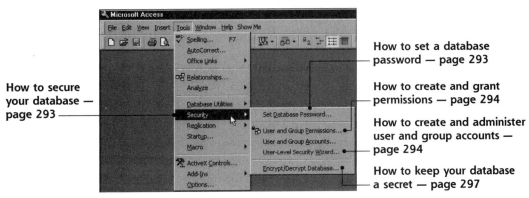

How to set a database
password — page 293

How to create and grant
permissions — page 294

How to create and administer
user and group accounts —
page 294

How to keep your database
a secret — page 297

TROUBLESHOOTING GUIDE

If You Run into Trouble

I don't know what it is about computers or electronic equipment in general, but if you start working with more than one piece of equipment at a time, it seems as though your problems increase exponentially. Sure, you know what I mean. You watch TV, and it's easy. You try to play a tape in your VCR, and suddenly you've got all kinds of complications. Two controllers. The "wrong" channel set on either the TV or the VCR. Your ten-year-old offering condescending advice. Then there's my favorite: The tape just doesn't seem to want to fit into the VCR — and then you notice that you're trying to put it in backwards.

Well, you can figure that at least once in your career you're going to have problems with Access. In my experience, you're likely to run into two kinds of problems. The first are operational kinds of problems: You try to do something and Access urps; the second kind of problem is where you try to get information out of your database, and the output device urps. What I want to do here is give you a pointer or two to help you on your way.

The Ol' Operational Problem

If you're working with your database and you try to do something that doesn't make sense to Access, it will show you a dialog box with a warning sign, such as the one shown in Figure T-1. The yellow triangle with an exclamation mark (!) in it is your clue that this is a warning. Also, you'll usually see three command buttons that let you tell Access what your intentions are. Click one, and Access will act accordingly.

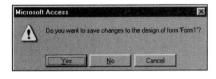

Figure T-1 A sample warning dialog box.

That's the quick and dirty solution. If you're having a more involved problem, such as when you think you're doing something correctly but Access isn't behaving as you think it should, then you may need to do some troubleshooting. Built into the Access Help system (which you learn about in Chapter 2, "When I Need Help, I Push the Button") is a whole bunch of troubleshooting topics.

The easiest thing I've found to do is to simply press the F1 key. When Windows pops up my Office Assistant, I type in a question. For example, in Figure T-2 you can see that I've asked Access to "tell me about troubleshooting databases."

Figure T-2   There's plenty of troubleshooting advice available.

From here, all you have to do is click one of the buttons or click See More to have Access display additional helpful information.

That Devil: The Printer

Sometimes in the office you get faced with unexpected pressure. I mean, you're sitting there, happily working away. You go to print something out on the printer — and blooey! Nothing comes out, or it comes out wrong. And this happens only because you needed to use two stupid pieces of equipment to work together for just a moment — for just a moment!

In case this ever happens to you, here's a troubleshooting checklist for your printer:

* Is the printer actually turned on?
* Does it have paper in it — in the proper place?
* Is the printer's Online or Ready light lit?
* Is anything jammed?
* Are all the printer's cables properly connected?
* If you're printing to a network printer, are you sure that you're printing to the "right" one?

One final word on printing: Most printers nowadays will let you print in what are called *portrait* and *landscape* modes. Portrait mode is where the paper is taller than it is wide. Paper in landscape mode, on the other hand, is wider than it is tall. Be sure that you're printing in the appropriate mode for your project or else your output won't appear properly on the printed page. You can adjust your printer's orientation by selecting Page Setup from the File menu, and then clicking on the Paper Size tab. You'll find the options for portrait and landscape orientation there.

INSTALLING ACCESS 97

Before you can begin your adventure with Access, you must have installed it on your hard disk. In this appendix, I show you how to do just that.

Access normally comes as part of Microsoft Office 97, a suite of related office productivity software. Access is the Office 97 database application. The other applications include a word processor (Word for Windows), a spreadsheet (Excel), presentation software (PowerPoint), and contact management software (Outlook).

If you've already installed Microsoft Office so that you can work with one of its other parts, you'd still be well-advised to read this appendix. That's because you can reinstall, or even change the software you installed (or its options) at any time after you performed the original installation.

TIP Installing Access is a simple process, but you'll want to pay close attention to the details.

NOTE I'm assuming here that you've bought the CD-ROM version of Microsoft Office 97. If so, you can follow right along with these instructions. If you've bought the floppy disk version instead, then the instructions will still work. There are only two differences:

✴ You'll insert your Microsoft Office 97 Disk #1 into your A: drive, instead of putting the CD-ROM into the CD-ROM drive.

✴ After you've made your choices as to what software and options to install, you'll be prompted to replace the disk in drive A: with successive disks.

Just keep your wits about you, and you'll have no trouble at all.

First Things First

Before you can start installing software, it's best to know that your computer has the room and capability to handle it. Here's what you need:

* At least a 486 computer running the Windows 95 operating system
* 8 megabytes of RAM
* Between 73 and 191 megabytes of room on your hard disk
* A VGA video card and monitor
* A CD-ROM would be nice

Installing Office and Access

Now let me run through the process of installing Microsoft Office 97 and Access with you. Office and Access are pretty intertwined, so we'll look at them together. Each part of Office — the word processor, the spreadsheet, and so on — has its own options. IDG Books Worldwide has published the Discover series to teach you about each application. So, for the purposes of this installation, I'll only talk about the options that pertain to Access in particular.

Office comes first

The first part of our discussion has to do with Microsoft Office.

To begin installation, follow these simple steps:

1. With your computer up and running, move your mouse cursor to the **Start** button. Click it and then select **Run**. Windows displays the Run dialog box, as shown in Figure B-1.

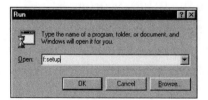

Figure B-1   This is the Run dialog box.

2. In this dialog box, there is a text box labeled Open. In it, type the letter of your CD-ROM drive (mine is F:) immediately followed by the word **setup**. When I did this, I typed **f:setup**, and then I clicked **OK**. Windows cooked for a moment and then displayed the Microsoft Office 97 Setup dialog box, as shown in Figure B-2.

3. Once you've read what the dialog box has to say — I like to mix my metaphors — click [**Continue**]. Windows asks for your name and organization in the — you guessed it — Name and Organization Information dialog box, which you can see in Figure B-3.

Figure B-2   The Microsoft Office 97 Setup dialog box.

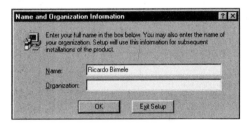

Figure B-3   The Name and Organization Information dialog box.

4. As you can see, I've typed my name in the dialog box, but I've left the Organization text box blank. Type your own name (and organization name, if you like) into the dialog's text boxes, then click [**OK**]. Windows asks for confirmation in another dialog box. If everything's okay, click [**OK**] in that dialog box too. Windows next asks for a CD Key number, as shown in Figure B-4.

Figure B-4   You'll need a number to enter here.

5. You'll find the number you need printed on a sticker that's on the back of the CD-ROM's jewel case (or other packaging if you're using floppy disks) in which your software was sold. (This is all part of a software anti-piracy protection scheme used by Microsoft.) Once you've entered your own number, click **OK**. Window displays the next Microsoft Office Setup dialog box, as shown in Figure B-5.

Figure B-5 Pick a place for your software.

6. By default, Windows wants to install your Office software into the C:\Program Files\Microsoft Office subdirectory. The reason it puts Office into that subdirectory — or any subdirectory other than the root directory, for that matter — is because that way you have fewer directories in your computer's root. Fewer directories means less confusion, a shorter list, and that kind of thing. I prefer to have my Office in its own directory though. Accordingly, I clicked on **Change Folder** and Windows displayed the Change Folder dialog box, as shown in Figure B-6.

Figure B-6 Insert the location you want in the Change Folder dialog box.

7. As you can see, I typed **Office97** in the Path text box. When I clicked
[**OK**], Windows showed me a dialog box telling me that directory didn't
yet exist, and asking whether it should create it for me. I clicked [**Yes**],
Windows cooked a minute, and then it displayed the Microsoft Office
Setup dialog box you see in Figure B-7.

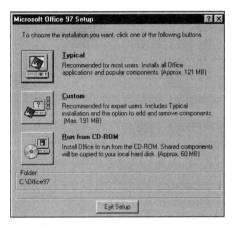

Figure B-7   Here's where we get serious.

8. You have a decision to make now about how to set up Office. Here's
what the options are and some ramifications of each.

* **Typical** works for most Microsoft Office users. If you click this button,
Windows installs Microsoft Office using the options its programmers
think will work well for most Office users. Normally, I'd say for you to
go ahead and use this option. In this case, however, I have to say no
— if you want to follow along all the examples in this book.

* **Run from CD-ROM** takes the least space on your hard disk, but it's
also likely to be the option that runs the slowest of these three.

* **Custom** gives you control over what gets installed during Office setup
and what doesn't. This is the option I'd like you to use. I'll go over the
options I want you to install in the next section of this appendix.

What Are My Options?

When you click the Custom button, Access displays the Custom dialog box, as
shown in Figure B-8. As I mentioned earlier, I won't go into all the options for
the other Office applications.

Here, I want to talk about only those options having to do with Access:

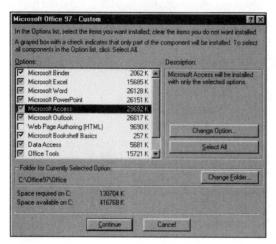

Figure B-8   The Custom dialog box.

1. Highlight the Microsoft Access option, as shown in Figure B-8, then click
   `Change Option`. Windows displays the Microsoft Office 97 — Microsoft
   Access dialog box, as shown in Figure B-9. The easiest thing for you to do
   at this point is to click `Select All`, and that's what I suggest.

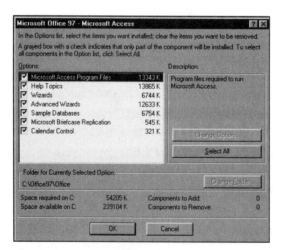

Figure B-9   You can Select All or choose other
Access options.

These are the options having to do with Microsoft Access:

* **Microsoft Access Program Files** are just that. You've got to have
  'em, so be sure this option is clicked.

* **Help Topics** are the Access part of the built-in Windows help system.
  You'll want these too.

- ✳ **Wizards** are a kind of intelligent program-within-a-program that guide you as you accomplish certain tasks. These include such procedures as creating complete databases, reports, and forms. We use wizards in this book, so you should check this item too.

- ✳ **Advanced Wizards** have to do with automatically documenting your database and such. While you don't need it now, you will eventually. Go ahead and check this item.

- ✳ **Sample Databases** are three complete databases put together by the people at Microsoft. We use two of these in this book, the Northwind database and the Developer Solutions database. The third, Orders database, is also useful as an example. You should definitely check this item.

- ✳ **Microsoft Briefcase Replication** has to do with making copies of your database to take with you on a laptop, for instance. We don't use it in this book, but you'll find it handy. Go ahead and check this item.

- ✳ **Calendar Control** is a facility you can put on your Access forms that gives you all the functionality of an electronic calendar. Again, it's not something we talk about in this book, but it is something you'll eventually find handy. I suggest clicking this item too.

2. Once you're done making your choices, click OK. Windows displays the Microsoft Office Setup dialog box again, and you can continue making choices for the other parts of Microsoft Office.

3. When you're done with all that, go ahead and click Continue. Windows cooks for several moments and finally displays the Microsoft Office 97 — Restart Windows dialog box, as shown in Figure B-10.

Figure B-10 Restart Windows, and you're on your way!

4. As it installs all this software, Windows puts files into directories and their names into its registry. Because Windows basically looks at its registry only when it first starts up, you have to restart Windows so it can recognize and use all the changes you just made. Go ahead and do so by clicking [**Restart Windows**]. Windows closes down for a moment and then restarts. Once it does so, you'll find all the Microsoft Office software you just installed available for you to use on the Program menu you see when you click the Start button.

Well, that's it! Now all you have to do is turn to the first chapter in this book and read away. It's an adventure you'll find valuable for the rest of your days. Enjoy!

BASICALLY WINDOWS

There are available a number of really good books on Microsoft Windows, and I recommend that you buy one or two. They'll give you the complete word on how Windows works. This appendix, on the other hand, will tell you a few things about Windows that are useful knowledge to someone working with the Microsoft Access database program.

Using the Mouse

Most computers running Microsoft Windows have attached to them — usually sitting right next to the keyboard — a small implement called a *mouse*. It gets its name from the connecting wire extending out of one end and from its often rapid and erratic movements as you push it around on your desk.

On the mouse you'll find from one to three flat surfaces you can press just like buttons. As a matter of fact, that's exactly what they are: buttons. When you press a mouse button, you might notice that it feels as though the button clicked. In the computer world, we've come to call the act of pressing a mouse button *clicking* it.

On your computer screen is a small arrow that moves in concert with your mouse. If you push your mouse up your desk, away from yourself, then the small arrow moves up too. When you move your mouse to the right or left, the small arrow moves right and left as well. We call that small arrow a *mouse cursor*.

The left mouse button is the one you'll most often click. If your mouse cursor is on an icon on your desktop, and you click the icon, it changes color; it's been *selected*. By that, Windows figures that you want to do something with the application represented by that icon. If you double-click the icon — click twice in rapid succession — then Windows automatically loads and runs the icon's program.

The right mouse button works to call up little context-sensitive menus. They work just like any other menus: You move your mouse cursor to the option you want to employ, and you press your left mouse button — what we in the biz call *left-clicking* your mouse.

As a matter of fact, you do much of your communicating with Access (or any other Windows-based program) by moving your mouse cursor over to and left-clicking something you see on your computer's screen.

It's All on Your Desktop

When you open Microsoft Windows, you see a screen something like Figure C-1. This screen is called a *desktop*, and it is a metaphor for the top of the desk on which your computer rests. The little pictures you see are called *icons*, and they each represent an individual Windows-based software program. You can have a whole bunch of icons on your Windows desktop.

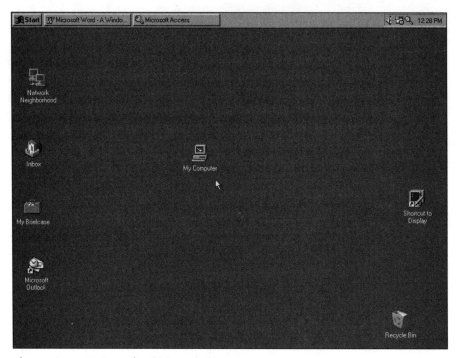

Figure C-1 A Microsoft Windows desktop.

On my desktop, I choose to have only those that are most important to my everyday work, just as I choose to have my office desk be as clean and neat as a pin, with nary a scrap of paper out of place or a computer keyboard not precisely aligned with the edge of my desk. (If you don't believe me, feel free to visit my office. Just give me a couple hours' notice to — um — "arrange my schedule." Yeah, that's it — "arrange my schedule.") Well, if I've made a good enough impression, I'll continue...

The two icons that are of most interest to us at this point are labeled My Computer and Network Neighborhood.

Network Neighborhood

Many people use Access on a network. That is, their computers are electronically connected with other computers. If yours is too, then you can double-click the

Network Neighborhood icon and see the names of other computers up and running on your network. That's what I did in Figure C-2. It's a picture of the network to which my computer is connected.

As you can see, it's not a very extensive network, consisting of only two computers at the moment, but it's a network nonetheless. In the small company where I work, we have only four computers that can be on the network. When all of them are "up," each of them can electronically communicate with all the others.

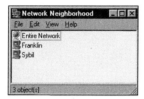

Figure C-2   Franklin is my desktop computer, and Sybil is my laptop.

Networks are important to people who use Access. When you run Access on computers that are connected to a network, everybody who uses those computers also has access to the Access data on your computer, tautologically speaking.

My very own computer

Whether your computer is on a network or not, chances are you'll be more interested in the My Computer icon. It is your entrée to the Microsoft Windows Explorer: its way of letting you figuratively look around in your computer. When I click the My Computer icon on my desktop, it shows what you can see in Figure C-3.

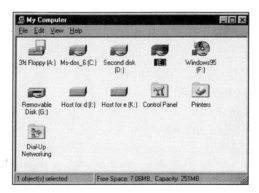

Figure C-3   My Computer shows my hard drives and some folders.

As you can see, I have a number of hard drives in my computer. The ones that have a small hand under them, looking as though they are being offered as a treat, are the ones that I'm sharing on the network. If I had an Access database on any of them, then anyone else on my network could work with the same database — at the same time, even.

When I click the drive icon labeled [E:], Windows shows me all the files and folders that it found on that drive, as shown in Figure C-4. The little file folder icons are an electronic metaphor for those old familiar manila folders we've all come to know and love. The other icons represent software applications on my E: drive. As you can see, Microsoft Access is right there, ready to be double-clicked and used.

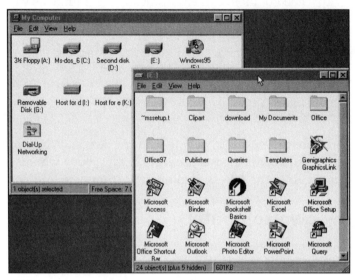

Figure C-4 On my computer, Access is on my E: drive.

If you want to, this would be a good time to click your own My Computer icon and look around the contents of your computer. It would also be a good time to find out where your copy of Access resides.

Get a Start on It

You can load and run any Windows application by working through the Windows Explorer, of course. You might find it faster, however, to use the Start button instead. By default, you find the Start button at the bottom left of your computer screen. When you click it, Windows displays a pop-up menu (which really pops upward!), much like the one in Figure C-5.

TIP If you don't have a keyboard that's been specially prepared for use with Windows, and you don't have a mouse, you can get to the Start menu by pressing Alt+S when only your desktop is visible. Then you can move up and down the menu by pressing the up-arrow key and the down-arrow key, respectively. When you get to an option you want to use, press Enter. To Windows, that's like clicking your left mouse button.

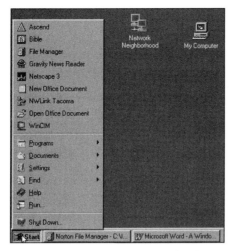

Figure C-5 The Start menu looks like this.

Once you see the Start menu, move your mouse cursor up to the Programs option. Windows pops up yet another menu. It looks like the one in Figure C-6. If you've installed Microsoft Access, then you will see its name on that menu. To load and run it then, all you need to do is to click its name.

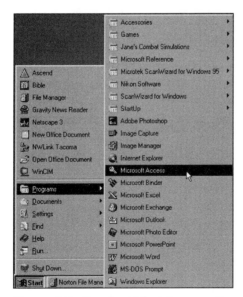

Figure C-6 You should find Access on the Programs menu.

My Mind Is a Sieve

As big as our computers are anymore, it's a wonder that we can find anything on them. Icons help, of course. They keep track of where their own piece of software is found. Every now and then, however, you come to the point where you need a file, but you don't know where to find it. Brother!

One of the options automatically built in to the Start menu is Find, as shown in Figure C-7.

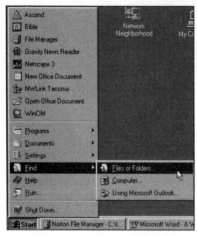

Figure C-7 Find what you want with Find.

There are three kinds of things you may want to find from time to time. These include:

* **Files or Folders** are the names of — well — files and folders to be found somewhere on one of your computer's hard disks or on another computer in your network.

* **Computer** is another computer on your network. Each one is listed by its name. On my company's network there are four computers: Franklin, Sybil, Bill, and Bob. You can call your computer anything you like, including cryptic numbers. Most people use humanly intelligible names, however, because they're easier to remember.

* **Using Microsoft Outlook** is available if you've installed Outlook as part of your Microsoft Office installation. It allows you to find particular words or phrases within files — just the thing if you know what you wrote, but you can't remember where you wrote it.

If You Need to Find Access

If you need to find Access and can't remember in which folder to find it, here's a quick way to do so:

1. Move your mouse cursor to the **Start** button and click it. Windows displays the Start menu.

2. Select the **Find** option on the Start menu. Windows displays the Find submenu.

3. Select **Files or Folders** from the submenu. Windows displays the Find Files dialog box.

4. Type **msaccess.exe** in the text box labeled <u>N</u>amed. Choose the drive where you think you put Access from those displayed in the combo box labeled <u>L</u>ook in:

5. Click the **Find Now** button. Windows opens the dialog box further to reveal a place where it puts a list of all the files it finds. You can see an example in Figure C-8.

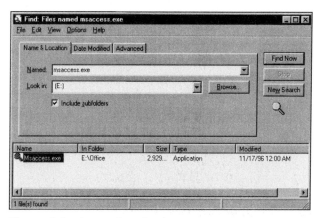

Figure C-8 Access: found at last!

When you see Access's program name among the files listed in the Find files dialog box, you can double click it to run it. If it's not listed, however, you can try looking in other drive letters. One way or another, if it's installed, you'll find it.

Help!

There's really no way you can "hurt" your computer by pressing its keyboard keys — that's "pressing" and not "banging on," mind you. As a matter of fact, pressing your computer's keys and playing with the software is the best and most-often-used method of learning computers.

When you get confused — and you *will* get confused — press F1. Windows knows "where you are" on your computer at all times, something we in the biz call your "context." So when you press F1, it uses that information to provide you with *context-sensitive help* (if it's available): help that is exactly targeted at what you're doing at that time.

There is an entire chapter on the Windows help system in this book. It's Chapter 2, called "When I Need Help, I Push the Button." It may even tell you more than you'll want to know about getting help while you're working with Access.

GLOSSARY

3-D graphic An image depicting objects in three dimensions: width from right and left, height up and down, and depth from the front and to the back.

Accessory An implement connected to your computer but that isn't really a part of it. For example, a mouse or a modem are used by your computer as accessories. See *peripheral*.

Active file The database file that is currently being accessed.

Alert box A dialog box that gives you a notice that what you are attempting to do may cause an error in your data.

Alt key A key found on IBM-PC compatible computers. It acts much like a Shift key, in that you press the Alt key in combination with an alphabetic key. In Access, you use the Alt+(some other key) combination as a keyboard shortcut that causes Access to perform some function.

Append To attach data to the end (last record) of a table.

Application A program on a computer that lets you perform some specific kind of work.

Argument A value used in an expression.

Arrow key One of four keys that cause your on-screen cursor to move to the right, left, up, or down.

ASCII An acronym for "American Standard Code for Information Interchange." It describes every alphabetic and control character in terms of a number.

Attribute A characteristic of an object. See *property*.

Backspace key A key that moves your on-screen cursor one space to the left, erasing any character that occupies that space. Also known as a destructive backspace.

Band In forms and reports, a rectangular area in which you place *controls*. Access bands include Header, Footer, and Detail.

Binary A number system in which there are only two numbers: 0 and 1. In the computer world, 0 means "off" and 1 means "on."

Bit A new word coined for computers from two other words: binary and digit. A bit can be either a 0 or a 1. Eight bits together form a *byte*.

Boolean algebra An algebra invented by George Boole, it is the way of computer logic. Numbers in Boolean algebra are limited to the value of 0 or 1. They can be combined through Boolean operators such as AND or OR as well as their opposites, NAND and NOR. For example, in Boolean algebra, 1 AND 1 = 1, 1 AND 0 = 0.

Bound A state in which a control on an Access form is connected to an underlying field. If it is bound, then the control displays the value of the underlying field. If not, then what the field displays is dependent on what you program it to display: a value calculated from the contents of other fields, for example.

Bug An error in the way a software application behaves. Sometimes also known as a feature.

Byte A group of eight binary digits, or bits. In computers, each letter or number is stored as a single byte.

Cache A part of memory that is logically close to your computer's *CPU* that holds often-used data.

CD-ROM An acronym for "Compact Disc - Read Only Memory," a device that stores data in a form that's readable by a small, low-powered laser beam.

Checkbox An Access object that has three states: yes (checked), no (unchecked), and maybe (grayed out). Checkboxes are often used to represent Boolean data.

Column A series of fields arranged vertically next to each other on a datasheet. Each column represents a single field present in all the records in a table.

Control An object such as a text box, command button, or label that you place on an Access object and that you can then manipulate to control Access or your data.

Control key A key that works much like a Shift key, in that you press it in conjunction with another key.

CPU An acronym for "Central Processing Unit," it's the "mind" of your computer contained within a chip; the CPU controls all the rest of your computer. The term is a holdover from mainframe computer days.

Data type A definition of a certain kind of data that describes what kind of values that data can comprise. For example, the text data type comprises all alphabetical characters as well as numbers (which are treated as text, not as their intrinsic values). Numeric data comprises number values.

Database A collection of data, arranged in columns and rows on tables. The data in a database can be selectively accessed, manipulated, and turned into useful information.

Database container A place in your Access window where all database objects (tables, queries, forms, reports, and the like) are stored by name.

Database tab A tab on the database container that you click to see its objects. For example, to see a list of all the queries in your database, you would click the Queries tab on the database container.

Delete key A key that moves your on-screen cursor one space to the right, erasing any character that occupies that space.

Delimiter A character that separates fields and characters in databases that have been exported as text files. Most commonly, a tab character is used to separate fields, and quote characters are used to enclose text (not numeric) data.

Desktop The area on your computer graphical interface on which you find program icons as well as windows.

Dialog box 1. A graphical window you use to communicate with and control Access. 2. A graphical window automatically displayed by Access to inform or warn you.

Distributed database A database whose various parts can be found on different computers on a network.

End key A key that when pressed moves your on-screen cursor to the right end of a line. Pressing Ctrl+End moves your on-screen cursor to the bottom of a file.

Enter key A key that when pressed causes a paragraph return character to be entered into a text field. Also known as a *Return key*.

Escape key A key that when pressed causes Access to stop what it's doing and wait for additional input or control.

Exclusive A mode in which you open a database; in exclusive mode the database's data is available only to you until you close the database.

Field An indivisible unit in a *record* that contains a value. Each record is made up of a number of fields.

Filename A set of letters and numbers that identify a particular data file.

Flat file A single-table database. A database that is the opposite of *relational*.

Front end The part of the computer or software that does the initial manipulation and processing on data or instructions. It usually contains any necessary humanly understandable user interface. The front end sends the results of its work to the "back-end" processor, which takes care of detailed processing and housekeeping (making sure the data is stored correctly, remembering where exactly the data was put, and so on).

GIGO An acronym for "Garbage In, Garbage Out." It's a statement that stands for the idea that bad data put into a database results in bad, useless, or inaccurate information coming out of the database.

Grid The regularly spaced dots found in the background of a form or report in Design view. They represent fixed points on the form or report to which controls can automatically snap, thereby making the alignment of those controls easier.

Hardware Your physical computer, mouse, printer, modem, and so on. *Software* (your computer's programs) runs on hardware.

Home key A key that when pressed moves your on-screen cursor to the left end of a line. Pressing Ctrl+Home moves your on-screen cursor to the top of a file.

Index A listing whereby Access keeps track of the order in which you want records in a table to be organized. Indexes make it easier (and therefor faster) for Access to find and retrieve individual records in a table.

Join In relational databases, a join is the connection made between two tables by using a field in each table that corresponds to a field in the other. For example, connecting a Social Security number field in each could join an employment table and an address table.

Key 1. A switch you press on your keyboard that is recognized by your computer as being an alphabetic, numeric, or control character. 2. The prime value in a record.

Landscape mode In printing, where the page is formatted so that it is wider than it is tall.

Legend A list of labels on a chart that tell you what each of the parts of the chart represent. In Access, a chart legend will usually include a small, colored box next to each of the legend's labels that corresponds with the color of that label's data item.

Link A connection between two objects: a table in one database and a table in another, for example.

Mail merge A process whereby names and addresses from within an Access database are included in documents created by using a word processor.

Memo field A field within Access that can contain 64 kilobytes of textual data.

Menu A list of options from which you select one to cause Access to perform its action.

Mouse A pointing device that you move with your hand, usually connected to your computer through a wire. As you do so, an on-screen mouse cursor moves in correlation with the mouse's movements.

Network A collection of individual computers that are electrically connected together so that they can communicate and share data.

Normalization A process in which each table in a database is checked to make sure that it is a small as possible, easy to understand and change, and each field in its records contains unique and non-repeating types of data. In practice, this means that if fields in a record are found to be common, then the table is divided until all its records contain unique data. When the tables cannot be further divided, then the database is said to be fully normalized.

Null A kind of placeholder entity that actually holds nothing.

Object A distinct entity on your computer's screen that you can "touch" with your mouse cursor.

Output The result of input.

Page footer A rectangular area at the bottom of a report page whereon you place fields that you want to appear on each page of the report.

Page header A rectangular area at the top of a report page whereon you place fields that you want to appear on each page of the report.

Page setup A selection on the File menu where you indicate how you want each page printed by default.

Parse To break up into its constituent parts, especially a string of words, so that it can be understood by a computer.

Peripheral A device connected to your computer that is controlled by the computer's microprocessor. Examples of peripheral devices include printers, modems, mice, keyboards, and monitors.

Pie chart A type of graph in which each constituent part (pie slice) is compared with the others in terms of their percentage of the whole.

Portrait mode In printing, where the page is formatted so that it is taller than it is wide.

Query A way of extracting data from your database so that it results in information.

Radio button An option button that works with a collection of related buttons much like the radio buttons in a car: You press one to select it, and that automatically deselects all the other related radio buttons.

RAM An acronym for "Random-Access Memory," it's your computer's scratch-pad memory. When you load a program from your hard disk, a duplicate of that program is put into your computer's RAM where it can be quickly accessed.

Record A basic unit within a database table. It comprises one or more records, each of which contains one or more fields.

Relational database A database comprising more than one table, where the tables can be joined together through common fields.

Report footer A rectangular area at the bottom of a report page whereon you place fields that you want to appear on the last page of the report.

Report header A rectangular area at the top of a report page whereon you place fields that you want to appear on first page of the report.

ROM An acronym for "Read-Only Memory," it's the low-level programs that are stored in your computer's motherboard chips, which are usually used to control parts of your computer's hardware.

Root directory The most basic part of a hierarchical disk directory.

Row A series of fields arranged next to one another, running from left to right on a datasheet. Each row represents a single record.

Search To seek out the value of a particular field or record in a database.

Software The programs that run on your computer.

SQL An acronym for "Structured Query Language," the data manipulation language that underlies Access.

String A data structure comprised of a string of alphabetic characters.

Subform An Access form that's embedded within another Access form. Most often, subforms come from queries in which you have two tables in a one-to-many relationship. The data from the one side of the relationship is depicted in the main form, while the data from the many side is depicted in the subform.

Subdirectory A directory that is under a root directory (or another subdirectory) in a hierarchical disk directory structure.

Subreport A normal report that's been inserted into another report — typically called the "main report."

Switchboard An Access form that is a kind of electronic pushbutton menu.

Tab key A key that when pressed moves your on-screen cursor from one field to the next. If the cursor is in the last field in a record, then pressing the Tab key causes Access to save the current record and open a new, blank record.

Table The basic container of data in Access. Data is arranged in tables in rows and columns; each row is a record and each column is a field.

Template Like an electronic framework for data. It's a description of the database you want to create with your computer.

Toolbar A collection of buttons that have pictures on them, each one representing an individual control, or a different action for Access to perform.

Type A blank database description.

Unbound A control on a form or report that is not connected to an underlying field.

User interface The part of a program that your user sees and employs to control the program. The easiest user interface element for a user to work with is a well-designed form.

View A mode of seeing and working with your database application. In Access, you can work in design view, form view, and print preview, among others.

Wildcard character A character that can stand in place of a number of other characters. Access wildcards include an asterisk (*), the number 9, and the number 0, among others.

Wizard A helper applet built into Access that guides you in creating reports, databases, forms, and queries.

INDEX

SYMBOLS & NUMBERS

& (ampersand)
   concatenation operator, 211
   in Microsoft Windows programming, 185–186
* (asterisk), wildcard, 136
; (semicolon), statement terminator, 264
, (comma), in SQL, 268
! (exclamation point), wildcard, 136
- (hyphen), wildcard, 136
[] (square brackets)
   in SQL queries, 265
   wildcard, 136
? (question mark), wildcard, 136
3-D area charts, 223
3-D bar charts, 223
3-D bubble charts, 223
3-D column charts, 223
3-D line charts, 223
3-D pie charts, 223

A

About Microsoft Access dialog box, 55
Access 97
   opening screen, 15
   starting, 1, 10–15
Access toolbar
   Close button, 70
   Left Align button, 209
   New button, 58
   Print button, 32, 203
   Right Align button, 206
   Save button, 26, 83, 130
   Show Table button, 129
   Zoom button, 203
Action queries, 126, 127, 153
Addresses form, 31–32
   entering into, 3
   illustrated, 4, 67
   moving around, 67
   Page buttons, 67
   Preview Fact Sheet button, 32
   scroll bar, 67
   See also forms
alignment
   left, 209
   page number, 210
   right, 206, 257
ampersand (&)
   concatenation operator, 211
   in Microsoft Windows programming, 185–186
analyzing performance, 103–104
   ideas, 104
   object types, 103
   recommendations, 104
   suggestions, 104
analyzing tables, 96–103
   duplicate fields and, 99
   explanation, 98
   poor design and, 100–103
   See also tables
AND, 134

applications, databases vs., 20
area charts, 223
arrow buttons, 72
AS keyword, 271
Assistants. *See* Office Assistants
asterisk (*), wildcard, 136
AutoForms, 173–181
   choosing, 175
   Columnar, 173, 175–176
   creating, 175
   Datasheet, 173, 177
   Tabular, 173, 176
   types of, 173, 175
   See also forms
Autonumber data type, 93
autonumber fields, 114–115
AutoReport, 200–210
   quick and dirty, 224–226
   starting, 201
   See also reports
Avg function, 160, 163

B

back end, 261
bar charts, 223
blank reports, 228–233
   design view, 228–229
   subreport in, 229
   See also reports
Boolean data, 254
bottom-up design, 89
bound controls, 255
bubble charts, 223
bytes, 245

IDG BOOKS WORLDWIDE REGISTRATION CARD

RETURN THIS REGISTRATION CARD FOR FREE CATALOG

Title of this book: **Discover Access 97**

My overall rating of this book: ❑ Very good [1] ❑ Good [2] ❑ Satisfactory [3] ❑ Fair [4] ❑ Poor [5]

How I first heard about this book:

❑ Found in bookstore; name: [6] _____

❑ Advertisement: [8] _____

❑ Word of mouth; heard about book from friend, co-worker, etc.: [10] _____

❑ Book review: [7] _____

❑ Catalog: [9] _____

❑ Other: [11] _____

What I liked most about this book:

_____

_____

_____

What I would change, add, delete, etc., in future editions of this book:

_____

_____

_____

Other comments:

_____

_____

Number of computer books I purchase in a year: ❑ 1 [12] ❑ 2-5 [13] ❑ 6-10 [14] ❑ More than 10 [15]

I would characterize my computer skills as: ❑ Beginner [16] ❑ Intermediate [17] ❑ Advanced [18] ❑ Professional [19]

I use ❑ DOS [20] ❑ Windows [21] ❑ OS/2 [22] ❑ Unix [23] ❑ Macintosh [24] ❑ Other: [25]_____
(please specify)

I would be interested in new books on the following subjects:
(please check all that apply, and use the spaces provided to identify specific software)

❑ Word processing: [26] _____

❑ Data bases: [28] _____

❑ File Utilities: [30] _____

❑ Networking: [32] _____

❑ Other: [34] _____

❑ Spreadsheets: [27] _____

❑ Desktop publishing: [29] _____

❑ Money management: [31] _____

❑ Programming languages: [33] _____

I use a PC at (please check all that apply): ❑ home [35] ❑ work [36] ❑ school [37] ❑ other: [38] _____

The disks I prefer to use are ❑ 5.25 [39] ❑ 3.5 [40] ❑ other: [41]_____

I have a CD ROM: ❑ yes [42] ❑ no [43]

I plan to buy or upgrade computer hardware this year: ❑ yes [44] ❑ no [45]

I plan to buy or upgrade computer software this year: ❑ yes [46] ❑ no [47]

Name: _____ Business title: [48] _____ Type of Business: [49] _____

Address (❑ home [50] ❑ work [51]/Company name: _____)

Street/Suite# _____

City [52]/State [53]/Zipcode [54]: _____ Country [55] _____

❑ **I liked this book!** You may quote me by name in future
IDG Books Worldwide promotional materials.

My daytime phone number is _____

IDG BOOKS

THE WORLD OF
COMPUTER
KNOWLEDGE

❑ YES!
Please keep me informed about IDG's World of Computer Knowledge.
Send me the latest IDG Books catalog.